PROGRESSIVE DYSTOPIA

MICHAEL OZGA

authorHOUSE®

AuthorHouse™
1663 Liberty Drive
Bloomington, IN 47403
www.authorhouse.com
Phone: 1-800-839- 8640

Published by AuthorHouse 5/10/2012

ISBN: 978-1-4670-4031-0 (sc)
ISBN: 978-1-4670-4032-7 (hc)
ISBN: 978-1-4670-4033-4 (e)

Library of Congress Control Number: 2011917778

This book is printed on acid-free paper.

For my parents, with love...

Contents

Preface

The following quotes will set the tone for this book. They provide the inspiration in writing this as well as a window to my core beliefs. They were also chosen for their relevance to current events:

ON GOVERNMENT...

"When the people fear the government its tyranny, when government fears the people there is liberty." [1]

Thomas Jefferson

"If the laws are to be trampled upon with impunity, and a minority is to dictate to the majority, there is an end put, at one stroke, to republican government, and nothing but anarchy and confusion is to be expected thereafter." [2]

George Washington

"He governs best who governs least." [3]

Founding Fathers

"In republics, it is a fundamental principle that the majority govern and the minority comply with the general voice..." [4]

Oliver Ellsworth

"A house divided against itself cannot stand." [5]

Abraham Lincoln

"Immediate necessity makes many things convenient" [6]

Thomas Paine

*"I know not what course others may take; but as for me,
give me liberty or give me death."* [7]

Patrick Henry

*"...that we were highly resolve that these dead shall not
have died in vain, that this nation, under God, shall
have a new birth of freedom, and that government of the
people, by the people, for the people, shall not perish from
earth."* [8]

Abraham Lincoln

*"...to see rising in America an empire of liberty, and the
prospect of two or three hundred millions of freemen,
without one noble or king among them"* [9]

John Adams

*"...They must be told that the ultimate authority,
wherever the derivative may be found, resides in the
people alone."* [10]

James Madison

*"From the nature of man, we may be sure that those who
have power in their hands will not give it up while they
can retain it. On the contrary, we know that they will
always, when they can, increase it."* [11]

George Mason

*"...We are indeed, and we are today, the last best hope of
man on earth."* [12]

Ronald Reagan

*"For we must consider that we shall be as a city upon a
hill. The eyes of all people are upon us."* [13]

John Winthrop

"Government is not reason, is not eloquence, it is force; like fire, a troublesome servant and fearful master. Never for a moment should it be left to irresponsible action." [14]

George Washington

"…A fire not to be quenched, it demands a uniform vigilance to prevent its bursting into a flame, lest, instead of warming, it should consume." [15]

George Washington

"The preservation of Freedom is the protective reason for limiting and decentralizing governmental power." [16]

Milton Friedman

"But in another sense, our new beginning is a continuation of the beginning created two centuries ago when, for the first time in history, government, the people said, was not our master, it is our servant: its only power that which we the people allow it to have." [17]

Ronald Reagan

ON RELIGION...

"Of all the dispositions and habits which lead to political prosperity, religion and morality are indispensable supports…" [18]

George Washington

"Sir, my concern is not whether God is on our side; my greatest concern is to be on God's side. For God is always right." "Intelligence, patriotism, Christianity, and a firm reliance on Him who has never forsaken this favored land, are still competent to adjust in the best way all our present difficulty." [19]

Abraham Lincoln

"I have lived, sir, a long time, and the longer I live, the more convincing proofs I see of this truth – that God governs in the affairs of men." [20]

Benjamin Franklin

"I am a real Christian, that is to say, a disciple of the doctrines of Jesus." [21]

Thomas Jefferson

"Thank you all very much and da blagoslovit vas gospod (God bless you)." Reagan to Soviet leaders 1986. [22]

Ronald Reagan

"Annuit Coeptis…He (God) has favored our undertaking" [23]

Official Seal of the United States of America

"…So help me God." [24]

George Washington April 30, 1789

"…We raise our voices to God who is the author of this most tender music. And may He continue to hold us close as we fill the world with our sound, in unity, affection and love, one people under God, dedicated to the dream of freedom that He has placed in the human heart, called upon now to pass that dream on to a waiting and hopeful world." [25]

Ronald Reagan January 21, 1985

"The American people have a great genius for splendid and unselfish action. Into the hands of America God has placed the destinies of an afflicted mankind." [26]

Pope Pius XII

"When the righteous are in authority, the people rejoice; but when the wicked beareth rule, the people mourn." [27]

PROVERBS 29:2

"It is the duty of all wise, free and virtuous governments to countenance and encourage virtue and religion." [28]
John Jay, Original Chief Justice U.S. Supreme Court

"...this is a religious people...this is a Christian nation" [29]
U.S. Supreme Court Church of the Holy Trinity v. United States 1892

"Our Constitution was made only for a moral and religious people. It is wholly inadequate to the government of any other." [30]

John Adams

"...There is no country in the world where the Christian religion retains a greater influence over the souls of men than in America." [31]

De Tocqueville

"...Natures God...Creator...unalienable rights... Supreme Judge...Divine Providence..." [32]
The Declaration of Independence

"In the Year of our Lord 1787" [33]

Constitution

"In God we Trust" [34]

National Motto

On Debt...

"To contract new debt is not the way to pay old ones." [35]
George Washington

"There is no practice more dangerous than that of borrowing money...it comes easy and is spent freely, and many things indulged in that would never be thought of if to be purchased by the sweat of the brow. In the

meantime, the debt is accumulating like a snowball in rolling." [36]

George Washington

"But what madness must it be to run in debt for these superfluities! …think what you do when you run in debt; you give to another power over your liberty…"[37]

Benjamin Franklin

"…We shall all consider ourselves morally bound to pay them ourselves; and consequently within the life expectancy of the majority…" [38]

Thomas Jefferson

"The principle of spending money to be paid by posterity, under the name of funding, is but swindling futurity on a large scale." [39]

Thomas Jefferson

"It must be done by all of us going forward with a program aimed at reaching a balanced budget. We can then begin reducing the national debt." [40]

Ronald Reagan

"I, however, place economy among the first and most important of republican virtues, and public debt as the greatest of the dangers to be feared." [41]

Thomas Jefferson

"We are spending more than we have ever spent before and it does not work…We have never made good on our promises…I say after eight years of this Administration we have just as much unemployment as when we started…and an enormous debt to boot!" [42]

Henry Morgenthau, Jr. Treasury Secretary under FDR

"…Tis hard for an empty bag to stand upright…"[43]

Benjamin Franklin

"No pecuniary consideration is more urgent than the regular redemption and discharge of the public debt; on none can delay be more injurious, or an economy of time more valuable."[44]

George Washington

ON SOCIAL WELFARE...

"The Utopian schemes of leveling and a community of goods are as visionary and impractical as those which vest all property in the Crown. These ideas are arbitrary, despotic, and in our government, unconstitutional."[45]

Samuel Adams

"Dependence begets subservience"[46]

Thomas Jefferson

"The Constitution only gives people the right to pursue happiness. You have to catch it yourself."[47]

Benjamin Franklin

"Federal aid in such cases encourages the expectation of paternal care on the part of the Government and weakens the sturdiness of our national character…"[48]

Grover Cleveland

"…I think the best way of doing good to the poor, is not making them easy in poverty, but leading or driving them out of it…that the more public provisions were made to the poor, the less they provided for themselves, and of course became poorer. And, on the contrary, the

less was done for them, the more they did for themselves,
and became richer." [49]

Benjamin Franklin

"Let not him who is houseless pull down the house of
another, but let him work diligently and build one for
himself, thus by example assuring that his own shall be
safe from violence when built." [50]

Abraham Lincoln

"The wise and correct course to follow in taxation and
in all other economic legislation is not to destroy those
who have already secured success but to create conditions
under which every one will have a better chance of being
successful." [51]

Calvin Coolidge

"To relieve the misfortune of our fellow creatures is
concurring with the Deity; it is godlike; but if we provide
encouragement for laziness…we had need be very
circumspect, lest we do more harm than good." [52]

Benjamin Franklin

"If we can prevent the government from wasting the
labors of the people, under the pretense of taking care of
them, they must become happy." [53]

Thomas Jefferson

"I have long been of your opinion, that your legal
provision to the poor in England is a very great evil,
operating as it does to the encouragement of idleness." [54]

Benjamin Franklin

ON FREE ENTERPRISE...

"Freedom to try, freedom to buy, freedom to sell, freedom to fail..." [55]

Adam Smith

"...the laws of supply and demand determines which products are desired and which are not." [56]

Adam Smith

"After all, the goddess of chance, as of justice is blind... the central principle of a market economy is co-operation through voluntary exchange." [57]

Milton Freedom

"...the market does in general; permit co-operation without conformity...the essence of a competitive market is its impersonal character." [58]

Milton Freedom

"What belongs to no one is wasted by every one." [59]

James Wilson

"Capitalism...is by nature a form or method of economic change and not only never is but never can be stationary...This process of Creative Destruction is the essential fact about capitalism..." [60]

Joseph Schumpeter

"Socialism is a philosophy of failure, the creed of ignorance and the gospel of envy; its inherent virtue is the equal sharing of misery" "The inherent vice of capitalism is the unequal sharing of blessing..." [61]

Winston Churchill

"Property is the fruit of labor…that some should be rich shows that others may become rich and hence is just encouragement to industry and enterprise…some will get wealthy…I don't believe in a law to prevent a man from getting rich; it would do more harm than good. That some achieve great success, is proof to all that others may achieve it as well." [62]

Abraham Lincoln

"Inequality would exist as long as liberty existed…It would unavoidably result from that very liberty itself." [63]

Alexander Hamilton

"…while democracy seeks equality in liberty, socialism seeks equality in restraint and servitude." "If you have any comprehension of my philosophy at all, you must know that one thing I stand for above all else is free trade throughout the world." [64]

Friedrich Hayek

"Here in America, as we reflect on the many things we have to be thankful for, we should take a moment to recognize that one of the key factors behind our nations great prosperity is the open trade policy that allows the American people to freely exchange goods and services with free people around the world." "…when Americans courageously supported the struggle for liberty, self-government and free enterprise throughout the world, and turned the tide of history away from totalitarian darkness and into the warm sunlight of human freedom." [65]

Ronald Reagan

The aforementioned quotes should set the tone for the book. From Adam Smith to Ronald Reagan, from Thomas Jefferson to Milton Friedman, from George Washington to Abraham Lincoln; the quotes should serve notice on our founding principles and how they have stood the test of time. The Founding Fathers looked to Adam Smith, Aristotle, Jesus, The Bible, John Locke, Polybius, Cicero, Sir William Blackstone, Charles de Montesquieu, Moses, et al…for direction and inspiration on laying the foundation for our country. The inherent beauty of our Constitution is its relevance to any point in time despite social or economic conditions. The Founding Fathers achieved this with the Constitution because it addresses something that has not changed and will not change--human nature. [66]

Washington, Jefferson, Franklin, Wythe, Clymer, Madison, et al…laid the foundation. Lincoln, Coolidge, Friedman, Reagan, et al…have carried the torch. As is evident by the quotes, The Founders were quite clear on where they stood with regard to governance, social welfare, debt, free markets and most importantly, religion. Progressives are entitled to their own opinions; however, they are not entitled to their own facts. This country was founded upon Judeo-Christian values; our civil law is based upon the Ten Commandments. The Founders were overwhelmingly religious men, more specifically Christian men. They believed in equal opportunity but not equal results. They believed in hard work, self-reliance, frugality, liberty and enumerated powers. They believed in the invisible hand of government and not the beneficent/paternal hand of government.

We are at a crossroads; a return to principles that made America the most prosperous, generous, industrious and most importantly, the most free people in the history of mankind. Or, we 'fundamentally transform' this country into something that The Founders and our children would not and will not recognize. The Founders warned against losing liberty as it will never be regained. Reagan spoke of embracing our destiny in 1974; "We cannot escape our destiny, nor should we try to do so. The leadership of the world was thrust upon us two centuries ago in that little hall in Philadelphia…We are indeed, and we are today, the last best hope of man on earth…" [67]

And finally...

"...These are the times that try men's soul..." [68]

Thomas Paine

Introduction

We *the People...*" Never have so few words meant so much to so many. It's the summation of our founding principles, beliefs and commitment to liberty. In these three words the founding principles of People's Law are clearly stated. The power to govern lies with the people, it flows from them and is delegated to those who govern. In other words, elected officials derive their just powers from the consent of the governed. Our rulers are servants of the people. The flow of power is from the people upward, not from the government downward. These three words represent: government by the people, creative destruction, initiative, self-reliance, competition, equal rights not equal things, the pursuit of happiness not the guarantee thereof, frugality, morality, virtue, thrift, hard work and compassion.

To quote Thomas Jefferson, "It is not by the consolidation or concentration of powers, but by their distribution that good government is effected." *"We the People..."* represents both vertical and horizontal separation of powers. The horizontal separation of powers exists between the Executive, Legislative and Judicial Branch of the Federal Government. A vertical separation of powers exists from the Federal Government, through State Government, through County Government, through Community, through Families and whose foundation lies with millions of individuals. *"We the People..."* is based upon the implicit confidence in the people.

The Founders recognized that human nature is a product of highs and lows, of shadow and sunshine. James Madison stated "As there is a degree of depravity in mankind, which requires a certain degree of circumspection and distrust, so there are other qualities in human nature which justify a certain portion of esteem and confidence."

Madison also stated … "if men were angels no government would be necessary…" [1] The Constitution is designed to bring the most happiness to the most people, in other words, majority rule and minority comply. It was designed to maximize prosperity, minimize poverty and make the entire nation rich. Human nature had to be accounted for when forming our republican government, and therein lies the inherent beauty of our Constitution. The Founders designed it to address human nature, something that has not and will not change.

The Progressive Movement has labored to subvert everything that *"We the People…"* represents. Progressives believe in a social utopia by means of Ruler's Law, which is a usurpation of liberty and depravity of human nature. Ruler's Law is monarchy, autocracy, plutocracy, aristocracy, oligarchy, etc…Government power is exercised by force, power, coercion or legislative usurpation. The power is concentrated in the ruler where the people are treated as subjects. Government is by rule of men rather than law. Unalienable rights do not exist. Fascism, National Socialism (i.e. Nazism), International Socialism (i.e. Communism), Progressivism, et al…represent Ruler's Law. [2]

Progressivism like its political DNA siblings (i.e., Fascism, Communism, National Socialism) advocates statism, absolute government, collectivism, populism, centralized state, interventional federal government, redistribution of wealth, a beneficent hand, social welfare, social engineering and a utopian belief in a community of goods. Juxtapose this to what the Founders intended with our Constitution. The principles of economy the Founders espoused for our country were based upon the writings of Adam Smith, who authored *Wealth of Nations*. The Constitution represents equal rights not equal things, it represents our instinctive will to succeed (i.e. compete), it represents supply and demand, free trade markets, and grants us the right to pursue happiness.

Albert Einstein said "thinking that doing more of the same will lead to a different outcome is a sign of insanity." [3] The collectivist, social utopian, progressive mindset is not new to this country or throughout the world for that matter. We have experienced this social/political depravity in our country throughout our history; Jamestown 1607, New Harmony, Indiana 1820's, Oneida, NY 1880's, TR, Wilson, FDR, LBJ, Clinton and now Obama. From 1607 to 2012, a period of 405 years, we have seen the progressive movement time and again. In each of its reincarnations it has not worked, does not work and will not work. Yet in their utopian/statist mind (i.e. insane) they continue their incessant push that they know what is in our best interest better than we do. The progressive movement is diametrically opposed to everything the Founders intended, fought and died for. [4]

Progressives want to "progress" past the Constitution. They want a perfect society (i.e. utopia) designed by an imperfect man. They want fiscal and social policy designed and implemented by central planners. Economist Thomas Sowell refers to these administrators as the "wise and knowledgeable few." These central planners, as Mr. Sowell points out are the most intelligent, best educated amongst us and have the power of government to enforce. Unfortunately, as history has shown, no one is smart enough to carry out social engineering. Central planning has been tried time and again throughout history with the identical results, failure. Unfortunately, Progressives appear to be impervious to the evidence of history. Economic and social policies planned by the wise and far sighted have always failed. Mr. Sowell poses the following question: how was it even possible that transferring decisions from elites with more education, intellect, data and power to ordinary people, could lead consistently to demonstrably better results?

Glenn Beck, of GBTV, poses an even better question; how can we progress past "We hold these truths to be self-evident, that all men are created equal, that they are endowed by their Creator with certain unalienable Rights that among them are Life, Liberty and the pursuit of Happiness?" Thomas Sowell points out the education and intellect of the "wise and knowledgeable few" may provide greater presumptions, but that just makes them more dangerous to the freedom as well as the well-being, of the people as a whole. Is the world a better place because of or in spite of central planners who designated themselves the 'wise and knowledgeable few'. Did mankind actually progress with elites such as Marx, Engels, Bismarck, Lenin, Stalin, Hitler, Mussolini, Ho Chi Minh, Mao Tse-tung, Pol Pot, et al…? Is America a better place because of policies designed and implemented by the "wise and knowledgeable few" of our past, Robert Owen, John Humphrey Noyes, FDR, Henry Morgenthau, Stuart Chase, LBJ, Carter, et al…? Will America be a better place because of policies designed and implemented by the current 'wise and knowledgeable few' Clinton, Obama, Sunstein, Geithner, Dodd, Frank, Bernancke, Sotomayer, Kagan, et al…? The questions of course are rhetorical as the answers are self-evident.

The central planners, or the "wise and knowledgeable few," have given us Social Security via the New Deal, which has current liabilities of $15.5 trillion. These "wise and knowledgeable few" have given us Medicare, via the Great Society, which has current liabilities of $88.5 trillion. These "wise and knowledgeable few" have given us Fannie Mae and Freddie Mac. The "wise and knowledgeable few" have given us sub-prime mortgages and the financial meltdown of 2008 due to social engineering on the part of Clinton, Cuomo, Cisneros, Frank, Dodd, et al. The "wise and knowledgeable few" have given us the Federal Reserve, designed to bring about economic stability and prosperity for the American people. Since the Fed was established in 1913, the real power/value of the dollar has decreased by 93%. The "wise and knowledgeable few" have given us the League of Nations, which was the predecessor to the United Nations. The UN, with 51 original members, was designed to end all wars, safeguard human rights, balance global interdependence, etc...The UN today is comprised of 192 nations and 44,000 employees and a yearly budget of $5 billion. The United States alone, via taxpayer money, funds approximately 22% of the budget, the remaining 190 countries fund the other 78%. We pay 22% of the budget for an organization, although well intended, has obvious socialist tendencies (i.e. ill-advised). [5]

The "wise and knowledgeable few" [6] under FDR and Keynesianism gave us well intended but ill-advised policies (i.e. prime the pump) that turned a mild recession into a Great Depression. The "wise and knowledgeable few" under Wilson gave us The Federal Reserve, a progressive tax system, etc...again, well intended but ill-advised. LBJ gave us Medicare and Medicaid, again well intended but ill-advised, as both account for trillions of dollars of unfunded liabilities. The "wise and knowledgeable few" repealed the Glass-Steagall Act in 1999, which contributed to the financial meltdown in 2008, well intended, ill-advised. The "wise and knowledgeable few" of today have given us TARP, The Stimulus, bailouts, nationalization of GM and Chrysler, Obamacare, Cap and Trade, The Dream Act, real unemployment of 17-18%, $5 trillion of additional debt, etc...If history is any judge, the central planners of today will be proven well intended but again ill-advised.

As American philosopher George Santayana said, "Those who cannot remember the past are condemned to repeat it." [7] The reader can judge based upon the facts of history whether Santayana's warning will come to fruition in America. The reader can decide whether the Presidents of this book represent Ruler's Law or People's Law. Whether they represent a concentration of power or the distribution thereof, whether they represent ruler down government or that which is governed from the people upward. The reader can judge whether TR, Wilson, FDR, Obama, et al...have been and are the "wise and knowledgeable few." Whether the policies of the past represent central planning or Constitutional principles based upon liberty. Thomas Jefferson and our Founders warned that a constant vigilance be maintained by an intelligent and informed electorate so as to preserve our Republic. Benjamin Franklin said "…a Republic, if you can keep it." Based upon their records, Theodore Roosevelt, Woodrow Wilson, FDR and now Obama were clearly Progressive in their political ideology. They were clearly advocates of Ruler's Law and clearly did not, and in the case of Obama, do not believe with the implicit confidence in the people, *__We the People…__*

CHAPTER 1

THEODORE ROOSEVELT

26TH PRESIDENT 1901-1909

"Personal property...is subject to the general right of the community to regulate its use to whatever degree the public welfare may require it. Every man holds his property subject to the general right of the community to regulate its use to whatever degree the public welfare may require it." [1]

Theodore Roosevelt

"The theory of the Communists may be summed up in the single sentence: Abolition of private property." [2]

Karl Marx

It's disturbing that someone who is carved in stone at Mount Rushmore as one of our greatest presidents and patriots is eerily similar in ideology to Karl Marx. It's not to suggest that TR was a Communist, it's meant to illustrate the blood lines (i.e. political DNA) that course through Progressivism, Fascism, National Socialism and Communism. TR was no less a statist/collectivist than Marx, Lenin, Stalin, Mussolini and Hitler. Whether it is tyranny by force (i.e. Lenin and Stalin) or tyranny by perfidy (i.e. TR, Wilson, FDR,

Obama) it is still tyranny. Soft tyranny, as Mark Levin suggests, is no less insidious than tyranny by force.

Roosevelt gave a speech in April 1912 describing "Who is a Progressive?" Included in the speech were the following statements: "...We of today who stand for the Progressive movement here in the United States are not wedded to any particular kind of machinery, save solely as means to the desired ends. Our aim is to secure the real and not the nominal rule of the people...For this purpose we believe in securing for the people the direct election of United States Senators...Every man is to that extent a Progressive if he stands for any form of social justice...The big business concern that is both honest and farsighted will, I believe, in the end favor our effort to secure thorough-going supervision and control over industrial big business, just as we have now secured it over the business of inter-State transportation and the business of banking under the National law...I stand for the adequate control, real control, of all big business...when I protest against unfair profits..." [3]

Roosevelt was proud of his Progressive ideology, which advocated social expediency over natural rights, redistributing private property in the name of social justice, expansion of national government, state control over numerous aspects of public life, nationalize private business, centralized and bureaucratic state, elastic view of the Constitution and secular in nature. Progressives like TR operate under the guise of altruism, righteousness, social justice and benevolent social control. Their elitist mindset and theoretical goal for some earthly utopia/panacea always decays into coercive legislation, depravity, usurping liberties and subverting the Constitution. The Constitution specifies general welfare, not special welfare.

Obama may have run a campaign based upon "Hope and Change," however, the roots for the welfare state/social justice politics was born more than a century ago and ushered into prominence by TR. Roosevelt took full advantage of the bully pulpit when president issuing 1081 executive orders. By comparison, his two predecessors, Presidents Cleveland and McKinley issued 122 combined. Article I, section I, paragraph I of the Constitution states, "All legislative or lawmaking powers granted by this Constitution shall be vested exclusively in the Congress of the United States." Despite this usurpation of enumerated powers, Roosevelt stated in defiance; "I decline to adopt the view that what was imperatively necessary for the Nation could not be done by the President unless he could find some specific authorization to do it. My belief was that it was not only his right but his duty to do ANYTHING that the needs of the Nation demanded unless such action was forbidden by the Constitution or by Law. Under this interpretation of Executive power I did and caused to be done many things not previously done by the President and the heads of the Departments. I did not usurp powers, but I did greatly broaden the use of Executive power." This set the precedent for Progressives (i.e. Wilson, FDR and Obama) to centralize power and usurp the Constitution under the guise of altruism. [4]

To put TR's incessant power grab into perspective, there were a combined 1262 executive orders issued from George Washington in 1789 through William McKinley in 1901. As stated above, Teddy Roosevelt issued 1081 from 1901 – 1909. Roosevelt set the precedent for fellow progressives Woodrow Wilson and FDR. Wilson issued 1803 executive orders during his tenure, 1913 – 1921. FDR issued an astonishing 3522 during his tenure, 1933 – 1945. These three presidents combined, TR, Wilson and FDR issued 6406 executive orders in 28 years of service. The remaining 41 Presidents served a total of 193 years and issued a combined 8803. The Founders warned against any consolidation or centralization of power in Washington particularly within the Executive Branch. TR, Wilson and especially FDR expanded the power of the Executive Branch based upon their own interpretation of constitutional powers. [5]

James Madison said… "The powers delegated by the proposed Constitution to the Federal Government are few and defined…" "…They must be told that the ultimate authority, wherever the derivative may be found, resides in the people alone." [6] "…If angels were to govern men, neither external nor internal controls on government which is to be administered by men over men, the great difficulty lies in this: you must first enable the government to control the governed; and in the next place oblige it to control itself." "I believe there are more instances of the abridgement of the freedom of the people by gradual and silent encroachments of those in power, than by violent and sudden usurpations…This danger ought to be wisely guarded against." [7]

George Washington said… "Government is not reason, it is not eloquence – it is force! Like fire, it is a dangerous servant and fearful master." [8] Alexander Hamilton also warned against abuse by those in authority; "For it is truth, which the experience of all ages has attested, that the people are commonly most in danger when the means of injuring their rights are in the possession of those toward whom they entertain the least suspicion." [9] The quotes illustrate the original intent of the Constitution, providing freedom from abuse by those in authority and to protect against the natural tendencies of perpetual expansion. Whether it was an exercise in self-aggrandizement, ego-mania or simply a reflection on human nature, it is very clear that the expansion of Executive powers via executive orders by TR, Wilson and FDR represents the usurpation of powers that the Founders warned against. Therein lies the genius of the Constitution; it was designed to control something which has not changed and will not change – human nature. [10]

Article I, Section I, Paragraph I of the Constitution states very clearly the lawmaking powers vested within the Constitution. Despite the lack of ambiguity and testament to his own ego and self-interpretation of powers granted, TR was defiant to the very end… "While President I have been President, empathically: I have used every ounce of power there was in the office and I have not cared a rap for the criticisms of those who spoke of my 'usurpation of power'; for I knew that the talk was all nonsense and that there was no usurpation." [11] The hallmark characteristic of Progressives is their paternalistic attitude towards the governed. It is an elitist, statist mindset born of arrogance not altruism. TR believed in the supremacy of the state, which in and of itself is a rejection of principles within the Declaration. TR viewed personal pursuits as an impediment to a utopian state. TR was an advocate of an all powerful central government and promoted what French historian Alexis de Tocqueville described as soft tyranny. [12]

President Howard Taft described TR as a "dangerous egotist" and a "demagogue." [13] A relative described TR as follows, "When Theodore attends a wedding, he wants to be the bride, and when he attends a funeral, he wants to be the corpse." [14] Whatever the description, TR was a politician first and foremost. As such, he pandered to the progressive/populist movement prominent during the early 20th century. Whether or not TR was a true ideologue like authors Upton Sinclair and Lincoln Steffens, he catered to their visions. These visions and other populist agitations affected law as government tinkering slowly progressed to government takeover. This agitation promulgated by populists led to law. Among these laws was the Interstate Commerce Act of 1887. Activism (i.e. populist agitation) may have given birth to legislation such as the ICC; it was progressives within (i.e. TR) that provided the teeth. [15]

In 1906, The Hepburn Act was enacted under TR which greatly enhanced the power of the ICC. These were landmark acts because it was the sentinel moment where bureaucratic regulation of private business at the federal level began. The ICC and Hepburn Act gave the federal government the power to decide what was unjust and unreasonable with regard to price. In other words, the government determined prices instead of the railroads and customers (i.e. producers and consumers). The government became a participant in the free market instead of a referee. Prior to the ICC and Hepburn Acts, and left to the free market, railroad prices decreased as profits increased. Following the ICC and particularly The Hepburn Act, profits for railroads decreased as prices increased. Once again policies that were well intended but ill-advised by the "wise and knowledgeable few." By 1909 under TR employees within the ICC grew fivefold from its inception in 1887. [16]

The tact used by TR was coercive power. This coercive use of power on the free market was viewed by economist Dr. Milton Friedman as the fundamental threat to freedom. The existence of a free market does not obviate the need for government. However, government should serve as a forum for determining the rules of the game and as umpire to interpret and enforce said rules. The government should not become an active participant, once this occurs the market loses its impersonal character via centralized authority. TR obviously chose central planning over private markets, top down vs. bottom up, socialism vs. capitalism. The entire premise of our founding was based upon the principle of limited and decentralized power. Government should serve as a means, neither to grant favors and gifts nor master to be blindly served. [17] The private sector is a check on the powers of government. TR drove us to centralization and was intent on extending the scope of the federal government. Again, as history as proven, men of good will and intentions are the first to rue its consequences.

Another example of TR's paternalistic exertion of power was his "wise and farsighted" approach to environmentalism. He declared tens of millions of acres of land be set aside for national parks. Thereby rendering these lands off limits to the private sector (i.e. mining, logging, and farming). The trade off here is between the "wise and knowledgeable few" (i.e. bureaucrats) and the less wise and less knowledgeable many (i.e. private owners). Rather than put trust in private stewardship, TR at the behest of environmentalist, put trust in the federal bureaucracy. The federal government became a means to an end for the progressive environmentalist, which continued throughout the 20th century and into the 21st. [18] This is another example of TR's incessant desire to exert power over others via an expansive and active central government, a hallmark of the progressive. TR's land grab was nothing more than redistributing private property in the name of social justice. TR, as part of his New Nationalism theme, called for the federal government to take an active role in economic policy through the superintending of private property. [19]

With regard to private property TR is quoted, "We grudge no man a fortune in civil life if it is obtained and well used. It is not even enough that it should have been gained without doing damage to the community. We should permit it to be gained only so long as the gaining represents benefit to the community. This, I know, implies a policy of a far more active governmental interference with social and economic conditions in this country than we have yet had, but I think we have got to face the fact that such an increase in government is now necessary." The reader can judge; does this quote represent top down or bottom up? Central planning or private markets? Socialism or capitalism? Collective right or individual right? The progressive mind set during this period which TR subscribed to can best be summed by Social Gospel advocate, Walter Rauschenbusch, "Socializing property will mean that instead of serving the welfare of a small group indirectly, and the public welfare only indirectly, it will be made more directly available for the service of all." [20]

Once again the underlying theme in both quotes is the belief in government expansion, benevolent social control, and coercive means in the name of altruism. The Progressive movement during the early part of the 20th century ran concurrent with TR's tenure in the

7

Whitehouse. Social advocates and fellow Progressives, Upton Sinclair, Lincoln Steffens, John Dewey, Jane Addams, Walter Rauschenbusch, Herbert Croly, Robert LaFollette, John Hopkins University, et al... were no doubt an influence on TR. Again, whether TR was indeed a true ideologue or simply a politician who pandered to the populist movement, the following quote from 1901 summarizes his elastic view of the Constitution and his 'altruistic' belief in a centralized, bureaucratic state, "The tremendous and highly complex industrial development which went on with ever accelerated rapidity during the latter part of the nineteenth century brings us face to face, at the beginning of the twentieth, with very serious social problems. The old laws, and the old customs which had almost the binding force of law, were once quite sufficient to regulate the accumulation and distribution of wealth. Since the industrial changes which have so enormously increased the productive power of mankind, they are no longer sufficient."

Altruistic or not, the overwhelming arrogance of this statement makes it very clear how TR and fellow progressives viewed the Constitution and the pernicious nature of their movement. Contrary to what TR and the Progressives believed, the Constitution is not an elastic document, it is static, a document relevant to any time. The Constitution was relevant in 1789, 1820, 1861, 1901, 1933, 1978, and 1999 and remains relevant in 2010 as we head in to 2012. The reason for its relevance, regardless of social and economic conditions, is the fact that it addresses something that never changes, human nature. Basic human nature is no different today under Obama, Clinton, Reid, Pelosi, et al...than it was under TR, Wilson, Croly, Chase, FDR, LBJ, et al... than it was under Washington, Jefferson, Adams, Franklin, Wythe, et al... Again, the inherent beauty and genius of our founding documents is their relevance to any point in history notwithstanding social and economic conditions.

TR did not feel bound by Article II of the Constitution, which defines enumerated powers of the Executive Branch. TR believed his powers to be plenary which he defined in his autobiography, "… insistence upon the theory that the executive power was limited only by specific restrictions and prohibitions appearing in the Constitution or imposed by the Congress under its Constitutional powers. My view was that every executive office, and above all every executive officer in high position, was a steward of the people bound actively and affirmatively to do all he could for the people, and not to content himself with the negative merit of keeping his talents undamaged in a napkin. I declined to adopt the view that what was imperatively necessary for the Nation could not be done by the President unless he could find some specific authorization to do it. My belief was that it was not only his right but his duty to do anything that needs of the Nation demanded unless such action was forbidden by the Constitution or by the laws." TR sums up not only his mindset but that of the progressives in this statement; they were and continue to be the self designated "wise and knowledgeable few." TR and the Progressives became self-appointed interpreters of the nation's needs. [21]

An example of TR's paternalism/progressivism occurred during the 1902 United Mine Workers strike. TR invoked the Sherman Anti Trust Act of 1890 during his mediation between striking miners and the Northern Securities Company. TR threatened to send in federal troops and nationalize the mine if the two parties could not come to agreement. TR intervened on behalf of the people with the coercive power of the federal government behind him. On which side did TR fall, central planning vs. free markets? Top down vs. bottom up? Socialism vs. capitalism? The government as umpire or active participant? The "wise and knowledgeable few" vs. the less wise and less knowledgeable many? The Founders based their economic principles on Adam Smith and *Wealth of Nations*. The over-riding principles being, freedom to try, buy, sell and fail. The Founders also agreed with Adam Smith that the greatest threat to economic prosperity is the arbitrary intervention of the government into affairs of private business. [22] The free market economics espoused by the Founders provided a climate that by 1905 the United States of America produced over 50% of all goods (i.e. clothes, food, houses). America became the richest industrial nation in the world despite being only 6% of its population.

The key point here is the very essence of Progressive (i.e. Statist, collectivist, communist, Marxist, Bolshevist, National Socialism, liberalism, totalitarianism) thought, that theory trumps reality. As Thomas Jefferson stated, "All theory yields to experience." Experience, whether it be in America, China or India is that free markets, spared of central planning (i.e. social engineering), works. The economies of both China and India, once they relied on the markets over central planning both increased dramatically. Progressivism took roots in Germany and spread to America via places of higher learning such as Johns Hopkins, founded specifically to proselytize the progressive theory. The theory is one of so called enlightenment by the "wise and knowledgeable few." There are no fixed truths in progressive ideology, and that all ideas change and evolve over time, this is relativism and historicism. Our Founders, on the other hand, laid the foundation of our country on fixed principles and self-evident truths. The following quote by TR in 1916 reflects his view on progressive theory: "I do not for one moment believe that the Americana of today should be a mere submission to the American ideals of the period of the Declaration of Independence, such action would be not only to stand still, but to go back. American democracy, of course, must mean an opportunity for everyone to contribute his own ideas to the working out of the future. But I will go further than you have done. I have actively fought in favor of grafting on our social life, no less than our industrial life, many of the German ideals." [23] Unfortunately, to many of our current "wise and knowledgeable few" American exceptionalism is a thing of the past as well.

TR and fellow progressives believed that government should continue to evolve and expand into all aspects of public life. Again not unlike today's version of the "wise and knowledgeable few." The theory of progressives at its heart is based upon Darwin and evolution (i.e. progress) as opposed to Newton and static (i.e. fixed truths). Progressives, like TR, want to make progress, want to evolve (i.e. no fixed truths). Unfortunately this requires, in their view, an administrative state, central planning, bureaucracies, rights created by government and the right of the collective vs. the individual. Another mainstay of progressive theory is the monumental shift in thought from equality of opportunity to equality of outcome. It is a redistribution of goods and benefits throughout society, a redistribution of wealth, a leveling of the playing field. As previously mentioned, TR pandered to the populist movement of the day that free markets, capitalism, private property and the individual pursuit of economic prosperity were at the roots of societies ills. Progressive theory was based upon egalitarianism, collective rights, social justice, entitlements, redistribution and central control by the "wise and knowledgeable few." These views were promoted by the prominent authors of the time, Herbert Croly, Upton Sinclair, Lincoln Steffens et al...and given teeth via policy and the "bully pulpit" by TR throughout his tenure as president. [24]

In 1910 TR gave his speech on "The New Nationalism," whereby the following references were made with regard to TR's desire to expand government power into the private sector. TR spoke of the "true friend of property" as one who insists on "property" as the "servant" of the "commonwealth." In this speech TR also advocates for "government supervision of the capitalization." TR also spoke of his desire of "national restraint upon unfair money." He believed wealth should be gained only if it represents "benefit to society." TR begrudges no man a fortune, so long as it is "gained" without "damage" to the "community." Keeping with progressive theory, TR also states that "governmental control" over economic conditions is now "necessary." TR proclaimed his belief in a "graduated income tax" on big fortunes as w graduated inheritance tax" on big fortunes. TR refers to "hı fare" when claiming that "every man holds his property su the general right of the community to regulate its use to whatever degree the public welfare may require it." What happened to Life, Liberty and the pursuit of Happiness? TR also speaks of the "right" to "regulate" the "use of wealth" in the "public interest." He also spoke of "wealth" in terms of the "interest" of the "public good." TR ends his speech by proclaiming "...we must have progress, and our public men must be genuinely progressive." [25]

Here are more references from a TR speech given in 1912: in comparing Progressives to the traditionalists, he refers to those not in line with progressive theory as "puzzle-headed" and "dull of mental vision." TR also refers to non-believers in progressive theory as "lacking social sympathy." TR also refers to "prosperity" through the "fair treatment of all." During this speech TR also spoke of a "period of change" and the necessity for "men of vision" all in the name of "justice" and "righteousness." TR referred to opponents as the representation of "brute power" and "ceded privilege." Given TR's family wealth and his use of the 'bully pulpit' and executive orders, this statement is quite disingenuous. TR refers to the "American citizen" who oppresses others by "great wealth." Again, TR was born into wealth and a beneficiary of privilege. TR spoke of "unfair profits" and "exploitation" by those very "beneficiaries of privilege." TR spoke of the progressive cause as the "cause of justice for all." Progressives may be many things; one thing for sure is their consistent message and incessant persistence. These quotes came from TR in 1912 but could seamlessly fit into a campaign speech by FDR, LBJ, Clinton and of course Obama. [26]

The "ends justify the means" was the rallying cry for all Progressives, whether early 20th century or today. Winston Churchill warned Europe and the rest of the world that "The day will come when it will be recognized without doubt throughout the civilized world that the strangling of Bolshevism at birth would have been an untold blessing to the human race." Unfortunately, TR was not as far sighted with regard to progressivism as Churchill was towards Communism. Whether it's Communism (i.e. bully) or Progressivism (i.e. nanny), it is still totalitarian. As one of the self designated "wise and knowledgeable few," it's astounding that TR was so blind to the cancer developing in the American blood stream. The Founders left a blueprint for success via the Declaration of Independence and the Constitution. Documents based upon virtue, morality, free markets, competition, self-reliance and individual rights. American Progressivism was imported from Germany and the welfare state established by Otto von Bismarck.

Bismarck is the patron saint of American Progressivism which espoused paternalism, eugenics, central planning, secularism, collective rights, social welfare, redistribution of wealth, enlightened social policy, top down socialism and kindergarten. TR believed the progressive mantra which Woodrow Wilson would later sum up, that the individual "marry his interest to the state." One way to accomplish this is indoctrination at an early age. In other words, kindergarten was transplanted from Bismarck's Germany into America to make public schools incubators of a national religion. One of the prominent voices of American Progressivism during TR's day was John Dewey who claimed that "the government is the true parent of the children; the state is sovereign over the family." Another influential thinker of the time and major influence on TR was Herbert Croly. Author of *The Promise of American Life* and founder of the "New Republic" are credited with being the brainchild of TR's "New Nationalism." Croly argued that "national life" should be like a "school" which at times required "coercive methods." "An individual has no meaning apart from the society in which his individuality has been formed." An opinion echoed by TR himself. [27]

The optimum way to put into perspective what the Progressives (TR, Croly, Dewey, et al) strove to achieve is to look at their statements and actions through the prism of our Founding Fathers (i.e. preface quotes). Thomas Jefferson and our Founders believed "that which governs least governs best," TR believed "government control" was in fact "necessary." Jefferson believed that "dependence begets subservience," TR believed in social welfare. Sam Adams believed, "The utopian schemes of leveling, redistributing wealth, and a community of goods, central ownership of production and distribution, are as visionary and impractical as those which vest all property in the crown. These ideas are arbitrary, despotic, and in our government unconstitutional." TR spoke of "property" as the "servant" to the "commonwealth." Of "human rights" and "wealth" in terms of the "public interest." Benjamin Franklin said, "The Constitution only gives people the right to pursue happiness, you have to catch it yourself." TR spoke of, a "period of change" where "justice" and "righteousness" would be imposed by "men of vision." [28] Adam Smith espoused the freedom to buy, try, sell and fail. TR spoke of the "right" of the government to "regulate" the "use of wealth." Dr. Milton Friedman believed that "competitive capitalism and freedom have been inseparable", that "private sectors are a check on government powers" [29] and finally, "voluntary co-operation" without "coercion." TR believed that the government should be an active participant as opposed to umpire when he threatened to nationalize mines in 1902.

The following is a list of prominent voices that were influential both home and abroad during the 19th century and early 20th century. Again, whether TR was a true ideologue or simply a politician that pandered to the populist movement, he was influenced by the key players listed. Whether the influence was direct or indirect the end result was the same, centralized control, social welfare, paternalism and totalitarianism. During the late 19th century, the original ideas of Marx and Engels were adapted and modified to fit many political circumstances. Social Darwinists found their voice, whereby eugenics could be utilized through central planning to create a pure race. The names may have changed, progressivism, fascism, communism, totalitarianism, but the end goal remains the same. As Mussolini stated "Everything in the State, nothing outside the State." [30] In other words, every action by the State is justified to achieve the common good. This premise is obviously openly hostile to individualism and goes against every principle of our Founding documents.

American Progressivism shares its political DNA with communism, which championed class, fascism, which championed nation and Nazism which championed race. [31] American progressivism was an attempt to modernize or Europeanize America through enlightened policies (i.e. Bismarck's top down socialism). In essence the common denominator between these political siblings is the individual marrying his/her interest to that of the state. This political philosophy is as far from the original intent of our Founders as one can imagine. Progressives were a convoluted mix of scientific utopianism, nationalism, socialism and Christianity. This mindset can best be summed by TR's words at the 1912 Progressive Party convention where TR stated, "Our cause is based on the eternal principles of righteousness...We stand at Armageddon, and we battle for the Lord." [32]

All presidents are swayed by the influential voices of their day. Whether the measures are overt in nature or covertly, all presidents listen due to ideology or as a matter of survival (i.e. political expediency). The following list of prominent voices influenced TR and his administration and also provide a foundation for the social and political dynamics of the day. Names such as Karl Marx,

Freidrich Engels, Charles Darwin et al are included due to their influence on the Socialist, Communist, Statist, Progressive ideology that dominated early 20th century politics. I believe TR catered to these enlightened despots for reasons of political expediency and his own pragmatism.

THE "WISE & KNOWLEDGEABLE FEW"

Jane Addams (1860-1935) Social worker, ardent feminist, peace activist...founder of Hull House in Chicago 1898 to serve the underprivileged. Hull House based on the settlement houses of London's East End. Awarded Nobel Peace Prize in 1931. [33]

Senator Albert Beveridge (1862-1927) Chief senatorial ally of TR, chief progressive within senate. Unsuccessful Progressive candidate for governor of Indiana 1912, chairman of National Progressive Convention in Chicago 1912, unsuccessful Progressive candidate for US Senate 1914...as chair of 1912 convention stated "God has marked us as His chosen people, henceforth to lead in the regeneration of the world". [34]

Otto Von Bismarck (1815-1898) "Iron Chancellor" who founded the German Empire in 1871. Introduced social legislation (i.e. social welfare) that introduced accident insurance, old age insurance and socialized medicine. Transformed Germany into the foremost military and industrial power in Europe. Exported progressive ideal (i.e. Bismarckian welfare) to America. Bismarck was a centralizer a uniter and viewed as a European Lincoln. Bismarck introduced top down socialism to Germany. This philosophy incorporated many of the entitlements progressives advocate; welfare state program, pensions, health insurance, 8 hour work days, etc...[35]

Herbert Croly (1869-1930) Intellectual leader of Progressive movement. Created "New Nationalism" philosophy, founder of progressive magazine *New Republic*, author of *The Promise of American Life* in 1909, which influenced TR as well as FDR. TR based his "New Nationalism" on Croly's progressive philosophy. Opposed the industrial society, advocated for "constructive discrimination" (i.e. redistribution of wealth) whereby the "weak" would be favored. Advocate of big government controlling big business. Actively promoted a strong central government, labor unions and nationalization of business. Wished for the eradication of individual liberties, opponent of small business and non-union workers. Authored *Progressive Democracy* in 1915 which espoused the Constitution as a living (i.e. Darwinism) document with no fixed truths. Thought the Constitution was obsolete as written and needed to evolve to fit the social issues of the time. [36]

Charles Darwin (1809-1882) Part of scientific expedition on HMS Beagle in 1831. Collaborated with Alfred Russell Wallace on evolution theory in 1858 and published *On the Origin of Species* in 1859. Darwin postulated evolution orthodoxy over creationism. Progressives used Darwinism (i.e. evolving) as analogous to government. Progressives viewed the Constitution as a living document that evolves with no fixed truths. The Constitution is static, progressives viewed government as dynamic and evolving. [37]

Eugene V. Debs (1855-1926) Prominent socialist early 20th century… organized American Railway Union 1893, jailed 1894 for his part in Pullman strike. Read works by Karl Marx while imprisoned, helped to form Social Democratic Party in 1897, ran for president in 1900 as SDP candidate. Later ran for president as candidate for the Socialist Party of America, which grew out of the SDP. Helped create the International Workers of the World movement. Arrested a second time in 1918 following his disparaging remarks over WWI and the Wilson administration. Debs felt WWI was motivated strictly by capitalism. Arrested under the provisions of The Espionage act of 1917, which made it illegal to speak out against the Wilson administration. Final run for presidency under the Socialist Party of America in 1920 while imprisoned at Atlanta Federal Penitentiary. [38]

John Dewey (1859-1952) Student of philosophy at Johns Hopkins University (i.e. founded in 1867 as Progressive institution) where he earned his doctorate. Influenced by the writings of Karl Marx, co-author of *Communist Manifesto*. Founder of Progressive education movement. Founding member of NAACP, and ACLU. Early member of Socialist Party of America and Progressive Party. Promoted alternatives to capitalism which he felt was obsolete and cruel. [39]

Richard T. Ely (1854-1943) Progressive economist educated at Columbia and University of Heidelberg in Germany. Taught at Johns Hopkins University and the University of Wisconsin. Founder of American Economic Association, helped create Wisconsin's progressive program of social reform legislation. Had great influence on TR. Advocated government ownership of public utilities, social reforms, labour movement, cooperative commonwealth, etc...Stated, "God works through the State in carrying out His purposes more universally than through any other institution." Authored many books and articles including, *Recent American Socialism* in 1885, *Social Aspects of Christianity* 1889, and *Socialism and Social Reform* in 1894. [40]

Friedrich Engels (1820-1895) Authored *Condition of the Working Class* in 1844 based upon cotton factory work in England. Contributor in 1844 to radical journal, *Franco-German Annals* which was edited by Karl Marx. He and Marx developed friendship based upon mutual hatred of capitalism. Established the Communist Correspondence

Committee in 1846 with Marx. Delegate to Communist League conference in London. Aim of Communist League was to overthrow the bourgeoisie, domination of the proletariat, abolish old bourgeois society based on class antagonisms, establish society void of classes and private property. Published *The Communist Manifesto* with Karl Marx in 1848. The *Manifesto* formulated a coming revolution and a society that would be established by the proletariat. According to Engels and Marx, the bourgeoisie were the owners of the factories and raw materials. The proletariat had very little and was forced to sell their labor to the capitalists. Expelled from Belgium with Marx following the *Manifesto* release. Co-founder of radical newspaper *New Rhenish Gazette* in Cologne. Continued life's work with Marx in London until their deaths. [41]

Washington Gladden (1836-1918) Minister, local politician, social reformer...prominent voice of early 20th century Progressive movement. Like his fellow Progressives, Gladden was quite intolerant of others with dissenting points of view. Helped to enact temperance laws in Columbus as city council member, 1900-1902. [42]

Samuel Gompers (1850-1924) Born in London...moved to America in 1863. Early labor leader, first member of Cigarmakers International Union 1864, elected president in 1875. Organized the Federation of Organized Trades and Labor in 1881...reorganized in 1886 as the American Federation of Labor, served as president 1886-1924. Conservative and accepted capitalism...distanced himself from the Industrial Workers of the World, which fought to abolish capitalism. Appointed by Wilson to the Advisory Council of National Defense 1917-1919. Appointed by Wilson to Commission on International Labor Legislation at Versailles Peace Conference. John L. Lewis formed the Committee for Industrial Organizations within the AFL in 1935. The two merged in 1955 to form the AFL-CIO. [43]

G.W.F. Hegel (1770-1831) Prominent German philosopher… influenced both Marx and Engels. Supporter of French Revolution… aim was to establish conceptual framework of philosophy, which encompassed his own beliefs as well as past philosophers. Right wing Hegelians were Christians…left wing Hegelians were atheist and included Marx and Engels. Final publication was *Philosophy of Right* (1821). Progressives based their belief in the organic state from the teachings of Hegel. Progressive's belief in the state as god based upon Hegel's *Philosophy of History*. Wilson used quotes from *Philosophy of Right* by Hegel in speeches. [44]

Johns Hopkins (1795-1873) Made fortune in the Baltimore and Ohio Railroad. Founded The Johns Hopkins University and The Johns Hopkins Hospital in 1867. The university founded specifically to teach progressive thought. The University staffed with professors schooled in Germany during Bismarck's reign. [45]

Harold L. Ickes (1874-1952) Chicago politician…supported TR and Progressive Party 1912. Supported Progressive candidates Charles Evans Hughes 1916, Hiram Johnson 1920 and 1924. Played prominent role in FDR's New Deal administration. [46]

Intercollegiate Socialist Society (ISS) (1905-1921) Formed in New York 1905 to support and spread socialist ideas on college campuses. Founded by Upton Sinclair, who also served as vice president, and included fellow progressives Jack London (president), Clarence Darrow, Harry Laidler et al. The ISS was byproduct of socialist club formed in 1901 at University of Wisconsin Madison and the Social Progress Club in 1905 at the University of California Berkeley. ISS spread throughout college campuses preaching the "New Gospel according to St. Marx." Renamed The League for Industrial Democracy in 1921. LID morphed into the Students for a Democratic Society (SDS) in Port Huron, Michigan 1960. Stated purpose of ISS was to "throw light on the world-wide movement of industrial democracy known as socialism." [47]

Robert LaFollette (1855-1925) As governor of Wisconsin in 1891 implemented his "Wisconsin Ideas" which became foundation of the Progressive movement. Founded *Lafollette's Weekly Magazine* in 1909 and the National Progressive Republican League in 1911 to advocate progressive ideas. Pushed for progressive reform as US Senator and ran unsuccessfully in 1924 presidential race on Progressive ticket. [48]

Harry Wellington Laidler (1884-1970) Economist and Socialist leader early 20th century…educated at Columbia. Founding member of ISS and secretary from 1910-1921. Served as executive director of League for Industrial Democracy 1921-1957. Socialist candidate for numerous public offices. [49]

Vladimir Lenin (1870-1924) Brother Aleksandr executed for his role in the assassination attempt on Emperor Alexander III. Lenin grew more rebellious at this time while attending college and upon graduation joined a group of Marxist revolutionaries. Part of Russian Social Democratic Party which was split between two parties: the Bolsheviks (radical Red Russians) and Mensheviks (moderate White Russians). Led Bolshevik split from Mensheviks in 1912 and into the 1917 Bolshevik Revolution. Lenin's Bolshevik Revolution promoted and financially backed by Germany. The irony here is that Russia would come to occupy Germany during WWII. "He who digs a pit will fall into it." Proverbs 26:27. Lenin denied the power of God, was an advocate of 'collective rule' and 'centralized power', and avowed anti-capitalist. Russian Communist Party responsible for tens of millions of deaths as well as the destruction of over 70,000 churches. [50]

Walter Lippman (1889-1974) Ardent supporter of Roosevelt, Wilson and the Progressive Party. Socialist and co-founder of the Harvard Socialist Club…close friends with John Reed, author of *Ten Days that Shook the World*. Reed buried at Kremlin Wall with fellow Bolshevik heroes. Worked as Lincoln Steffens secretary in 1911, authored *A Preface to Politics* in 1913, joined with Herbert Croly and Walter Weyl to found New Republic. Worked as assistant to Wilson's Secretary of War…assistant to Wilson in drafting Fourteen Points Peace Programme. Member of Wilson's delegation to Paris Peace Conference in 1919…assisted Wilson with League of Nations covenant. [51]

Jack London (1876-1916) Converted to socialism at early age after reading *The Communist Manifesto*…known as boy socialist of Oakland. Mayoral candidate of Oakland on Socialist ticket 1901. Worked with the Social Democratic Federation in London 1902. Member of American Socialist Party and joined the ISS in 1905, served as President. Ardent supporter of TR. [52]

Karl Marx (1818-1883) Influential socialist thinker of the 19th century who advocated the revolutionary overthrow of capitalism. Emigrated to France in 1843 whereby he became a communist and developed life long friendship with Friedrich Engels. Both Marx and Engels expelled from Paris in 1844, moved to Brussels and published *The German Ideology*, predicting the collapse of industrial capitalism while being replaced by communism. Published *The Communist Manifesto* in 1848 with Engels. Sought refuge in London in 1849 where he remained until his death. Published *Capital* in 1867, which again advocated for and predicted the collapse of industrial capitalism. Described by Engels during eulogy, as a revolutionist whose mission in life was to contribute to the overthrow of the capitalist society and to liberate/emancipate the modern proletariat. [53]

Benito Mussolini (1883-1945) Moved to Switzerland in 1902 due to poor employment prospects in Italy. Became involved with socialist politics during his stay, returned to Italy in 1904 and joined the socialist press. Broke with the socialist and formed the Fascist Party in 1919. Organized the "Black Shirts" of 1921 which served as armed squads that terrorized political opponents. Self-proclaimed dictator of Italy in 1925, with the support of "Black Shirts." Ruled through strong state control and took the title "Il Duce." Formed Pact of Steel with Nazi Germany in 1939 and allied with Germany and Japan during WWII. [54]

Walter Rauschenbusch (1861-1918) The preeminent prophet for Social Gospel during the Progressive Era. Ordained in 1886 as pastor in New York's infamous Hell's Kitchen where he formulated his views that questioned laissez-faire capitalism. Formulated theology of Christian socialism and authored *Christianity and the Social Crisis*, *Christianizing the Social Order*, *A Theology for the Social Gospel*, and *Prayers for the Social Awakening*. [55]

John Reed (1887-1920) American journalist and poet, born in Oregon to a wealthy family whose father was a great admirer of TR. After traveling abroad, Reed began his journalist career at leftist magazines, *New Review* and *The Masses*. Organized several strikes on behalf of labor movements. Covered the Mexican Revolution for *Metropolitan Magazine* and *World*. Authored *Insurgent Mexico* in 1914 after spending months with Pancho Villa covering the Mexican Revolution. Covered WWI for *Metropolitan Magazine* and authored *The War in Eastern Europe* in 1916. Traveled to St. Petersburg and covered the Bolshevik Revolution for "The Masses." Reed was close personal friends with Lenin, identified himself with the Bolshevik movement and was pro-Communist. Wrote for *The New Communist Voice of Labour* in 1919. Authored *Ten Days That Shook the World* in

1920 which chronicled the Bolshevik Revolution. Died, buried and honored in Russia as Bolshevik hero. John Reed clubs established throughout United States in his honor. [56]

Margaret Sanger (1883-1966) Feminist, women's rights activist, member of Socialist Party with fellow Progressives: John Reed, Upton Sinclair, Eugene Debs, Norman Thomas, et al. Founded American Birth-Control League, co-founder of Workers Birth Control Group. Advocate of eugenics. [57]

Upton Sinclair (1878-1968) American novelist, described by TR as "muckraking journalist." Ardent reader of socialist classics and read the socialist weekly *Appeal to Reason*. Member of socialist party and board member of ACLU. Published novel *The Jungle* in 1906, which chronicled the life of an immigrant who is exploited by Chicago stockyard owners. TR received 100 letters per day demanding reforms. Subsequent legislation, Pure Food and Drug Act 1906, was direct result of Sinclair's novel. Sinclair established the socialist commune Helicon Home Colony in New Jersey which served as a commune for left wing writers. Published novel *Boston* in 1928, which was sympathetic to anarchists Sacco and Vanzetti. Ran unsuccessfully as socialist for governor of California in 1934. Ardent believer in socialism until his death in 1968. [58]

Joseph Stalin (1879-1953) As a young man, was sent to a seminary in Tbilisi by mother, to study to become a priest. Stalin dropped out of seminary study and chose revolutionary circles instead. Stalin was a hands on revolutionary unlike Lenin and Trotsky who were the intellectual leaders, often living abroad. Stalin held a life long distrust of educated intellectuals. Appointed to General Secretary of the Communists Party Central Committee in 1922. Following Lenin's death in 1924, Stalin became de facto leader as a result of his purging as General Secretary. Stalin continued to "purge" the Soviet Union of its founding fathers (i.e. Trotsky) and labeled them enemies of the people. Anyone with higher education suspected of being a threat to the revolution. Forced collectivized agriculture which reduced millions to serfs once again. [59]

Lincoln Steffens (1866-1936) Most famous of the American muckraker journalists from 1903-1910. Born to wealth in California, educated at the University of California Berkeley. Subsequent education in Germany and France. Returned to America and began writing for the New York *Evening Post*, became editor of *McClure's Magazine*. Articles *The Shame of St. Louis* and *The Shame of Minneapolis* brought him fame. Derided by President Theodore Roosevelt as "muckrake" journalism. Wrote articles supporting radical revolutionaries following the Mexican Revolution in 1910. Viewed American capitalism as a corrupting factor and capitalism as a whole as causing social corruption. Admired the Bolshevik Revolution and following his travels to Russia stated "I have seen the future, and it works." Advocated for a Communist revolution to "save" the United States. [60]

Ida Tarbell (1867-1944) One of the muckraking journalists of the early 20th century. Authored 19 part series for *McClure's Magazine* 1902-1904, *The History of the Standard Oil Company*. Series was expose on Standard Oil and Rockefeller's business practices... described by Tarbell as "open disregard of decent ethical business practices by capitalists." Described Rockefeller as "money mad"...a "hypocrite"...and "our national life is on every side distinctly poorer, uglier, meaner, for the kind of influence he exercises." [61]

Norman Thomas (1884-1968) Politician, social reformer, joined Socialist Party 1915, co-founder of ACLU, served as co-director for League for Industrial Democracy (founded as ISS) from 1922-1937. Socialist candidate for mayoral race of New York 1925, for governor

1924 and U.S. president in 1928-1948. Studied political science at Princeton during Woodrow Wilson's tenure as professor. Contributor to the Nation and World Tomorrow. [62]

Walter Weyl (1874-1919) Sympathetic to labor movement…assisted Robert Lafollette with research. Called for the redistribution of wealth, described personal wealth as social surplus. Described wealth as product of society and dismissed the notion of personal wealth. Authored *The New Democracy* in 1912…assisted Herbert Croly and Walter Lippman with production of the *New Republic* in 1914. [63]

CHAPTER 2
WOODROW WILSON
28TH PRESIDENT 1913-1921

*"...we are not bound to adhere to the doctrines held by
the signers of the Declaration of Independence."* [1]

Woodrow Wilson

*"Government is not a machine, but a living thing, it
falls not under the Newtonian theory of the universe, but
under the Darwinian theory of organic life."* [2]

Woodrow Wilson

*"Government...does now whatever experience permits or
the times demand."* [3]

Woodrow Wilson

*"No doubt...a lot of nonsense has been talked about the
inalienable rights of the individual, and a great deal that
was mere vague sentiment and pleasing speculation has
been put forward as fundamental principle."* [4]

Woodrow Wilson

It's clear by these disparaging remarks that Wilson held our
Founding documents and their authors in contempt. According
to Wilson and fellow progressives, the Declaration of Independence

and the Constitution held no relevance to early 20ᵗʰ century America and in fact were obsolete. Wilson believed we as a nation had to 'progress' past these documents if we were to truly evolve as a society. Wilson and fellow progressives believed we had to ascend to a higher level of society, led of course by them. The Constitution was, in the eyes of Wilson, an impediment to this vision of "progress." Wilson acknowledged the original intent and structure of the Constitution. Unfortunately, the concept of checks and balances, limited and enumerated powers and individual rights were restrictive and obsolete according to Wilson and fellow progressives. Wilson was an elitist, an academic, someone who valued theory over experience. Or as Thomas Sowell would describe social engineers in general, one of the "wise and knowledgeable few."

Wilson viewed the masses as "tools" and "clay in the hands of the consummate leader," referred to "artificial" barriers within the Constitution and described our Founding documents as "antiquated." During a speech at Princeton, Wilson told an audience, "Our problem is not merely to help students to adjust themselves to world life. . but to make them as unlike their fathers as we can." This paternalistic statism was also present at the time with the creation of kindergarten in America. Bismarck introduced kindergarten into German society, which was designed to indoctrinate children. John Dewey introduced kindergarten into American society with the same intention, to shape the apples before they fell from the trees. [5] Wilson in fact described the welfare state implemented by Bismarck in Germany as an "admirable system…the most studied and most nearly perfected." One of the influential progressive thinkers of the time was author Herbert Croly. Like Wilson, Croly was an admirer of Bismarck's welfare state in Germany. Like Wilson, Croly was an advocate of "severe coercive measures" in managing society. Like Wilson, Croly believed in the "beneficent activities of expert social engineers." [6]

Otto von Bismarck introduced his top down socialism into German society during the latter part of the 19th century. Wilson described him as a "commanding genius" who displayed a "keenness of insight, clearness of judgment and promptness of decision." Bismarck's model made the middle class dependent on the state, or as Wilson described progressivism…the individual "marry his interest to the state." [7] The emphasis here is one of collectivism over individualism; the good of the whole over that of the individual, a direct contradiction of the original intent of our Founding documents. Wilson was the consummate statist and advocate of social justice, redistribution of private property, social welfare, indoctrination of children, indoctrination of the masses and collectivism. Wilson viewed himself and other progressive thinkers as part of the intelligent minority. They were advocates of a centrally planned society managed by the elites. Early 20th century progressivism shared its political DNA with communism, fascism and National Socialism. The progressive movement in early 20th century America paralleled the aforementioned political movements that were developing throughout Europe. Although they differed in name, they all shared in the common belief of a collective society, centrally planned and managed by elites.

Wilson, like TR, believed the Constitution restricted his ability to transform society from one of individualism to one of collective will. TR usurped the power of the Legislative Branch by issuing 1081 executive orders during his tenure, 1901-1909. Wilson took this to a new level by issuing 1803 executive orders during his eight year tenure as president. [8] Once again, to put this expansive abuse and coercive use of power into perspective, there were 1262 executive orders issued from George Washington in 1789 through William McKinley in 1901. Wilson's coercive use of power was, like TR before him, consistent with the progressive philosophy of the ends justifying the means. No less insidious than Italian Fascism under

Mussolini or Russian Bolshevism under Lenin. Wilson, TR and other progressives viewed themselves as the intellectual minority responsible for managing the masses within an evolving society. A society that was better organized based upon trail and error (i.e. Darwinian evolution). Once elected in 1912, Wilson declared to "pick out progressives and only progressives" for his administration. Wilson also claimed, "If you are not a progressive…you better look out." [9]

As previously mentioned, Wilson was an advocate of the social welfare system adopted by Bismarck in Germany. In 1887, Wilson published an essay titled "The Study of Administration." The essay was based upon Wilson's study of the Prussian bureaucracy of which he held in high regard. Wilson described his theory of the evolution (i.e. progress) of government and broke it down into three periods of growth. The first period was one of absolute rulers or despotism. The second period of growth was one of constitutional rule whereby absolute rule was replaced by popular control (i.e. America). The third period of growth was that of "administrative" control. This was the system adopted by the Prussian bureaucracy under Bismarck. Wilson viewed the Prussian model as the "most nearly perfected" form and deemed the administrative rule as enlightened. It's abundantly clear that Wilson held our Constitution in disdain and was a fervent believer in the European model of rule by administration, particularly that of Germany under Bismarck. Wilson was elected president 25 years after publishing his essay on Administration. As part of the oath of office he promised to uphold the Constitution, which was the very document he abhorred and held in disdain, as he felt it was a hindrance on progress. Wilson placed our constitutional rule into his second period of growth, which by implication renders our system obsolete.

Wilson viewed our history of governance, under Constitutional rule, as one that is designed to curb executive (i.e. administrative) power. In his view, our system of legislative oversight was a hindrance and not progress. Wilson felt the need to break the chains of our Constitution in the name of progress and ascendancy. The checks and balances, enumerated powers and limits on the federal government were viewed as archaic and counterproductive. America, in Wilson's view had to unleash, energize and empower its administrative side. The underlying principle of progressives and the essay by Wilson is that government is a living entity, both dynamic and evolving. In other words, Darwinian (i.e. evolving and dynamic) over Newtonian (i.e. fixed and static principles). To this end Wilson described our Constitutional rule in his essay as machinery; this machine being driven by old (i.e. obsolete) boilers, bands, belts, wheels, joints and valves. Wilson was an advocate of installing new parts, or transplanting foreign systems into our country, namely that of the Prussian bureaucracy.[10] The essay promoted the European style of government, or as Wilson described it, "master of masterful corporations." In other words, a centrally planned society whereby the intellectual minority ruled. The underlying condescension here is present during the essay as Wilson describes the people as "selfish, ignorant, timid, stubborn or foolish." Hence the need for an enlightened administration. [11]

As previously noted, Wilson usurped the Legislative Branch by issuing 1803 executive orders during his tenure as president. Wilson imposed administrative law through executive orders on virtually every aspect of American life. The Food Administration, the Grain Corporation, the War Trade Board, the Committee on Public Information was established through executive order without specific authorization from Congress. Wilson issued these on the basis of "implied authority." [12] The original intent of our Founders via the Constitution was to limit the power of the federal government and specifically that of the executive branch. The enumerated powers within the Constitution gave the executive branch responsibility for the following: chief of state over all Americans, commander in chief over the military, chief executive officer over the executive branch, chief diplomat in foreign affairs, chief architect for needed legislation and conscience of the nation in granting pardons or reprieves. TR and Wilson initiated the phase whereby the office of the president ruled by "implied authority." As a result, the president is now responsible for maintaining the workforce, agricultural prosperity, national housing, underwriting loans, providing federal assistance, administer national welfare programs, administer social security, administer Medicare and Medicaid, allocate billions for education, arbiter of labor disputes, regulate major industries, regulate broadcasting, supervisory control of energy development, supervisory control of nearly 40% of nations land mass, etc...

The "implied authority" phase of the executive branch was facilitated by TR, taken to a new level by Wilson and further expanded upon throughout the 20th century under FDR (i.e. New Deal) and LBJ (i.e. Great Society). We are witness to the same "implied authority" today under Obama (i.e. nationalization of industry, banks, healthcare and insurance companies). The strict interpretation of Article I, Section I of the Constitution was forever altered by the presidencies of TR and Wilson. TR, Wilson and later with FDR, LBJ and through Obama, the office of the president "evolved" past the doctrine of enumerated powers whereby the president felt he had "implied authority" to do anything not specifically prohibited by the Constitution. [13]

Under the Constitution the government was a checks and balance system whereby the three branches of government were co-equals. No one branch was to be elevated above the other; furthermore, Article II of the Constitution both empowered and limited the president by enumerated powers. By "implied authority," Wilson viewed the presidency as having powers that were plenary and dictated by the needs of the time. Wilson, like TR before him, viewed the separation of powers as obsolete and advocated for the presidency to be elevated above the other two branches thereby transcending the separation of powers. [14] Wilson and fellow progressives viewed themselves as "enlightened experts that would rise above partisan politics and regulate for the common good." [15] Wilson advocated a power shift from a Constitutional Republic to his version of an administration, in other words, a government run by educated elites. Whether the intentions here were altruistic or not is beside the point. Wilson's version of progressive governance was paternalist, in other words, arrogant, condescending, dismissive and elitist. Not unlike what we are experiencing to date with Obama. By implication, progressive ideology viewed the masses as, for lack of a better word, dumb. In his own words Wilson viewed the masses as "tools" and "clay in the hands of a consummate leader."

The following are excerpts from *The New Freedom* released by Wilson in 1913. Wilson was critical of our Constitutional Republic due to the limits placed upon the executive branch. He viewed progressivism as visionary and evolutionary. Wilson claims to be "forced to be a progressive" as a means of keeping up with society's needs. He felt America was falling behind, namely behind Europe. Keep in mind, Wilson was a lifelong academic and based his principles on theory over experience. In his view the Constitution was obsolete and needed to be replaced by a European form of enlightened governance. Wilson stated "...that the Constitution of the United States had been made under the dominion of the Newtonian Theory." "They speak of the "checks and balances" of the Constitution, and use to express their idea the simile of the organization of the universe, and particularly of the solar system, how by the attraction of gravitation the various parts are held in their orbits; and then they proceed to represent Congress, the Judiciary and the president as a sort of imitation of the solar system." [16]

In addition Wilson states "The Constitution was founded on the law of gravitation. The government was to exist and move by virtue of the efficacy of checks and balances." "The trouble with the theory is that government is not a machine but a living thing. It falls, not under the theory of the universe, but under the theory of organic life. It is accountable to Darwin, not to Newton. It is modified by its environment, necessitated by its tasks, shaped to its functions by the sheer pressure of life." "All that progressives ask or desire is permission, in an era when development, evolution is the scientific word, to interpret the Constitution according to Darwinian principle; all they ask is recognition of the fact that a nation is a living thing and not a machine." [17] Wilson goes on to state, "The Declaration of Independence…is of no consequence to us unless we can translate its general terms into examples of the present day and substitute them in some vital way for the examples it itself gives, so concrete, so intimately involved in the circumstances of the day in which it was conceived and written." Wilson's condescension towards the Founding documents and thorough disdain is made abundantly clear in his statements. The Constitution was fine for its time, The Declaration of Independence has no use unless it can be adopted to fit our current needs.

The Constitution begins with "We the People"…and was designed to "form a more perfect union" and "secure the blessings of liberty to ourselves and our posterity." Two of the broad objectives of the Constitution are to provide safety and security, "insure domestic tranquility" and "provide for the common defense." These broad objectives were also designed to promote and foster prosperity under the rule of law, "establish justice" and "promote the general welfare." The Constitution is a statement of purpose and remains as relevant today as it was in 1787. There is nothing obsolete or irrelevant within the document. Wilson viewed the Constitution as stagnant because it was based upon these static and fixed truths. The

Constitution was structured so that government derives its power from the consent of the governed. This was an anathema to Wilson who viewed government as a top down structure. The Founders believed in unalienable rights, Wilson and progressives believed that government dispenses our rights. The Founders believed the strength of a republic relied upon a well informed electorate. Progressives relied upon an uninformed electorate.

Wilson's legacy includes but is not limited to the following: Amendment XVI, Amendment XVII, Amendment XVIII, Espionage Act of 1917, Sedition Act of 1918, Federal Reserve, League of Nations. These policies exemplify Wilson's elitism, narcissism, condescension and utter disdain for our Founders. Wilson believed in the beneficent hand of social engineering; he believed we needed to progress past our founding documents as they were obsolete. In his own words:

> *"Remember that God ordained that I should be the next president of the United States. Neither you nor any other mortal or mortals could have prevented this."*
>
> **Woodrow Wilson**

> *"While we are followers of Jefferson, there is one principle of Jefferson's which no longer can obtain in the practical politics of America. You know that it was Jefferson who said that the best government is that which does as little governing as possible...but that time has passed. America is not now and cannot in the future be a place for unrestricted individual enterprise."*
>
> **Woodrow Wilson**

> *"The people of the United States do not wish to curtail the activities of this Government; they wish, rather, to enlarge them; and with every enlargement, with the mere growth, indeed, of the country itself, there must come, of course, the inevitable increase of expense...it is not*

> *expenditure but extravagance that we should fear being*
> *criticized for."* [18]
>
> **Woodrow Wilson**

The aforementioned quotes put Wilson's elitism and governing philosophy into context. The following policies do the same.

AMENDMENT *XVI*
RATIFIED FEBRUARY 3, 1913

The Congress shall have the power to lay and collect taxes on incomes, from whatever source derived, without apportionment among the several States, and without regard to any census or enumeration. [19]

Signed by Wilson into law on October 3, 1913, it was used as a means to grow revenue and later as an excuse to fund WWI. The goal of Wilson in the end was the redistribution of wealth. At this laws inception, 98% of Americans were exempt. Within a few short years the top rate for the wealthy increased to 77%. Prior to the 16th Amendment, our government generally relied upon duties, excise taxes and land sales as a means of revenue. This limited source of revenues was designed to limit the power and scope of the federal government. The nefarious legacy of the 16th Amendment is that of a progressive tax system, which is the second principle of the Communist Manifesto. With an increased source of revenue via the new tax code the federal government was free to pursue its goal of wealth redistribution and social justice. By punishing the most productive in society via the new tax law, the 16th Amendment led to a growth in central government. Under Wilson the gross domestic product did increase by 126%, unfortunately our National Debt grew by an incredible 722% despite tax increases. [20]

AMENDMENT XVII
RATIFIED APRIL 8, 1913

The Senate of the United States shall be composed of two Senators from each state, elected by the people thereof, for six years; and each Senator shall have one vote. The electors in each State shall have the qualifications requisite for electors of the most numerous branch of the State legislatures.

When vacancies happen in the representation of any State in the Senate, the executive authority of such State shall issue writs of election to fill such vacancies: Provided, That the legislature of any State may empower the executive thereof to make temporary appointments until the people fill the vacancies by election as the legislature may direct.

This amendment shall not be so construed as to affect the election or term of any Senator chosen before it becomes valid as part of the Constitution. [21]

Article 1, section 1, paragraph 1 of the Constitution provides for the makeup of Congress. The Congress will consist of two chambers, one upper and one lower. The House of Representatives are the lower house and represent the people. The Senate is the upper house and represents the States. This was designed as a checks and balance on legislative power. The House of Representatives elected by the people was balanced against the Senate, elected by state legislatures. The House represents the many (i.e. masses), the Senate represents the few (i.e. the states). This formed a balance of power or double security between the House and Senate.

The 17th Amendment provided for the popular election of Senators by the people, identical to that of Congressman. This eliminated the balance of power and virtually eliminated the sovereign power of the States, as they no longer had someone in Washington to protect their rights and sovereignty. The legacy of the 17th Amendment permanently usurped the rights of the States and undermines the inherent genius of the Framers & Founders intent, one of balanced powers. This balance of power was designed with the purpose of slowing down the legislative process by the very balance of powers enumerated in Article 1.

> *"The legislative body should be divided into two branches, in order that the people might have a double security..."* [22]
>
> *James Iredell*

> *"In the legislature, promptitude of decision is oftener an evil than a benefit. The distinction of opinion, and the jarring of parties in that department of government, though they may sometimes obstruct salutary plans, yet often promote deliberation and circumspection, and serve to check excesses in the majority."* [23]
>
> *Alexander Hamilton*

> *"The accumulation of all powers, legislative, executive, and judiciary, in the same hands, whether of one, a few, or many, and whether hereditary, self appointed, or elective, may justly be pronounced the very definition of tyranny."* [24]
>
> *James Madison*

AMENDMENT *XVIII*
PROHIBITION
RATIFIED JANUARY *16*, *1919*

Section 1. After one year from the ratification of this article the manufacture, sale or transportation of intoxicating liquors within, the importation thereof into, or the exportation thereof from the United States and all territory subject to the jurisdiction thereof for beverage purposes is hereby prohibited.

Section 2. The Congress and the States shall have concurrent power to enforce this article by appropriate legislation.

Section 3. This article shall be inoperative unless it shall have been ratified as an amendment to the Constitution by the legislatures of the several States, as provided in the Constitution, within seven years from the date of the submission hereof to the States by the Congress. [25]

The 18th Amendment is one of the best examples of reform, social engineering, or "noble experiments" as Progressives would describe it. Not only was Prohibition viewed as reform, it was sold to the public as patriotic. Anti-German sentiment was rampant following WWI, as many domestic breweries were owned by German families (i.e. Pabst, Busch, Piels). Like many Progressive reform measures, Prohibition was "well intended but ill advised." The 18th Amendment drove the liquor business underground, led to rampant corruption, placed enormous stress on law enforcement and helped facilitate the growth of organized crime in this country. The Democrats actually split between "Wets" and "Drys." The "Wets" looked to repeal Prohibition, the "Dry" were advocates of the amendment. The leading proponent of the "Drys" was Wilson's Treasury Secretary who would become Wilson's son-in-law, William MacAdoo.[26] The 18th Amendment also strained relations both north and south of the border as bootleg was transported from Mexico and Canada. [27] Prohibition was an abysmal failure and was finally repealed on December 5, 1933. Its legacy was that of uncontrolled graft and crime.

ESPIONAGE ACT OF *1917* & SEDITION ACT OF *1918*

The irony of Progressives (i.e. liberals) is their supposed fidelity to liberty. When in truth Progressives are nothing but totalitarian. No better proof exists than the Espionage Act of 1917 and the Sedition Act of 1918. These acts made it illegal to profess any and all criticism of the government whether in public or private. Any breach of this could earn one a lengthy prison sentence. Tens of thousands were arrested during Wilson's administration by the Department of Justice for such actions. The following quote is found in a letter issued by the Wilson administration addressed to U. S Attorneys with regard to criticism by the general public "...Obey the law; keep your mouth shut." The Justice Department actually created a separate branch called the APL or American Protective League. The APL was in charge of cracking down on "seditious street oratory." [28] Amendment I of the Constitution guarantees the Freedom of Religion, Speech the Press and Assembly and Petition. Furthermore, Congress shall make no law...abridging the freedom of speech, or of the press, or the right of the people to assemble, and to petition the Government for a redress of grievances. Wilson's Espionage and Sedition Acts are as far removed from the 1st Amendment and the intent of the Founders as possible.

The Sedition Act actually banned "uttering, printing, writing, or publishing any disloyal, profane, scurrilous, or abusive language about the United States government or the military." Like Germany under Bismarck, the Wilson administration utilized propaganda especially aimed at our children. The Committee on Public Information (i.e. CPI) under Wilson, issued the following pledge children were asked to sign; titled *A Little American's Promise*, which proclaims:

> *At table I'll not leave a scrap*
> *Of food upon my plate,*
> *And I'll not eat between meals but*
> *For supper time I'll wait.*
> *I make that promise that I'll do*
> *My honest, earnest part*
> *In helping my America*
> *With all my loyal heart*

For children to young to read, the following proclamation was issued:

> *Little Boy Blue, come blow your horn!*
> *The cook's using wheat where she ought to use corn*
> *And terrible famine our country will sweep,*
> *If the cooks and the housewives remain fast asleep!*
> *Go wake them! Go wake them! It's now up to you!*
> *Be a loyal American, Little Boy Blue!* [29]

Targeting children for propaganda was the same tactic used by Bismarck in Germany with the implementation of kindergarten. Wilson himself believed that education should serve to make children as unlike their fathers as possible. One of the tenets of any totalitarian regime is propaganda aimed at children. Wilson himself believed that … "government's goal is to polish the apple before it falls from the tree, to make children as unlike their fathers as possible…" [30]

41

FEDERAL RESERVE ACT *1913*

The Federal Reserve Act was a knee-jerk reaction to the financial panic of 1907. This panic, preceded by those in 1873, 1884, 1890 and 1893, was facilitated by banks inability to convert deposits into currency, or a run on banks. The Federal Reserve was designed as a hedge on bank runs (i.e. providing banks with liquidity) and as a backup to the gold standard, which was prevalent throughout the world. By the end of WWI, many countries dropped the gold standard in favor of central banks. This elevated the Federal Reserve to one of financial authority in this country, giving it discretionary power over the US monetary quantity. This created a ripple effect throughout the world's financial markets. [31] Another example of a well intended policy that was ill advised. The legacy of the Federal Reserve; in 1913 one $20 bill could buy one $20 gold piece. Today, it would take 50 $20 bills to buy the same $20 gold piece. Instead of safeguarding our currency, the dollar has lost 98% of its value courtesy of the Federal Reserve.

The Federal Reserve was designed to be the "lender of last resort" which would be controlled by Congress and facilitate financial stability. In effect, the Federal Reserve issued fiat money. Fiat currency is not backed by either gold or silver. It is simply a piece of paper backed only by the word of the government or central back that issues it. Under Article 1, Section 8, Clause 5 of the Constitution, "The people of the states empower the Congress to coin money and regulate the value thereof and also of foreign coins," "The people of the states empower Congress to fix the standard of weights and measures." [32] These provisions were enacted to prevent the federal government from printing paper money (i.e. fiat or bills of credit). The Founders were adamantly opposed to fiat money (i.e. paper currency) due to the Continental dollars. These were issued during the Revolutionary war and eventually used by the English to flood the colonies with counterfeit dollars. Inflation made the Continentals worthless. The same situation occurred during the Civil War when Congress issued greenbacks (i.e. fiat money). Once again, the money supply was inflated, counterfeiting was rampant and the dollar lost its value.

These two situations are precisely why the Founders were so adamantly opposed to the issuance of paper (i.e. fiat) money. To put this into perspective and to clarify the fears of our Founders, from 1789 – 1913 the dollar's value increased by 13%. With the inception of the Federal Reserve, from 1913 on, the value of the dollar has decreased by an astonishing 93%.[33] Again the Federal Reserve was established to offer liquidity to banks. Unfortunately it evolved into the primary arbiter of our nation's money supply. Eventually usurping the power vested in Congress under Article 1, Section 8, Clause 5 of the Constitution. The formation of the Federal Reserve occurred in 1910 by covert means with representatives from financial titans Morgan, Rockefeller and Rothschild. To quote Wilson after he signed the Federal Reserve into law, the Act would "supplant the dictatorship of the private banking institutions" as well as "stabilize the inflexibility of the national bank notes." [34] The Federal Reserve would exist as a private entity and would be answerable to Congress. However, the federal government itself would not have an equity position within the Reserve itself.

The Federal Reserve has morphed into a private entity vested with the power to control our nation's money supply (usurping the power of Congress). Although it is obligated to report to Congress twice each year, the federal government has no auditing power over the Federal Reserve. In effect, the Fed Chairman can tell Congress anything he/she wants with immunity as Congress is powerless to substantiate the claims. [35] As the Federal Reserve charges the federal government interest on each note it prints, notes printed from thin air, the Fed is incentivized to print money in spite of the fact this fiat currency is backed by nothing. The legacy of the Federal Reserve, well intended but ill advised, is pernicious to say the least. Although the original intent was to ensure Reserve notes would be redeemable in gold, this lasted only until 1933. From 1934 onwards, the Federal Reserve promised to redeem the notes in silver, than in 1973 the Reserve notes were not redeemable in any precious metals. At this point our dollar was declared "legal tender" in 1973 by Congress, backed by nothing more than the word of the government. Since 1973, our currency has fluctuated in the world market and traded like any other commodity. [36]

Article 1, Section 8, Clause 5 of the Constitution was added to avoid precisely what the Federal Reserve Act created, which is fiat money. Wilson allowed Congress in 1913 to procreate a deal with private bankers that essentially usurps the power of Congress and vests all power in our nation's money supply in the hands of private bankers. Bankers, who in their own self interest make money by printing worthless notes. The resultant inflation drives up the cost of consumer products and devalues our own savings, 401K plans, etc...Our Founders warned against this practice, which facilitated Article 1, Section 8, Clause 5 of the Constitution. Noted economist F. A Hayek also warned against this practice, "To put it in the hands of an institution which is protected against competition, which can force us to accept the money, which is subject to incessant political pressure, such an authority will never give us good money." [37] Another legacy of the Federal Reserve Act was its action, or more appropriately, inaction during the crash of 1929. The Reserve was designed to prevent a major contraction by pumping liquidity into banks and providing stability during a systemic run. The Federal Reserve sat idly by during the 1929 crash which precipitated the Great Depression. The Reserve could have prevented the massive contraction by simply providing liquidity, which was exactly the sole purpose for its existence; Progressive policies at their best...

THE LEAGUE OF NATIONS

Wilson addressed Congress in January 1918 and proposed his "Fourteen Points" plan for peace. The "Fourteen Points" was Wilson's view of international life after WWI. This view included a "peace without victory." Wilson called for peace without punitive measures taken against Germany. Wilson described his Fourteen Points as "The program of the world's peace, therefore, is our program; and that program, the only possible program, as we see it." The Fourteenth and final Point was "A general association of nations must be formed under specific covenant for the purpose of affording mutual guarantees of political independence and territorial integrity to great and small nations alike." [38] European leaders did not, however, agree with Wilson and rejected his Fourteen Points at Paris. The Fourteen Points were as polarizing at home as they were abroad. TR described the Fourteen Points as "fourteen scraps of paper." Fourteen Senators comprised of both Democrats and Republicans formed the "irreconcilables" that opposed Wilson's call for a League of Nations. The Fourteen Points offered by Wilson was an armistice that did not include unconditional surrender. European leaders as well as TR called for unconditional surrender.

Wilson called for a "peace without victory;" European leaders disagreed and settled on a vengeful peace through The Treaty of Versailles. Although his Fourteen Points were rejected at home and abroad, The Treaty of Versailles did include the League of Nations Covenant. The League of Nations represented Wilson's idealistic view of a global government and global police force. Part of the League of Nations covenant included Article X which allowed The League to commit US troops to foreign wars without Congressional approval. Wilson agreed with this, Congress did not. After a lengthy battle, Congress finally voted to reject The Treaty, which included The League of Nations covenant. [39] Wilson's Fourteen Points, particularly

XIV, and his cherished League of Nations was nothing more than a Progressive attempt to circumvent the Constitution and cede U.S. sovereignty to global governance.

There are common traits that bind together all elitists: arrogance, condescension and dismissiveness. Whether it's Progressivism (i.e. liberalism), Fascism, National Socialism or Communism, another common denominator shared by the statist is an inherent lust for power. In his book *Congressional Government,* Wilson states his view on power, "I cannot imagine power as a thing negative and not positive." Wilson often referred to the masses as 'tools' or 'clay', to be molded by those in power. Wilson also invoked the name of God while president stating that opposition to his agenda was tantamount to blasphemy. Wilson saw himself as the right hand of God. [40] Another trait Wilson shared with TR was his views on race. Wilson is alleged to have said, "It is like writing history with lightening"… "and my only regret is that it is all so terribly true." These statements attributed to Wilson came after viewing The Birth of a Nation in 1915, which was a pro KKK movie. Wilson's alleged endorsement was used by the KKK to revive their movement.

Aside from his words, Wilson's action like those of TR speaks volumes. In 1906, TR discharged without honor 167 blacks who were members of the 25th infantry regiment. The black soldiers were being framed in a murder, TR sat idly by until after the current election cycle. Only than did TR issue his dishonorable discharge notice for all 167 soldiers. Wilson himself was no less a bigot during his tenure as president. Upon taking office Wilson replaced 15 of 17 blacks within the administration with whites. He also replaced black ambassadors to Haiti and Santo Domingo with whites as well as issuing orders to the Treasury to segregate their departments. [41] When viewed in totality, Wilson's tenure as president was an abysmal failure and a sad legacy to say the least. Amendment XVI, XVII, XVIII, Espionage and Sedition Acts, Federal Reserve, League of

Nations, his record on national debt and race leave nothing to be desired.

THE "WISE & KNOWLEDGEABLE FEW"

The presidencies of TR and Wilson were swayed by many of the same influential voices. With the exception of a few additions, the following list of enlightened despots is identical to that which influenced TR. Included in the list are those that were ardent supporters of both TR and Wilson. Unlike Roosevelt, Wilson was motivated by pure ideology as he was a true believer in the Progressive movement and the need for a centrally planned existence governed by the intellectual minority.

Jane Addams (1860-1935) Social worker, ardent feminist, peace activist…founder of Hull House in Chicago 1898 to serve the underprivileged. Hull House based on the settlement houses of London's East End. Awarded Nobel Peace Prize in 1931. [42]

Senator Albert Beveridge (1862-1927) Chief senatorial ally of TR, chief progressive within senate. Unsuccessful Progressive candidate for governor of Indiana 1912, chairman of National Progressive Convention in Chicago 1912, unsuccessful Progressive candidate for US Senate 1914…as chair of 1912 convention stated "God has marked us as His chosen people, henceforth to lead in the regeneration of the world." [43]

Edward L. Bernays (1891-1995) Nephew of Sigmund Freud… master of propaganda, father of public relations. Combined political persuasion and advertising to construct "necessary illusions…filtered to the masses as "reality." Appointed to the Committee on Public Information by Wilson in 1917. Instrumental in swaying public opinion during WWI, provided Wilson with PR methods that facilitated "social persuasion and control." CPI utilized techniques that disseminated propaganda on large scale...typically used by totalitarian regimes. The CPI was instrumental in passing the Espionage Act of 1917 and the Sedition Act of 1918. CPI enjoyed censorship power...and was used by Wilson to manipulate the collective attitudes. Bernays served as press officer for Wilson in Europe following WWI. Author of *Crystallizing Public Opinion* (1923) and *Propaganda* (1928). Joseph Goebbels adopted Bernays techniques for Nazi propaganda. [44]

Otto Von Bismarck (1815-1898) "Iron Chancellor" who founded the German Empire in 1871. Introduced social legislation (i.e. social welfare) that introduced accident insurance, old age insurance and socialized medicine. Transformed Germany into the foremost military and industrial power in Europe. Exported progressive ideal (i.e. Bismarckian welfare) to America. Bismarck was a centralizer a uniter and viewed as a European Lincoln. Bismarck introduced top down socialism to Germany. This philosophy incorporated many of the entitlements progressives advocate: welfare state program, pensions, health insurance, eight-hour work days, etc...[45]

William Jennings Bryan (1860-1925) Ran for president 1896, 1900, 1908...Secretary of State 1912 under Wilson, resigned in protest 1915. Reformer, liberal, advocate of income tax (16th Amendment), popular election of senators (17th Amendment), Depart of Labor, Prohibition (18th Amendment), woman's suffrage. Defended creationism in 1925 Scope Monkey Trial vs. Clarence Darrow. [46]

George Creel (1876-1953) Appointed by Wilson to spearhead the Committee on Public Information (CPI), the propaganda arm of Wilson administration during WWI. Aim was to garner public support for Wilson's entry into WWI. Recruited approx. 75,000 individuals who gave approx. 7.5 million speeches throughout the country during the war years. The 75,000 were called "Four Minute Men", which was reference to the average attention span of most individuals. Ran against Upton Sinclair for governorship of California. [47]

Herbert Croly (1869-1930) Intellectual leader of Progressive movement. Created "New Nationalism" philosophy, founder of progressive magazine *New Republic*, author of *The Promise of American Life* in 1909, which influenced TR as well as FDR. TR based his "New Nationalism" on Croly's progressive philosophy. Opposed the industrial society, advocated for "constructive discrimination" (i.e. redistribution of wealth) whereby the "weak" would be favored. Advocate of big government controlling big business. Actively promoted a strong central government, labor unions and nationalization of business. Wished for the eradication of individual liberties, opponent of small business and non-union workers. Authored *Progressive Democracy* in 1915, which espoused the Constitution as a living (i.e. Darwinism) document with no fixed truths. Thought the Constitution was obsolete as written and needed to evolve to fit the social issues of the time. [48]

Charles Darwin (1809-1882) Part of scientific expedition on HMS Beagle in 1831. Collaborated with Alfred Russell Wallace on evolution theory in 1858 and published *On the Origin of Species* in 1859. Darwin postulated evolution orthodoxy over creationism. Progressives used Darwinism (i.e. evolving) as analogous to government. Progressives viewed the Constitution as a living document that evolves with no fixed truths. The Constitution is static, progressives viewed government as dynamic and evolving. [49]

Eugene V. Debs (1855-1926) Prominent socialist early 20th century... organized American Railway Union 1893, jailed 1894 for his part in Pullman strike. Read works by Karl Marx while imprisoned, helped to form Social Democratic Party in 1897, ran for president in 1900 as SDP candidate. Later ran for president as candidate for the Socialist Party of America, which grew out of the SDP. Helped create the International Workers of the World movement. Arrested a second time in 1918 following his disparaging remarks over WWI and the Wilson administration. Debs felt WWI was motivated strictly by capitalism. Arrested under the provisions of The Espionage act of 1917, which made it illegal to speak out against the Wilson administration. Final run for presidency under the Socialist Party of America in 1920 while imprisoned at Atlanta Federal Penitentiary. [50]

John Dewey (1859-1952) Student of philosophy at Johns Hopkins University (i.e. founded in 1867 as Progressive institution) where he earned his doctorate. Influenced by the writings of Karl Marx, co-author of *The Communist Manifesto*. Founder of Progressive education movement. Founding member of NAACP, and ACLU. Early member of Socialist Party of America and Progressive Party. Promoted alternatives to capitalism, which he felt was obsolete and cruel. [51]

Richard T. Ely (1854-1943) Progressive economist educated at Columbia and University of Heidelberg in Germany. Taught at Johns Hopkins University and the University of Wisconsin. Founder of American Economic Association, helped create Wisconsin's progressive program of social reform legislation. Had great influence on TR. Advocated government ownership of public utilities, social reforms, labour movement, cooperative commonwealth, etc…Stated, "God works through the State in carrying out His purposes more universally than through any other institution." Authored many books and articles including, *Recent American Socialism* in 1885, *Social Aspects of Christianity* in1889 and *Socialism and Social Reform* in 1894. [52]

Friedrich Engels (1820-1895) Authored *Condition of the Working Class* in 1844 based upon cotton factory work in England. Contributor in 1844 to radical journal, *Franco-German Annals* which was edited by Karl Marx. He and Marx developed friendship based upon mutual hatred of capitalism. Established the Communist Correspondence Committee in 1846 with Marx. Delegate to Communist League conference in London. Aim of Communist League was to overthrow the bourgeoisie, domination of the proletariat, abolish old bourgeois society based on class antagonisms, establish society void of classes and private property. Published *The Communist Manifesto* with Karl Marx in 1848. *The Manifesto* formulated a coming revolution and a society that would be established by the proletariat. According to Engels and Marx, the bourgeoisie were the owners of the factories and raw materials. The proletariat had very little and was forced to sell their labor to the capitalists. Expelled from Belgium with Marx following *The Manifesto* release. Co-founder of radical newspaper *New Rhenish Gazette* in Cologne. Continued life's work with Marx in London until their deaths. [53]

Washington Gladden (1836-1918) Minister, local politician, social reformer...prominent voice of early 20th century Progressive movement. Like his fellow Progressives, Gladden was quite intolerant of others with dissenting points of view. Helped to enact temperance laws in Columbus as city council member, 1900-1902. [54]

Samuel Gompers (1850-1924) Born in London...moved to America in 1863. Early labor leader, first member of Cigarmakers International Union 1864, elected president in 1875. Organized the Federation of Organized Trades and Labor in 1881...reorganized in 1886 as the American Federation of Labor, served as president 1886-1924. Conservative and accepted capitalism...distanced himself from the Industrial Workers of the World, which fought to abolish capitalism.

Appointed by Wilson to the Advisory Council of National Defense 1917-1919. Appointed by Wilson to Commission on International Labor Legislation at Versailles Peace Conference. John L. Lewis formed the Committee for Industrial Organizations within the AFL in 1935. The two merged in 1955 to form the AFL-CIO. [55]

G.W.F. Hegel (1770-1831) Prominent German philosopher... influenced both Marx and Engels. Supporter of French Revolution... aim was to establish conceptual framework of philosophy, which encompassed his own beliefs as well as past philosophers. Right wing Hegelians were Christians...left wing Hegelians were atheist and included Marx and Engels. Final publication was *Philosophy of Right* (1821). Progressives based their belief in the organic state from the teachings of Hegel. Progressive's belief in the state as god based upon Hegel's *Philosophy of History*. Wilson used quotes from *Philosophy of Right* by Hegel in speeches. [56]

Johns Hopkins (1795-1873) Made fortune in the Baltimore and Ohio Railroad. Founded The Johns Hopkins University and The Johns Hopkins Hospital in 1867. The university founded specifically to teach progressive thought. The University staffed with professors schooled in Germany during Bismarck's reign. [57]

Intercollegiate Socialist Society (ISS) (1905-1921) Formed in New York 1905 to support and spread socialist ideas on college campuses. Founded by Upton Sinclair, who also served as vice president, and included fellow progressives Jack London (president), Clarence Darrow, Harry Laidler et al. The ISS was byproduct of socialist club formed in 1901 at University of Wisconsin Madison and the Social Progress Club in 1905 at the University of California Berkeley. ISS spread throughout college campuses preaching the "New Gospel according to St. Marx." Renamed The League for Industrial Democracy in 1921. LID morphed into the Students for a Democratic Society (SDS) in Port Huron, Michigan 1960. Stated purpose of ISS was to "throw light on the world-wide movement of industrial democracy known as socialism." [58]

Robert LaFollette (1855-1925) As governor of Wisconsin in 1891 implemented his "Wisconsin Ideas" which became foundation of the Progressive movement. Founded *Lafollette's Weekly Magazine* in 1909 and the National Progressive Republican League in 1911 to advocate progressive ideas. Pushed for progressive reform as US Senator and ran unsuccessfully in 1924 presidential race on Progressive ticket. [59]

Harry Wellington Laidler (1884-1970) Economist and Socialist leader early 20th century…educated at Columbia. Founding member of ISS and secretary from 1910-1921. Served as executive director of League for Industrial Democracy 1921-1957. Socialist candidate for numerous public offices. [60]

Vladimir Lenin (1870-1924) Brother Aleksandr executed for his role in the assassination attempt on Emperor Alexander III. Lenin grew more rebellious at this time while attending college and upon graduation joined a group of Marxist revolutionaries. Part of Russian Social Democratic Party, which was split between two parties: the Bolsheviks (radical Red Russians) and Mensheviks (moderate White Russians). Led Bolshevik split from Mensheviks in 1912 and into the 1917 Bolshevik Revolution. Lenin's Bolshevik Revolution promoted and financially backed by Germany. The irony here is that Russia would come to occupy Germany during WWII. "He who digs a pit will fall into it." Proverbs 26:27. Lenin denied the power of God, was an advocate of "collective rule" and "centralized power," and avowed anti-capitalist. Russian Communist Party responsible for tens of millions of deaths as well as the destruction of over 70,000 churches. [61]

Walter Lippman (1889-1974) Ardent supporter of Roosevelt, Wilson and the Progressive Party. Socialist and co-founder of the Harvard Socialist Club...close friends with John Reed, author of *Ten Days that Shook the World*. Reed buried at Kremlin Wall with fellow Bolshevik heroes. Worked as Lincoln Steffens secretary in 1911, authored *A Preface to Politics* in 1913, joined with Herbert Croly and Walter Weyl to found New Republic. Worked as assistant to Wilson's Secretary of War...assistant to Wilson in drafting Fourteen Points Peace Programme. Member of Wilson's delegation to Paris Peace Conference in 1919...assisted Wilson with League of Nations covenant. [62]

Jack London (1876-1916) Converted to socialism at early age after reading *The Communist Manifesto*...known as boy socialist of Oakland. Mayoral candidate of Oakland on Socialist ticket 1901. Worked with the Social Democratic Federation in London 1902. Member of American Socialist Party and joined the ISS in 1905, served as President. Ardent supporter of TR. [63]

Karl Marx (1818-1883) Influential socialist thinker of the 19th century who advocated the revolutionary overthrow of capitalism. Emigrated to France in 1843 whereby he became a communist and developed life long friendship with Friedrich Engels. Both Marx and Engels expelled from Paris in 1844, moved to Brussels and published *The German Ideology*, predicting the collapse of industrial capitalism while being replaced by communism. Published *The Communist Manifesto* in 1848 with Engels. Sought refuge in London in 1849, where he remained until his death. Published *Capital* in 1867, which again advocated for and predicted the collapse of industrial capitalism. Described by Engels during eulogy, as a revolutionist whose mission in life was to contribute to the overthrow of the capitalist society and to liberate/emancipate the modern proletariat. [64]

William Gibbs McAdoo (1863-1941) U.S. Senator, Secretary of Treasury under Wilson 1913-1918…member of first Federal Reserve Board. Married Wilson's daughter 1914…Ran for Democratic nomination for President in 1920 and 1924, endorsed by KKK in 1924. Part of "Dry" Democrats who supported Prohibition. [65]

Benito Mussolini (1883-1945) Moved to Switzerland in 1902 due to poor employment prospects in Italy. Became involved with socialist politics during his stay, returned to Italy in 1904 and joined the socialist press. Broke with the socialist and formed the Fascist Party in 1919. Organized the "Black Shirts" of 1921 which served as armed squads that terrorized political opponents. Self-proclaimed dictator of Italy in 1925, with the support of "Black Shirts." Ruled through strong state control and took the title "Il Duce." Formed Pact of Steel with Nazi Germany in 1939 and allied with Germany and Japan during WWII. [66]

Walter Rauschenbusch (1861-1918) The preeminent prophet for Social Gospel during the Progressive Era. Ordained in 1886 as pastor in New York's infamous Hell's Kitchen where he formulated his views that questioned laissez-faire capitalism. Formulated theology of Christian socialism and authored *Christianity and the Social Crisis, Christianizing the Social Order, A Theology for the Social Gospel* and *Prayers for the Social Awakening.* [67]

John Reed (1887-1920) American journalist and poet, born in Oregon to a wealthy family whose father was a great admirer of TR. After traveling abroad, Reed began his journalist career at leftist magazines, *New Review* and *The Masses.* Organized several strikes on behalf of labor movements. Covered the Mexican Revolution for *Metropolitan Magazine* and *World.* Authored *Insurgent Mexico* in 1914 after spending months with Pancho Villa covering the Mexican Revolution. Covered WWI for *Metropolitan Magazine* and authored

The War in Eastern Europe in 1916. Traveled to St. Petersburg and covered the Bolshevik Revolution for *The Masses*. Reed was close personal friends with Lenin, identified himself with the Bolshevik movement and was pro-Communist. Wrote for *The New Communist, Voice of Labour* in 1919. Authored *Ten Days That Shook the World* in 1920 which chronicled the Bolshevik Revolution. Died, buried and honored in Russia as Bolshevik hero. John Reed clubs established throughout United States in his honor. [68]

Margaret Sanger (1883-1966) Feminist, women's rights activist, member of Socialist Party with fellow Progressives John Reed, Upton Sinclair, Eugene Debs, Norman Thomas, et al. Founded American Birth-Control League, co-founder of Workers Birth Control Group. Advocate of eugenics. [69]

Upton Sinclair (1878-1968) American novelist, described by TR as "muckraking journalist." Ardent reader of socialist classics and read the socialist weekly *Appeal to Reason*. Member of socialist party and board member of ACLU. Published novel *The Jungle* in 1906, which chronicled the life of an immigrant who is exploited by Chicago stockyard owners. TR received 100 letters per day demanding reforms. Subsequent legislation, Pure Food and Drug Act 1906, was direct result of Sinclair's novel. Sinclair established the socialist commune Helicon Home Colony in New Jersey, which served as a commune for left wing writers. Published novel *Boston* in 1928, which was sympathetic to anarchists Sacco and Vanzetti. Ran unsuccessfully as socialist for governor of California in 1934. Ardent believer in socialism until his death in 1968. [70]

Joseph Stalin (1879-1953) As a young man, was sent to a seminary in Tbilisi by mother, to study to become a priest. Stalin dropped out of seminary study and chose revolutionary circles instead. Stalin was a hands on revolutionary unlike Lenin and Trotsky who were the intellectual leaders, often living abroad. Stalin held a life long distrust of educated intellectuals. Appointed to General Secretary of the Communists Party Central Committee in 1922. Following Lenin's death in 1924, Stalin became de facto leader as a result of his purging as General Secretary. Stalin continued to "purge" the Soviet Union of its founding fathers (i.e. Trotsky) and labeled them enemies of the people. Anyone with higher education suspected of being a threat to the revolution. He forced collectivized agriculture which reduced millions to serfs once again. [71]

Lincoln Steffens (1866-1936) Most famous of the American muckraker journalists from 1903-1910. Born to wealth in California, educated at the University of California Berkeley. Subsequent education in Germany and France. Returned to America and began writing for the *New York Evening Post*, became editor of *McClure's Magazine*. Articles *The Shame of St. Louis* and *The Shame of Minneapolis* brought him fame. Derided by President Theodore Roosevelt as "muckrake" journalism. Wrote articles supporting radical revolutionaries following the Mexican Revolution in 1910. Viewed American capitalism as a corrupting factor and capitalism as a whole as causing social corruption. Admired the Bolshevik Revolution and following his travels to Russia stated; "I have seen the future, and it works." Advocated for a Communist revolution to "save" the United States. [72]

Ida Tarbell (1867-1944) One of the muckraking journalists of the early 20th century. Authored 19 part series for *McClure's Magazine* 1902-1904, *The History of the Standard Oil Company*. Series was expose on Standard Oil and Rockefeller's business practices... described by Tarbell as "open disregard of decent ethical business practices by capitalists." Described Rockefeller as "money mad"...a "hypocrite"…and "our national life is on every side distinctly poorer, uglier, meaner, for the kind of influence he exercises." [73]

Norman Thomas (1884-1968) Politician, social reformer, joined Socialist Party 1915, co-founder of ACLU, served as co-director for League for Industrial Democracy (founded as ISS) from 1922-1937. Socialist candidate for mayoral race of New York 1925, for governor 1924 and U.S. president in 1928-1948. Studied political science at Princeton during Woodrow Wilson's tenure as professor. Contributor to the Nation and World Tomorrow. [74]

Walter Weyl (1874-1919) Sympathetic to labor movement… assisted Robert Lafollette with research. Called for the redistribution of wealth, described personal wealth as social surplus. Described wealth as product of society and dismissed the notion of personal wealth. Authored *New Democracy* in 1912…assisted Herbert Croly and Walter Lippman with production of *New Republic* in 1914. [75]

CHAPTER 3
FRANKLIN DELANO ROOSEVELT
32ND PRESIDENT 1933-1945

One could argue that FDR was perhaps the worst president in our nation's history. Certainly there have been worse based upon shear incompetence (i.e. Carter, Obama). However, when viewed in terms of malicious behavior (i.e. attempts to pack the Supreme Court), record on unemployment, record on national debt, record on deficit spending, abuses of power (i.e. NRA), legacy of social security (i.e. trillions of unfunded liabilities), legacy of Fannie Mae, ceding Eastern Europe to Communism following WWII, arrogance, condescension, dismissiveness, etc...one would be hard pressed to find a president that was more damaging during his tenure and left behind a legacy that America is still digging out from than FDR. The following quotes provide a reasonable summary on FDR's legacy.

> *"...we have tried spending money. We are spending more than we have ever spent before and it does not work... We have never made good on our promise ...I say after eight years of this Administration we have just as much unemployment as when we started...and enormous debt to boot!"* [1]

> *Henry Morgenthau, Jr.*

> *"....thinking that doing more of the same will lead to a different outcome is a sign of insanity..."* [2]
>
> **Albert Einstein**

> *"The country needs and...demands bold, persistent experimentation. It is common sense to take a method and try it. If it fails, admit it frankly and try another. But above all, try something."* [3]
>
> **FDR**

Perhaps FDR and the country would have been better served if he had acknowledged Morgenthau, took the advice of Einstein or for that matter his own. Morgenthau was not a partisan Republican; he was in fact FDR's Treasury Secretary and part of FDR's brain trust in developing The New Deal agenda. Despite all evidence to the contrary, FDR, more often than not, is remembered as perhaps one of our greatest presidents. FDR ignored his own words and that of Einstein and continued his Progressive (i.e. New Deal) agenda throughout the 1930's despite all evidence suggesting it was not working. His own Treasury Secretary stated as much. Despite the abysmal failure of FDR policies, history, or more accurately, the liberal view of history, remembers FDR as a hero. *The American Pageant* describes FDR as a "gifted leader," one who was tapped on the shoulder by destiny. *The American Pageant* goes on to describe FDR's decisive action in implementing his New Deal agenda of "relief, recovery and reform." [4]

The American Pageant also describes FDR's "Hundred Days" as frantic but long overdue. The Hundred Days included the implementation of many Progressive entitlement programs. Entitlement programs that have saddled future generations with trillions of unfunded liabilities. The history book goes on to describe FDR as the "greatest of American conservatives, as both "Hamiltonian" and "Jeffersonian." [5] *The Pageant* describes FDR's balance sheet as "managing" the economy and providing "a fairer distribution of the national income," "balancing the human budget," averting the total collapse of the "American economic system," and "Demonstrating anew the value of powerful presidential power." [6] *The American Pageant* includes a quote by FDR from his acceptance speech at the Democratic convention in 1936, "Governments can err; presidents do make mistakes...but better the occasional faults of a Government that lives in a spirit of charity than the consistent omissions of a Government frozen in the ice of its own indifference." [7] Unfortunately, FDR's mindset is diametrically opposed to that on which the country was founded. Quoting Benjamin Franklin... "The Constitution guarantees us the right to pursue happiness', its up to us to catch it." This country was not founded on the premise that the federal government should serve as the "beneficent hand" (i.e. charity). The legacy of FDR is one of dependence which does nothing but lead to subservience.

The Century describes the tenure of FDR in terms of his "extraordinary accomplishments." [8] The book goes on to describe FDR as "...a buoyant, audacious spirit brimming with a captivating confidence..." Although FDR had no remedy, he provided "a supreme sense of confidence" and promised a "balanced budget and curb on government spending." *The Century* describes The New Deal administration as... "Intellectuals and social workers both, they were casting government anew, government as social engineer, executing Roosevelt's belief that the public sector not only had a mandate to dabble in the economy but was also charged with meeting people's social needs." Creative destruction, open markets, free trade and enterprise were being replaced by government management (i.e. central planning) under FDR. [9]

The legacy of FDR is based upon but not limited to the following accomplishments, or lack thereof: unemployment, TVA, CCC, NRA, WPA, social security, supreme court nominations, national debt, deficit spending, gold standard, Poland, etc...These "extraordinary accomplishments" are courtesy of the "buoyant" and "audacious" "intellectuals" that comprised the FDR administration.[10] The New Deal slogan is nothing but a euphemism for "priming the pump," "statism," "tax & spend," or as Judge Andrew Napolitano describes, the "legacy of lunacy." [11] The New Deal under FDR was the "hope and change" of the 1930's. During a 1932 convention speech, FDR is quoted "I pledge to you, I pledge myself to a new deal for the American people."[12] The "pledge" for a "new deal" is as non-specific and generic as "hope and change" was for Obama in 2008. Unfortunately, the American electorate bought into the non-specific pledge by FDR as they did for Obama in 2008. Another successful tactic the two politicians had in common was in blaming their predecessor. Another parallel between FDR and Obama, they both poured gasoline on a fire and made bad situations worse. To wit...

UNEMPLOYMENT

October 29, 1929 is known as "Black Thursday." On this day the Dow Jones Industrial Average drops from 261 to 230. Although substantial, a 12% loss was not historic when viewed in context of the 22% drop in 1987. Unfortunately, the way the loss in 1929 was handled or more accurately mishandled, led to a recession, subsequent election of FDR, 12 years of tyranny and a Great Depression. Just a little more than a month prior, the DOW actually hit an historic high at the time of 381. Many Progressives viewed the crash of 1929 as an indictment on the failures of capitalism. The 12% drop of 10/29/29 was nothing more than the market correcting itself. Hoover, and subsequently Roosevelt, took it upon themselves to implement the beneficent hand (i.e. central planning) of government which turned a slight recession into a Great Depression. This lack of faith in free enterprise was a strategic disaster for the United States. If the federal government under Hoover and FDR had not intervened, the US economy would have recovered and averted the Great Depression. Countries throughout the world saw their respective economies contract, however, unlike the United States they recovered much faster with much less government intervention.

President Calvin Coolidge was an ardent believer, as was his Treasury Secretary Andrew Mellon, in Adam Smith's philosophy of the invisible hand of government. This was opposed to the beneficent hand (i.e. central planning) that Hoover, FDR and fellow progressives believed in. Under Coolidge, unemployment never exceeded 5%, hit 3.2% in 1925 and actually dipped to the 1% range during his final years in office.[13] By the year's end of 1929 under Hoover, unemployment was hovering around the 5% mark.[14] By September of 1931, unemployment hit the 17% mark with the DOW hovering around 140. [15] By February of 1932 the DOW dropped to the 50's. Near the end of 1933, FDR's first year in office, the DOW was back up to around 93 but unemployment hit 23%. [16] FDR's record for unemployment from 1933-1940 was abysmal, which his own Treasury Secretary acknowledged. The numbers were, by any objective standard, horrific despite his pledge to create jobs:

- 1933 unemployment stood at 24.9%
- 1934 unemployment stood at 21.7%
- 1935 unemployment stood at 20.1%
- 1936 unemployment stood at 17.0%
- 1937 unemployment stood at 14.3%
- 1938 unemployment stood at 19.0%
- 1939 unemployment stood at 17.2%
- 1940 unemployment stood at 14.6% [17]

As part of his First Inaugural Address in 1933 FDR states, "Our greatest primary task is to put people to work. This is no unsolvable problem if we face it wisely and courageously." [18] FDR goes on to say the situation "...can be helped by national planning..." and "We must act, and act quickly." FDR also states, "I shall ask the Congress for the one remaining instrument to meet the crisis, broad executive power to wage a war against the emergency as great as the power that would be given me if we were in fact invaded by foreign foe." [19] Despite FDR seeking and being granted overreaching powers by Congress unemployment averaged 18.6% from 1933-1940. Despite FDR's own words in trying something and if it fails, admit it and move on, unemployment averaged 18.6% from 1933-1940. Despite the TVA, WPA, NRA, deficit spending, priming the pump, the frantic 'Hundred Days', et al...unemployment averaged 18.6% from 1933-1940. Despite this record of failed policies, FDR is lionized by the left in this country. Put into context, unemployment under George W. Bush averaged 5.25% from 2001-2009, yet the left depicts him as a failure.

GOLD STANDARD

Much of Europe was abandoning the gold standard during the 1920's. As a result, gold flooded the U.S. economy. The primary goal of the Federal Reserve and its reason for existence is to provide liquidity and stability, which would prevent a subsequent run on banks. In other words, the Fed's job is to prevent a major contraction of our economy. By 1931 the U.S. gold stock and gold reserves held by the Fed were at an all time high. Despite this, the Federal Reserve refused to pump cash into the economy which resulted in further contraction. [20] The Progressive argument for the Federal Reserve or any central bank for that matter is the need for government intervention. The intervention, or central planning, Progressives argue are necessary to mitigate the inherent instability of a private free enterprise economy, which by its very nature will have cycles of boom and bust. The mismanagement began under Hoover; FDR continued to mismanage the economy and turned a moderate contraction into a major catastrophe. [21] While Progressives will argue the Great Depression was an indictment on the free market system, the truth is the Great Depression was caused by government meddling and an abandonment of free market principles (i.e. self correction).

FDR began his experiment with gold not long after taking office in 1933. His goal was to reestablish a new international standard for gold after the U.S. dollar had reset itself. The truth is FDR and his brain trust were in over their collective heads. FDR manipulated gold prices on a whim; when asked why he raised the price of gold by 21 cents, FDR responded "It's a lucky number" and "because it's three times seven." Morgenthau himself said "If anybody knew how we really set the gold price through a combination of lucky numbers, etc., I think they would be frightened." [22] The worth of the U.S. dollar was set by the price of gold, which in turn set the price for whatever the dollar purchased. FDR experimented with the price of gold, took us off the gold standard, put us back on the gold standard, forced private citizens to sell their gold back to the U.S. government, invalidated the gold clause in private contracts by refusing to honor the governments own gold clause. The resultant effect of FDR's experiment (i.e. mismanagement) was a redistribution of wealth to the tune of $200 billion. [23]

The point here is not to make an argument for or against the gold standard, silver standard, bi-metal standard or any precious metal for that matter. The point here is that FDR and his 'brain trust' or more appropriately his "brain dead trust" had no clue on how to handle the economic situation in this country or the economic instability abroad. The experimentation and subsequent oscillation on behalf of the FDR administration made a weak U.S. dollar weaker, further contracted the ailing economy and turned a recession into a Great Depression. The very principle of a free market is its inherent ability to self correct. Unfortunately, The New Deal abandoned this free market principle in favor of a centrally planned economy (i.e. government intervention). The very premise of The New Deal is to advocate for bigger government. FDR and his fellow progressives viewed government as the answer, hence bigger is better. The handling or mishandling of the gold standard was based upon theory and in many cases, the whim of FDR. The New Deal approach to the economy was based upon Keynesianism, which advocated for experimentation and government spending (i.e. priming the pump). [24]

True to his Progressive roots, FDR did not let a serious crisis go to waste with regard to gold. Executive Order 6102 issue April 5, 1933 states: [25]

All persons are hereby required to deliver on or before May 1, 1933, to a Federal Reserve Bank or a branch or agency thereof or to any member bank now owned by them or coming into their ownership on or before April 28, 1933...

Whoever willfully violates any provision of this Executive Order or of these regulations or of any rule, regulation or license issued thereunder may be fined not more than $10,000, or if a natural person, may be imprisoned for not more than ten years, or both.

FDR's handling of gold was not part of any coherent strategic plan (i.e. vision). The on again off again gold standard and subsequent executive order was nothing more than experimentation. FDR himself is quoted as saying, "We seldom know, six weeks in advance, what we are going to do." [26]

CIVILIAN CONSERVATION CORPS

Passed by Congress March 29, 1933 to establish some 250,000 jobs for young men 18-25 and part of the infamous first 'Hundred Days' mandate. The CCC did put hundreds of thousands to work in some 1000 camps throughout the country. The CCC also created parks, bridges and roads, planted some 3 million trees and employed many that would have remained jobless save for the CCC. Although it had a stabilizing effect; the CCC was another example of throwing enough money, creating enough legislation to provide the illusion of recovery. The CCC was essentially make work subsidized by the federal government (i.e. taxpayers) and did not create private sector long-term employment. Unemployment leads to a drop in both salaries and prices. Unfortunately, the FDR 'brain dead trust' failed to acknowledge that government does not add value to the economy, it detracts value. [27] In short, the CCC was a band aid that did little if anything to address long term unemployment in the United States. It served to remove hundreds of thousands from the private workforce through the beneficent hand of social planners. [28] The CCC was eerily similar to 'youth camps' implemented by Hitler in Nazi Germany and Mussolini in Fascist Italy. [29] In fact, it was the Nazis who coined the phrase, 'work makes you free,' [30] or ARBEIT MACHT. [31]

TENNESSEE VALLEY AUTHORITY

Passed by Congress May 18, 1933. Implemented during the frantic and infamous 'Hundred Days' of the New Deal, the TVA was designed to produce jobs for dam construction; which would produce new cities, control flooding, and provide hydroelectric power. The Tennessee Valley region incorporates seven states and some 40,000 square miles through Tennessee, Kentucky, Georgia, Alabama, North Carolina, Virginia and Mississippi. [32] As part of The New Deal, the TVA was a public sector project designed to help an ailing economy. What the TVA actually did was to suppress capital within the private sector, in this case the private utilities company of Commonwealth and Southern and its subsidiary, Alabama Power. The TVA was based upon the mindset that utilities, particularly electricity was too valuable an asset to leave to the private sector. The only way to properly manage and distribute utilities, in this case electricity, was by government control. FDR was making the case that utilities could be run more efficiently by the public sector. FDR argued that the private sector was bereft of both capital and goodwill when it came to utilities. [33] The TVA was nothing more than a shining example of the right of the individual being usurped by that of the collective.

The TVA was another example of a progressive utopia, well intended but typically ill advised. The TVA promised to provide more Americans with electricity, lower the cost of electricity, raise our overall standard of living and form a more prosperous society. The TVA was a quintessential example of central planning by the intellectual few. The TVA was subsidized by public capital (i.e. taxpayers) and did not pay taxes which allowed it to out compete the private sector utilities. In essence creating a government monopoly and destroying private wealth by rendering shares in private utilities virtually worthless. [34] FDR actually had plans to expand the TVA throughout the country and designate regional capitals to manage and dispense utilities. Areas of the country under consideration were Philadelphia, Detroit, Baltimore, Cleveland, Cincinnati, Knoxville, Nashville, Atlanta, Chicago, St. Louis, New Orleans, Dallas, St. Paul, Slat Lake City, LA, San Francisco, Duluth and Portland.

The TVA, like much of The New Deal agenda and Progressive ideology in general, was a canard. Spend enough money, pass enough laws and the impression will be one of recovery. The Obama administration of today relies upon just the same strategy. Unfortunately, nothing is truly solved by simply giving the impression that it is, as true for Obama as it was for FDR. The utilities industry, the Tennessee Valley and the economy in general would have been much better served if the FDR administration had not been so heavy handed with regard to regulations. By its own meddling, the FDR administration simply froze private capital. The TVA, while creating jobs and providing electricity would have created more jobs and provided electricity at cheaper rates if the private sector had been left alone to compete with each other and not the federal government. FDR invoked a WWI power project in defending the TVA, "This power development of war days leads logically to national planning." [35] Eleanor Roosevelt herself believed in a "benevolent dictator." [36] The TVA, via government meddling in the private sector, actually suppressed competition and froze private capital. [37]

AGRICULTURAL ADJUSTMENT ADMINISTRATION

Created May 19, 1933 with the explicit promise to increase prices for farmers by artificially decreasing the output. Yet another example of "brain dead trust" policies, well intended but ill- advised. Governments do not add value to the economy; governments simply establish the rules of the game and serve to enforce. Free trade enterprise will dictate supply and demand. In an attempt to artificially manipulate the market (i.e. supply and demand), FDR and "The New Deal" regime ordered farmers to slaughter 6 million piglets. The thought process here, or lack thereof, was to limit the supply side thereby increasing demand, which would increase the price of pork. The AAA established production controls, taxed the distributor to fund itself, paid farmers to produce less and tinkered with supply and demand. On balance, the AAA had little to no effect on the price of pork and despite the ill advised "tinkering" with supply and demand the price for commodities remained at 40% below pre crash highs. Destroying 6 million piglets also left millions hungry. [38] The AAA serves as a perfect example on government intrusion into the free market; freedom is restricted and resources are wasted. The consumer has also paid twice, once in taxes to subsidize the program and second by paying a higher price for food. [39]

NATIONAL RECOVERY ADMINISTRATION

Signed into law on June 16, 1933 and the culmination of the first "One Hundred Days." The NRA is yet another shining example of Progressive policies (i.e. meddling), well intended but ill advised. Central planning at its best, which through its very existence and bureaucratic vagaries did nothing but inhibit growth by freezing private capital.[40] FDR himself promoted the NRA as a program to "put people back to work." The premise behind the NRA was that bigger was better, hence millions of workers and companies were saddled by the NRA's 500 plus codes. Codes that set the price of labor, the price of goods, production quotas, etc... which did nothing but artificially manipulate the market. Not at all what the federal government should be doing. The cost of labor and the price of goods should be determined by free trade, by producers and consumers. Government should not be involved in the artificial manipulation of the economy. The NRA is a prime example of FDR's antipathy towards the individual in favor of the collective. With regard to the NRA, FDR states "Must we go on in many groping, disorganized, separate units to defeat or shall we move as one great team to victory?" [41]

By the end of the NRA's first year, some 700 plus codes were enacted that resulted in some 10,000 pages of legislation. To put into perspective, the entire federal statue law to date was comprised of slightly more than 2,700 pages. The NRA, like the entire New Deal, was nothing but a canard. Spend enough money, create enough new laws, and give the masses the impression that the country is recovering, eerily similar to the Obama administration. [42] The price-fixing mandates of the NRA, well intended they may be, actually damaged small business throughout the country. Through government regulations (i.e. meddling), the NRA disrupted the natural laws of any free market, that of competition and profits. [43] The very nature and existence of the NRA, central government planning, ran counterintuitive to free market principles. The free market is impersonal, it is tolerant of diversity, and it is based on the customer deciding what is in the customer's best interest; which is not the government's responsibility. [44] The inherent beauty of a free market is that it separates economic efficiency from irrelevant characteristics. [45]

The free market is impersonal and actually serves as a check on political power. The exchange between consumer and producer is voluntary cooperation, both parties benefit from the transaction. This free exchange is done so without central planning or coercion. The price fixing mandates of the NRA are centrally planned and coercive. This coercive force via the NRA is a concentration of power between economic and political, which precludes the free market from serving as a check to political power. The very power to coerce through legislation (i.e. NRA) is itself a threat to freedom. Freedom of exchange is what the free market thrives on and not centrally planned coercion. The freedom of exchange between consumer and producer is what protects the consumer from producer and producer from consumer. Neither acts as a coercive force on the other. The government's responsibility in the free exchange is to serve as umpire, not as an active participant (i.e. coercive force) between consumer and producer. [46] Because of its coercive nature, the NRA was dubbed by some economists of the 1930's as the "National Retardation Affair," as in retarding growth. [47]

By mid 1934, The Supreme Court had ruled against the NRA in a number of cases. In rejecting the authority of the NRA one justice states, "Extraordinary conditions may call for extraordinary remedies. But the argument necessarily stops short of an attempt to justify action which lies outside the sphere of constitutional authority. Extraordinary conditions do not create or enlarge constitutional power." The justice went on to describe the NRA as a "...coercive exercise of the law-making power." [48] Another justice defended the unanimous decision against the NRA by stating "...We live under a written Constitution...fortunate or unfortunate, it is fact." Another justice stated that the decision was "...the end of this business of centralization."[49] The Supreme Court decision against the NRA did indeed sound the death knell for the legislative behemoth. With time the NRA and its codes faded and some 500 plus cases were dropped against defendants charged with NRA violations. FDR in defiance claimed the decision sent us back to "the horse and buggy age." [50] Despite its promise to create jobs through a federal bureaucracy, industrial production under the NRA actually fell by 25%. [51] In May 1935, the Supreme Court ruled against the NRA in Schechter Poultry v. U.S. The decision was a fatal blow to the NRA with regard to interstate commerce, wage and price controls. [52]

PUBLIC WORKS ADMINISTRATION

Established June 16, 1933 as part of the National Industrial Recovery Act as well as the finale to the first "Hundred Days." The epitome of the New Deal "prime the pump" mentality. No hidden agenda here as the program was designed to spend big money on big projects. Billions, approximately $6 billion, were budgeted for public construction projects, approximately 34,000. Projects included dams, airports, schools and hospitals. Despite the size and scope of the PWA, it had little to no effect on the overall industrial production rates or unemployment. Despite make-work projects such as the PWA and WPA, unemployment hovered around the 20% mark. [53] Like other New Deal initiatives the PWA relied upon the illusion of recovery.

WORKS PROGRESS ADMINISTRATION

The WPA, another prime the pump initiative, courtesy of FDR and Keynesianism. Created under executive order May 6, 1935 and was implemented to throw money at projects such as reforestation, highways, building construction, slum clearance, etc...The WPA ran for eight years and was terminated in 1943, mainly due to the prosperity that WWII provided with regard to jobs. The WPA employed 8.5 million during its eight year run and built over 650,000 miles of highways and roads. Also responsible for constructing or repairing over 120,000 bridges, 125,000 public buildings, 8000 plus parks and 800 plus airport landing fields. The eight-year run included work on over 1.4 million projects at a cost of $11 billion. The other legacy of the WPA includes a bloated government bureaucracy where confusion and waste were rampant. The WPA also included programs such as the Federal Writers Project, Federal Arts Project and Federal Theater Project. These employed writers, actors and musicians. These programs evolved into lobbying arms of the New Deal as writers hired under the Federal Writers Project actually published articles that highlighted the success of New Deal programs. [54] FDR was nothing if not consistent with his New Deal vision; spend enough money, create enough laws and agencies and give the impression of recovery. The WPA certainly fits the bill.

SOCIAL SECURITY

Economist Thomas Sowell describes Social Security as follows: Social Security has been a pyramid scheme from the beginning. Those who paid in first received money from those who paid in second--and so on, generation after generation. This was great so long as the small generation when Social Security began was being supported by larger generations resulting from the baby boom. But, like all pyramid schemes, the whole thing is in big trouble once the pyramid stops growing. When the baby boomers retire, that will be the moment of truth--or more artful lies. [55] Amendment V of The Constitution, Protection of Rights to Life, Liberty, and Property states; "No person...be deprived of life, liberty or property without due process of law; nor shall private property be taken for public use, without just compensation." [56] What Social Security does is impose a tax, which forces us to sacrifice our personal property (i.e. money) without due cause. [57] Rexford Tugwell was a member of FDR's "brain dead trust," who later became a Professor at Columbia Law School. Tugwell himself described the New Deal agenda; which included Social Security, "To the extent that these New Deal policies developed, they were the tortured interpretations of a document (i.e. the Constitution) intended to prevent them." [58]

Signed into law on August 14, 1935, The Social Security Act was sold as a retirement plan. Social security is, in fact, a ponzi scheme that would make Bernie Madoff proud. Enacted at a time when the retirement age of 65 also happened to be the average life expectancy. FDR himself described the true nature of social security... "They are politics all the way through. We put those payroll contributions there as to give the contributors a legal, moral, and political right to collect their pensions...With those taxes in there, no damn politician can ever scrap my Social Security program. Those taxes aren't a matter of economics, they're straight politics." [59] The proverbial lock box (i.e. trust fund) does not exist; money flows in and is spent just as rapidly, all in the name of political expediency. The first beneficiary of social security was Ida May Fuller, a resident of Vermont. Ms. Fuller contributed for three years prior to retirement; her total contribution was $24.75. Ms. Fuller retired at age 65 in 1939 and collected benefits from 1940-1975. Over the course of her retirement Ms. Fuller was paid a total of $24,888.92. In other words, her return on investment was 1000 fold. The insolvency of social security was evident from the very beginning. [60]

Social security is nothing more than a contract by coercion. We as private citizens are forced by law to purchase old age insurance (i.e. retirement plan) subsidized through payroll taxes. Social security is income redistribution; it is the nationalization of an annuity program. Social security taxes the young to subsidize the old, social security is not self-financing, social security is paternalism (i.e. benevolent tyranny). Social security does not compete with private annuities; we are compelled by the federal government to participate. Social security represents in large part collectivism over individualism. Social security deprives the private citizen a percentage of their income by compulsion. Economist Milton Friedman describes the distinguishing virtue of this paternalistic annuity as arrogance. Social security is another example of the Progressive policy being well intended but ill advised. By nationalizing the provision of annuities, social security represents central planning. Or as economist Thomas Sowell describes, "the wise and knowledgeable few" taking care of the less wise and less knowledgeable many. Benevolent it may be, it is tyranny none the less. [61] Let social security compete with the private sector. A competitive free market will dictate which annuity best serves the individual, a government program that is compulsory or a private alternative.

Starting in 2010, social security will pay out benefits that exceed revenues (i.e. payroll taxes). At its inception, the ratio of pay in to pay out was approximately 40-1. The approximate ratio today of those who pay in to those that receive is 3-1. Today's retirement age of 65 is the same as it was in 1933 when social security was signed into law. Unfortunately, today's life expectancy is approximately 80 compared to 65 in 1933. The system is insolvent. As of this writing, social security represents approximately $50 trillion of unfunded liabilities. Just as unfortunate, social security also represents the third rail of politics. Neither party has the political will to change a system that is outdated, ill advised, insolvent, etc...Which is exactly what FDR intended in his role as beneficent dictator. The sacred cow of entitlement programs; which FDR boldly claimed... "no damn politician can ever scrap my Social Security program."

Marketed as an old age reserve account, social security was government insurance for senior citizens. Social security tapped into the undercurrent of fear within the American public; the implication being that an annuity with the government was safer than those through private banks. Private companies already paying into a pension plan for their employees were forced to cooperate and pay twice, once into their existing pension plan and once into a compulsory government sponsored plan. Social security was never afforded the opportunity to stand on its own and compete in the marketplace; central planners forced the private sector to cooperate in the name of social welfare. Many companies were not able to afford the cost of subsidizing both private pensions and government sponsored pensions (i.e. social security). Many companies abandoned their private pensions, eerily similar to what Obamacare will do to healthcare. Why should private companies pay the cost of pensions or healthcare if the government will do so for them? Secretary of Labor Frances Perkins drafted the bill that became social security and in her own words described it as "...just a teeny weeny bit of socialism." [62]

As a matter of political expedience, social security was sold to the public as a right. Prior to the 1936 election, pamphlets were sent to the general public by the newly formed Social Security Board. The pamphlet stated the government would "set up a Social Security Account for you"... "From the time you are old and stop working, you will get a government check every month of your life. This check will come to you as your right." In other words, if you opposed FDR, his New Deal agenda and Social Security, you were trampling on the rights of others. [63] Sold under the guise of social welfare, social security was nothing more than a political quid pro qou; votes for entitlements. The Declaration of Independence states that we are endowed by our Creator with certain unalienable Rights. Jefferson made no mention of social security, government pensions, or annuities as rights. FDR and fellow Progressives believed that rights were granted and can thereby be revoked by government. This is not what Jefferson described in the Declaration as 'unalienable'. Social Security is yet another example of FDR's "legacy of lunacy." [64]

EXECUTIVE ORDERS

The New Deal itself provides the perfect segue for FDR's use, or misuse, of executive orders. FDR himself, during his inaugural address, stated that he sought "unimagined power." From 1789 under George Washington through 1932 under Herbert Hoover there were just over 4000 executive orders issued during this 143 year period. FDR himself issued 3522 in the twelve years of his presidential tenure, 1933-1945. Perhaps nothing exemplifies the true nature or vision of the New Deal, than FDR's abuse of executive orders. The underlying vision of the New Deal was that FDR truly envisioned himself as our benevolent dictator, or as Thomas Sowell describes, the "wise and knowledgeable few" acting on behalf of the "less wise and less knowledgeable many." FDR's use of executive orders underscores the true nature of the New Deal and is best described by Amity Shlaes in *The Forgotten Man*, the gamble by FDR was that by spending enough money and creating enough new laws, his administration could give the impression that the United States was indeed on the road to recovery. Unfortunately, the electorate bought the ruse for twelve years. The country is following the same path under Obama, one that relies upon theory over experience and the illusion of recovery. [65]

NATIONAL DEBT

The national debt stood at $22,538,672,560 when FDR took office in 1933. At the end of his twelve-year tenure as President in 1945, the national debt under FDR and his New Deal stood at $258,682,187,410 or an increase of 1047%. True to his Progressive roots and belief in Keynesianism economics, FDR and the "brain dead trust" of his New Deal administration did spend, spend and spend adnauseam. A spending record Obama himself would be proud of. The beauty in the Progressive/Keynesianism argument with regard to spending, if massive spending does not provide the desired results, you simply did not spend enough. It's a built in argument for Progressives, the answer to every problem is spending, when it does not work, just spend more. The best way to sum up the failure of the New Deal is to quote one of its architects and FDR's Treasury Secretary Henry Morgenthau "...we have tried spending money. We are spending more than we have ever spent before and it does not work...We have never made good on our promises...I say after eight years of this Administration we have just as much unemployment as when we started...and enormous debt to boot!" FDR, and the country, would have been better served by following the advice of our Founders:

"To contract new debt is not the way to pay old ones." [66]
George Washington

"There is no practice more dangerous than that of borrowing money...it comes easy and is spent freely, and many things indulged in that would never be thought of if to be purchased by the sweat of the brow. In the meantime, the debt is accumulating like a snowball in rolling." [67]

George Washington

"But what madness must it be to run in debt for these superfluities! ...think what you do when you run in debt; you give to another power over your liberty..." [68]

Benjamin Franklin

TAXES

Andrew Mellon was a venture capitalist who served as Treasury Secretary to Presidents Harding, Coolidge and Hoover. His views on taxes were simple, tax (i.e. charge) "what the traffic will bear." [69] The point here is that over taxation inhibits growth, freezes capital and decreases revenue to the federal government. The higher the taxes, the more loopholes will be created to avert them, which of course lead to less tax revenues. Mellon goes on to state his views on over taxation "...when initiative is crippled by legislation or by a tax system which denies him the right to receive a reasonable share of his earnings, then he will no longer exert himself and the country will be deprived of the energy on which its continued greatness depends." [70] As Treasury Secretary under Coolidge, the tax rates were lowered, tax revenues increased, and the country moved into a surplus. [71] Under Coolidge the national debt was lowered from $24 billion to $16 billion. With regard to taxes, Coolidge states "the wise and correct course to follow in taxation and all other economic legislation is not to destroy those who have already secured success but to create conditions under which every one will have a better chance to be successful." [72] Unemployment under Coolidge dropped to 3.2% in 1925 and was decreased further to fewer than 2% during the late 1920's. [73]

In response to the 1929 crash, rising unemployment and the ailing economy, Hoover signed into law the Revenue Act of 1932. This was designed to increase taxes on industry and commerce. What it did was to raise the maximum rate to above 60%, inhibit small business growth, inhibit new hires and compound the deflation problem.

During the Democratic National Convention in 1932 FDR stated, that "governments be made solvent." With regard to high taxes, FDR stated "...governments cost too much." [74] FDR also proclaimed the Coolidge years of prosperity as "an era of selfishness" and claimed the masses "look to us for guidance and for more equitable opportunity to share in the distribution of national wealth."[75] In January of 1933, Rex Tugwell, professor of economics at Columbia and financial adviser to FDR, states the plans of the New Deal, "drastically higher income and inheritance taxes." [76] FDR took a bad situation he inherited from Hoover and proceeded to poor gasoline on the fire. The experimental policies implemented under FDR and the New Deal terrified business, froze capital, inhibited growth and hiring, further suppressing an ailing economy. To counteract private businesses holding onto cash instead of reinvesting, FDR passed the undistributed profits tax. Not only did FDR fail to properly manage the recession he inherited from Hoover, his policies created the Great Depression by suffocating growth. [77]

By the summer of 1935 FDR was speaking out against the "great accumulation of wealth" and proposed new taxes to level the playing field. Amongst these were estate taxes, inheritance taxes and a graduated corporate tax. [78] By August of 1935, the new tax laws (Revenue Act) were signed by FDR which raised the top rate to 79% as well as lowering the thresholds so that more people would pay more taxes. Keep in mind FDR's statement at the 1932 Democratic National Convention with regard to taxes "...governments cost too much." [79] Not only was FDR going after (i.e. punishing) the family by raising the top rate and threshold, he was also going after (i.e. punishing) business through the graduated corporate tax and newly implemented dividend tax. The new tax burdens did not have the desired effect of stimulating the economy. To the contrary, New Deal policies froze capital and growth, exacerbated the deflationary spiral and deepened the depression. The very entity (i.e. private sector) that would have staved off a depression if left to market adjustments was being choked by New Deal legislation in the name of social justice and income redistribution. The undistributed profits tax was particularly heinous, and based on nothing more than socialist tenets. Instead of allowing private companies to hold onto earnings as a hedge against economic downturns, the FDR administration punished companies via the undistributed profits tax. Private companies were no longer investing in new equipment nor retaining employees. [80]

Throughout the 1920's two-thirds of companies were profitable. Under FDR and the New Deal, only one-third of companies were profitable. Prior to FDR, the per capita income of the United States was one-third larger than that of Great Britain. By the late 1930's under FDR, the per capita incomes were virtually identical. The Economist in London described FDR's policies as "institutional obstruction to a free flow of capital." [81] The New Deal was identity politics at its best (i.e. worst). The proletariat vs. the bourgeois was the war cry of the Bolsheviks; FDR followed the same tact by imposing tax laws that were prohibitive and specifically designed to punish the rich. FDR made the following claim during a 1932 campaign speech, "I shall use this position of high responsibility to discuss up and down the country, in all seasons, at all times, the duty of reducing taxes, of increasing the efficiency of government…and getting the most public service for every dollar paid by taxation. This I pledge you and nothing I have said in the campaign transcends in importance this covenant with the taxpayers of this country." [82] As previously mentioned, the top rate went to 79% (from 25%) under FDR, the bottom rate went from 1.1% to 4% and finally 19%.

Nothing epitomizes the statist, centrally planned mindset by the "wise and knowledgeable few," more than FDR's coercive use of taxes. Economist Milton Friedman describes the economic situation during the 1930's under FDR as the "Great Contraction." [83] FDR left no stone unturned with regard to taxes, the Marijuana Tax

Act passed in 1937 and took effect October 1, 1937. [84] Like most progressives FDR was no stranger to hypocrisy. Roosevelt railed against "the great accumulation of wealth," raised the top bracket to 79%, he passed estate taxes, inheritance taxes, corporate taxes and undistributed profits taxes. As for Roosevelt himself, he filed an ambiguous return in 1937 and claimed, "I am unable wholly to figure out the amount of the tax for the following reason…as this is a problem of higher mathematics." The common denominator of progressives, do as I say not as I do. [85]

JAPANESE INTERNMENT CAMPS

Executive Order 9066 was signed into law by FDR on February 19, 1942. EO9066 sent 100,000 plus Japanese-Americans to internment camps that were scattered throughout the western United States. Of the 110,000, 64% of these were American citizens, many of which were 2nd and 3rd generation Americans. [86] The rational behind the internment camps was a rampant fear that Japanese-Americans would act as saboteurs. [87] In 1944, The Supreme Court ruled that the internment camps were indeed constitutional. Japanese-Americans forfeited millions of dollars in property and earnings as a result of the internment. As heinous as the internment camps were, EO9066 has been for the most part white washed by historians. Author James M. McPherson describes the event in *To the Best of my Ability* as being "less playful." The internment camps are not even mentioned when McPherson lists the "few political missteps" by FDR during his tenure. [88]

The Century by Peter Jennings and Todd Brewster mentions the internment in passing. *The Century* devotes an entire sentence to the internment, simply stated as "cruel and unconstitutional." [89] *Witness to America* by Stephen Ambrose and Douglas Brinkley devote 34 pages to FDR and WWII. *Witness* does not feel obliged to mention, even in passing, the incarceration of 110,000 Japanese-Americans, two-thirds of which were American citizens.

Fast forward to September 11, 2001 and imagine the treatment of George W. Bush if he had acquiesced to public sentiment towards Muslim-Americans in the same fashion as FDR treated Japanese-Americans in 1942. Bush would have been vilified by the professional left, the mainstream media, the ACLU, etc…It will be interesting to see if history is as kind to George W. Bush with regard to Guantanamo, the Patriot Act, etc…as it was towards FDR with regard to Japanese internment.

EASTERN EUROPE & POLAND

FDR was part of "The Big Three" during WWII, the term used to describe FDR, Churchill and Stalin. FDR, Stalin and Churchill met at two summits, the first was November 28-December 3, 1943 in Tehran. The second was February 4-11, 1945 in Yalta (Crimea region of the Ukraine); the third summit took place in July-August 1945 in Potsdam and included Churchill, Stalin and Truman. The Yalta Conference was to establish the treatment of Germany and how Eastern Europe would be divided post WWII. Both Churchill and FDR made concessions to Stalin during the conference by appeasing him with regard to Eastern Europe. The concessions to Stalin by Churchill and FDR were made in an attempt to induce Stalin to assist with the war against Japan. The Yalta Conference also called for the establishment of a United Nations. [90]

The Yalta Conference in 1945 was simply an affirmation on what "The Big Three" had already agreed upon in Tehran 1943. Churchill had already pressed for "an independent and strong Poland." However, he and FDR finally appeased Stalin on the partition of Eastern Europe. Stalin did promise "a strong, free, independent and democratic Poland." [91] FDR swallowed the bait and met separately with Stalin in Tehran to determine the fate of Poland. FDR agreed to partition Poland but asked Stalin to keep this private. FDR did not want his stance in Tehran 1943 to be made public as 1944 was an election year. FDR feared he would lose the Polish-American vote. The end result of this political expediency (i.e. treachery) by FDR sentenced Poland to forty plus years of communist rule, all in the name of getting re-elected. [92] British Field Marshall Montgomery was honest enough to state that Churchill and FDR sold out Poland.[93] FDR defended his actions by stating Eastern Europe and Poland were already lost, "so better to give them up gracefully." [94] The pernicious behavior on the part of FDR is part of his legacy. Not only did he condemn Poland to communist rule but Eastern Europe as a whole.

SUPREME COURT

January 7, 1935, Supreme Court finds section 9c of the National Industry Recovery Act unconstitutional in Panama Refining v. Ryan. May 27, 1935, Supreme Court finds National Industry Recovery Act unconstitutional in Schechter Poultry v. United States. On May 27, 1935, the Supreme Court finds FDR did not have executive authority to dismiss William Humphrey (Hoover appointee) from Federal Trade Commission. January 6, 1936, Supreme Court strikes down Agriculture Administration Act as unconstitutional. June 1, 1936, Supreme Court strikes down minimum wage law as unconstitutional in Morehead v. New York ex rel. Tipaldo. February 5, 1937, in response to unfavorable decision by the Supreme Court, FDR plans to "pack" the court by announcing his Federal Court Reorganizing bill. FDR hoped to add an additional six justices to the Supreme Court bringing the total to 15. The six additional justices would obviously be appointed based upon their acquiescence to the New Deal policy.

Roosevelt argued that the current Supreme Court Justices were overworked and were too old. Six of the current justices were over 70 with four older than 75. FDR referred to the repudiation of his New Deal policies as "those dark days." FDR claimed the "dangers of 1929 are again becoming possible," and the current justices were unable to handle "our modern economic conditions." Roosevelt spoke of "new blood" on the court and the need to "save the Constitution from the Court and the Court from the Constitution." Roosevelt claimed the four justices could have "thrown all the affairs of this great nation back into hopeless chaos" by not supporting his experimentation with gold. The court-packing scheme by Roosevelt was specifically aimed at four justices that in most cases did not agree with the New Deal agenda. The Four Horsemen as they were referred to are Justices Pierce Butler, Willis Van Devanter, George Sutherland and James McReynolds. "The Four Horsemen" label was a reference to the Four Horsemen of the Apocalypse. FDR proposed the Federal Court Reorganization bill on February 5, 1937. Fortunately, sanity prevailed and the bill died on the House floor as Congress failed to support the court-packing scheme. Although FDR lost his court-packing scheme he found solace with regard to his first nomination to the Court. Roosevelt nominated and received approval from Congress for Senator Hugo Black to replace retiring Justice Van Devanter. Hugo Black was a former KKK member and showed particular vehemence towards Catholics. [95]

CRASH OF *1937*

Autumn 1937, almost five years into FDR's New Deal agenda and eight years after the infamous Crash of 1929. Despite billions spent to 'prime the pump', despite numerous agencies (i.e. AAA, TVA, CCC) designed to create both jobs and wealth, despite the central planning on behalf of the 'brain trust', the U.S. economy experienced another

major contraction from August – December 1937. The Dow was hovering at 190 in early August, slides to 114 in November and settles at 119 in late December, unemployment also rose to 1931 levels. Despite close to five years of New Deal 'perpetual experimentation', the United States was increasingly seen as unreliable with regard to business. Foreign companies were pumping capital into American stocks at approximately $1 billion per year during the 1920's. That level dropped by a factor of 20 to approximately $50 million per year under FDR during the 1930's. History has excoriated Herbert Hoover for the Crash of 1929, deservedly so. Hoover mishandled the October 29, 1929 crash by turning a correction into a recession via his intrusive policies. Hoover's intervention, Smoot-Hawley, higher taxes and wage controls were disastrous. FDR promised a New Deal, jobs, prosperity, social entitlements, etc...what he delivered was no less disastrous than Hoover. Yet somehow, history has given him a pass. Adolf Berle, one of FDR's intellectual "brain trust," made the following statements in the fall of 1937 regarding the depression within a depression, "Yesterday the 1929 panic was really repreated with more to come today"... "The Stock Market people are most bewildered and frightened"... "plain now that business is dropping as well as the market--in other words, we're in for a rather bad winter."
96

FEDERAL NATIONAL MORTGAGE ASSOCIATION (FANNIE MAE)

Founded in 1938 as part of Roosevelt's New Deal and another example of well intended but ill-advised policies by the "wise and knowledgeable few" that sacrificed common sense for utopian schemes. Fannie Mae was a GSE or government sponsored enterprise. It was created specifically to encourage and expand home ownership as a "social entitlement" as opposed to something earned. [97] Fast forward to 2008, Fannie Mae and her sister agency Freddie Mac (Federal Home Loan Mortgage Corporation) are at the center of our financial meltdown. The legacy here is definitely one of lunacy as Fannie and Freddie guaranteed sub-prime mortgages to high risk individuals. The end result, taxpayers absorb tens of billions of dollars in losses. [98] Not only were 401K savings depleted, home values spiraled downward as the housing bubble burst. The problem with this GSE, the federal government guarantees a bailout should it fail. Of course, bailout is a euphuism for gouging the taxpayers. Fannie is labeled a quasi-government agency, which translates to a private-public company. The problem is that it operates without federal control while benefiting from government benefits. Fannie Mae is exempt from SEC guidelines, tax exempt, has lax capital requirements and sells its debt to the U.S. Treasury. [99] Like Social Security, TVA, AAA, PWA, WPA, CCC, et al., FNMA is yet another example of progressive policies and the unintended consequences of central planning.

Abraham Lincoln once said, "Property is the fruit of labor. Property is desirable, is a positive good in the world. That some should be rich shows that others may become rich, and hence is just encouragement to industry and enterprise." [100] The point here, home ownership is not a right but a privilege. Home ownership is the result of hard work and savings, of self-reliance and frugality. Home ownership is not a social entitlement, it is something earned. The Constitution guarantees the right to life, liberty and the pursuit of happiness, however, as Benjamin Franklin said, it's up to us to chase it.

The Presidencies of TR, Wilson and FDR were swayed by many of the same influential voices. With the exception of a few additions, namely FDR's "brain trust," the following list of enlightened despots is identical to that which influenced TR and Wilson. The list includes many who supported TR, Wilson and FDR. Aside from the individuals listed below, the common thread that binds TR, Wilson and FDR is a shared belief in a centrally planned existence governed by the intellectual minority. By any objective measure, the "New Deal" under FDR was an abysmal failure. Many of the following played important roles during FDR's tenure and contributed to his centrally planned "New Deal" agenda, either by direct participation within the administration or indirectly via their teachings, writings, etc…

THE "WISE & KNOWLEDGEABLE FEW"

Roger Baldwin (1884-1981) Peace activist, progressive and founder of American Civil Liberties Union. Attended Harvard during birth of American Progressive movement. Founded ACLU in 1920, promoted progressive causes and socio-economic polices via ACLU. Prominent voice in American Union Against Militarism convicted of violating the Selective Service Act and imprisoned during WWI. Member of the International Workers of the World prior to founding ACLU. Life partner, Evelyn Preston, was close family friend to Roosevelts. Friend and ally to Margaret Sanger. Also served as civil liberties consultant under General Douglas MacArthur in Japan 1947. [101]

Adolf A. Berle (1895-1971) Harvard grad, professor of corporate law at Columbia. One of the original three that comprised the 'brain trust' in 1932 that helped FDR frame the New Deal agenda. Major force in developing federal farm and home owner's mortgage programs. Published numerous works on social and economic issues. Best known work is *The Modern Corporation and Private Property* published in 1932. In his work, Berle argued that the means of production were concentrated in the hands of approximately 200 companies. With this concentration of power, the companies essentially separated themselves from the forces of a free market society due to their monopoly standing. The economic concentration rendered true competition obsolete. Berle advocated that these large companies fulfill their 'responsibilities' to society and not just to shareholders. "Responsibilities" to society of course meant redistribution of wealth. Berle wrote FDR's 1932 speech *Commonwealth Club Address* where Berle (via FDR) advocates for government control (i.e. central planning) of economic policy. [102]

Brain Trust Term given to the intellectuals who consulted FDR during 1932 presidential campaign. The original group of academic advisors was comprised of three Columbia professors: Raymond Moley, Rexford Guy Tugwell and Adolph A. Berle. The group was later joined by Basil O'Connor, Samuel Rosenman and Hugh Johnson. During the infamous "First Hundred Days," the "brain trust" assisted FDR in developing the foundation of the "New Deal." One of the underling principles of the "New Deal" was described by Berle as a "new economic constitutional order." [103]

Whittaker Chambers (1901-1961) Member of American Communist Party 1924-1938; also served as Soviet spy until 1938. Defected from communist party and later testified before the House of Un-American Activities Committee. While serving as editor for *Time*, Chambers testifies before the Committee and accuses Alger Hiss of being part of communist cell in the 1930's. Hiss served in the FDR administration within the Departments of Agriculture, Justice and State throughout the 1930's. Chambers authored *Witness*, published in 1952. In *Witness* Chambers argues that the New Deal is a form of secular liberalism and nothing more than a "watered down version" of Communist ideology. The Venona transcripts of the KGB during WWII were released in 1996. The transcripts confirmed the accusation by Chambers that Hiss did in fact act as a Soviet spy throughout the 1930's and until 1945. [104]

Stuart Chase (1888-1985) Prominent economics writer and part of FDR's infamous 'kitchen cabinet'. Educated at MIT and Harvard, member of Harvard Fabian Society. Authored book in 1932 titled *New Deal*, given credit for coining the phrase later co-opted by FDR. Not part of FDR's "brain trust" but was advocate of New Deal policies and promoted them in his writings. Claimed "New Deal" was "victory for collectivization" in magazine article 1934. Part of 1927 junket to Russia and wrote glowingly of the Russian experiment. Called for the departure from the free-market and claimed "Russia, I am convinced, will solve for all practical purposes the economic problem." Advocate of central planning and stated, "Why should Russians have all the fun remaking a world." Went on to serve on planning commission in 1950's Connecticut. Ardent supporter of LBJ's Great Society. Was advocate of strong central government, deficit spending to fund social programs, strong executive branch, nationalization of banking, nationalization of housing, nationalization of health care, nationalization of industry, state controlled communications, progressive taxes, social security, government control of energy, natural resources, transportation and agricultural. [105]

Winston Churchill (1874-1965) On his death bed said, "The journey has been enjoyable and well worth making --- *once*!" Born to English father and American mother. Prodigious writer and artist who authored 40 books as well as thousands of articles for newspapers and magazines, as well as hundreds of paintings. Served as British Officer in military, as war correspondent, as First Lord of the Admiralty, as Member of Parliament, as Secretary of War and Air, as Chancellor of Exchequer (Treasury Secretary) and Prime Minister. Member of "Big Three" during WWII, which included Stalin and FDR. Attended Tehran Conference in 1943, Yalta in 1945 with Stalin and FDR. Attended Potsdam in 1945 with Stalin and

Truman. Distrusted Stalin and warned FDR against his treachery. Unfortunately for Eastern Europe and Poland, FDR was oversuspicous of Churchill and undersuspicous of Stalin. Anti-communist, anti-socialist, warned Europe early on of Bolshevik Revolution, stating, "Of all the tyrannies in history, the Bolshevik tyranny is the worst." Opposed economic polices of Keynes; which FDR adopted as part of New Deal agenda.[106]

Father Charles E. Coughlin (1891-1979) Host of radio program, Hour of Prayer, leader of anti-Semitic Christian Front. Served in Royal Oak, Michigan at the Shrine of the Little Flower. Ardent supporter of FDR early on and promoted "New Deal" policies on radio program. Advised listeners to vote for FDR during 1932 presidential campaign. Coughlin was powerful voice during the 1930's as his radio program reached tens of millions each week. FDR took full advantage of this and used Coughlin to promote the "New Deal" and attack those in opposition. Coughlin turned on FDR in 1935 as it became clear that FDR had no plans for Coughlin in his administration. From 1935 on, Coughlin used his program to attack FDR. Formed political action group, the National Union for Social Justice in 1935. Founded journal *Social Justice* in 1936 to promote his ideology. Eventually promoted fascism and dictatorships in general as the sole cure for capitalism. Admirer of Benito Mussolini. Fell out of public favor for his anti-Semitic views and for blaming WWII on the Jews. [107]

Herbert Croly (1869-1930) Intellectual leader of Progressive movement. Created "New Nationalism" philosophy, founder of progressive magazine *New Republic*, author of *The Promise of American Life* in 1909, which influenced TR as well as FDR. TR based his "New Nationalism" on Croly's progressive philosophy. Opposed the industrial society, advocated for "constructive discrimination" (i.e. redistribution of wealth) whereby the "weak" would be favored. Advocate of big government controlling big business. Actively promoted a strong central government, labor unions and nationalization of business. Wished for the eradication of individual liberties, opponent of small business and non-union workers. Authored *Progressive Democracy* in 1915 which espoused the Constitution as a living (i.e. Darwinism) document with no fixed truths. Thought the Constitution was obsolete as written and needed to evolve to fit the social issues of the time. [108]

John Dewey (1859-1952) Student of philosophy at Johns Hopkins University (i.e. founded in 1867 as Progressive institution) where he earned his doctorate. Influenced by the writings of Karl Marx, co-author of *The Communist Manifesto*. Founder of Progressive education movement. Founding member of NAACP, and ACLU. Early member of Socialist Party of America and Progressive Party. Promoted alternatives to capitalism, which he felt was obsolete and cruel. [109]

Alger Hiss (1904-1996) Graduate of Johns Hopkins University, founded as progressive school in late 19th century. Served in FDR's administration in the Departments of Agriculture, Justice and State. Joined FDR in Yalta conference with Stalin and Churchill 1945. Accused by Whittaker Chambers in 1948 of knowingly providing classified State documents that eventually were transmitted to Soviet Union. Hiss charged and bought to trial in 1949, retried in 1950. 1949 trial ended in hung jury, Hiss convicted in 1950 trial. Served three years of five year sentence. In 1996, the Soviet Union released classified documents from WWII that provided evidence of Hiss's guilt. [110]

Harold LeClaire Ickes (1874-1953) Attended University of Chicago. Worked for Teddy Roosevelt's Progressive Party during 1912 campaign. Worked for Progressive campaigns of Charles Hughes in 1916 and Hiram Johnson in 1920. Served as Secretary of Interior for FDR in 1933, where he oversaw activity for the Public Works Administration. Served as president of Chicago NAACP and wrote for the *New Republic* from 1946-1952. *New Republic* was progressive magazine founded in early 20th century. [111]

Hugh Samuel Johnson (1882-1942) Graduate of West Point, distinguished military career, worked on FDR's campaign team in 1932. Became part of FDR's "brain trust," comprised of Raymond Moley, Rexford Tugwell, Johnson, Samuel Rosenman and Basil O'Connor. Johnson appointed administrator of FDR's National Recovery Administration in 1933, resigned in 1934. [112]

John Maynard Keynes (1883-1946) Like his father, Keynes was an economist who taught at Cambridge. Attended Eton College and King's College. Associated with members of the Fabian Society, which included George Bernard Shaw. Pacifist and worked in Treasury Department for England during WWI. Part of British delegation that attended the Versailles Peace Conference in 1919. Authored *The Economic Consequences of the Peace* in 1919. The work argued that the reparations imposed upon Germany were extreme and would eventually lead to further conflict. Became editor of *The Nation* in 1923 and argued against the Conservative British government's economic policies, which at the time included Winston Churchill who was serving as Chancellor of the Exchequer (Treasury Secretary). Published *The End of Laissez-Faire* after visiting Soviet Union in 1926. Published articles in 1929 that advocated for "the management of the economy" by government as well as advocating governments to "spend its way out of the depression." Keynes continued to publish works throughout the 1920's and into the 1930's that promoted government's role in 'managing an economy'. Keynes advocated for the abandonment of the gold standard, increased government expenditures and a planned economy. Keynes was advisor to the British government throughout the 1920's and 1930's and attended the Bretton Woods Conference in 1944. Met with FDR in May of 1934, and was major influence with regard to New Deal policy making as it related to a centrally planned economy. The basic premise behind Keynesianism is perpetual experimentation. This was certainly applied by FDR as part of New Deal implementation. Keynes approved of all the New Deal spending on behalf of the FDR administration. After meeting with FDR, Keynes stated, "With one dollar paid out for relief or public works or anything else you have created four dollars worth of national income." Keynes was advocate of putting cash in the hands of the consumer, which was part of FDR's undistributed profits tax. This tax essentially punished private companies for their surplus and forced them to spend or issue dividends. [113]

Harry Wellington Laidler (1884-1970) Economist and Socialist leader early 20th century…educated at Columbia. Founding member of ISS and secretary from 1910-1921. Served as executive director of League for Industrial Democracy 1921-1957. Socialist candidate for numerous public offices. [114]

Walter Lippman (1889-1974) Ardent supporter of Roosevelt, Wilson and the Progressive Party. Socialist and co-founder of the Harvard Socialist Club…close friends with John Reed, author of *Ten Days that Shook the World*. Reed buried at Kremlin Wall with fellow Bolshevik heroes. Worked as Lincoln Steffens secretary in 1911, authored *A Preface to Politics* in 1913, joined with Herbert Croly and Walter Weyl to found *New Republic*. Worked as assistant to

Wilson's Secretary of War...assistant to Wilson in drafting Fourteen Points Peace Programme. Member of Wilson's delegation to Paris Peace Conference in 1919...assisted Wilson with League of Nations covenant. [115]

Raymond Moley (1886-1975) Columbia Ph.D. graduate, taught at Columbia's Barnard College. Part of original three Columbia professors that comprised FDR's "brain trust." The other two were Adolf Berle and Rexford Tugwell. Major advisor and speech writer for FDR through 1936. Later disillusioned with anti-business policies of the New Deal. He served as editor of *Today Magazine* which later became *Newsweek*. He served as senior advisor to campaigns of Wendell Willkie, Barry Goldwater and Richard Nixon. [116]

Henry Morgenthau, Jr. (1891-1967) Attended Exeter Academy and Cornell University. Served as FDR's Treasury Secretary from 1934-1945. Also served as Chairman of the New York State Agricultural Advisory Committee for Governor Roosevelt in 1929. Advocated for the undistributed profits tax that forced private companies to either pay dividends or spend their surplus cash. Essentially a plan to "choke" income out of private companies and redistribute cash into the hands of consumers. The plan coincided with the election year of 1936; Morgenthau estimated the tax would redistribute approximately $4.5 billion to the consumer. Responsible for the successful war bonds program that amounted to approximately $1 billion in distributions. Attended the Bretton Woods Conference in 1944. Morgenthau himself provides the best summary of the New Deal agenda in which he played an integral role, "We have tried spending money. We are spending more than we have ever spent before and it does not work...We have never made good on our promise...I say after eight years of this Administration we have just as much unemployment as when we started ...and enormous debt to boot." [117]

Benito Mussolini (1883-1945) Moved to Switzerland in 1902 due to poor employment prospects in Italy. Became involved with socialist politics during his stay, returned to Italy in 1904 and joined the socialist press. Broke with the socialist and formed the Fascist Party in 1919. Organized the "Black Shirts" of 1921, which served as armed squads that terrorized political opponents. Self-proclaimed dictator of Italy in 1925, with the support of "Black Shirts." Ruled through strong state control and took the title "Il Duce." Formed Pact of Steel with Nazi Germany in 1939 and allied with Germany and Japan during WWII. Popular figure in America as well as globally, during FDR's rise to the presidency. Both *Time* and *Forbes* magazines featured Mussolini at one time. NRA under FDR was in emulating Mussolini's Italian model of merging industry, labor and government into one entity. [118]

Basil O'Connor (1892-1972) Attended Dartmouth and Harvard, became legal advisor to FDR in early 1920's. Formed law firm with FDR that existed from 1924-1933. Founded Georgia Warm Springs Foundations with FDR in 1927. Founded National Foundation for Infantile Paralysis with FDR in 1938 which later became March of Dimes. Served as Chairman for American Red Cross. Became part of FDR's "brain trust" in 1933 with Hugh Johnson and Samuel Rosenman, as well as the original three members that included Berle, Tugwell and Moley. [119]

George Peek (1873-1943) Attended Northwestern University. Was FDR's first Administrator of the Agricultural Adjustment Administration (AAA). Joined with Hugh Johnson in advocating the McNary-Haugen Farm Relief Bill that would have established the first price supports for agriculture. Forced to resign his post due to disagreements over implementation of the AAA. Fought with Henry Wallace and was opposed to production quotas which he viewed as socialist. He advocated for large cartels of producers and food processors. He resigned in December of 1933. [120]

Frances Perkins (1880-1965) Attended Mount Holyoke and Columbia, served as FDR's Secretary of Labor for 12 years. First woman to hold cabinet position. Advocate of labor movement, social justice, suffrage movement, member of Socialist Party and supported Wilson in 1912 presidential campaign. Played major role in legislation that became Wagner Act, Fail Labor Standards Act and Social Security Act. Professor at Cornell after serving FDR; taught in the School of Industrial and Labor Relations. [121]

Samuel Irving Rosenman (1896-1973) Attended Columbia law school, advisor and speech writer for FDR. Became part of FDR's "brain trust" in 1933 joining Hugh Johnson and Basil O'Connor; as well as original three members that included Berle, Tugwell and Moley. Drafted many of FDR's speeches promoting the New Deal policy including FDR's first inaugural address. [122]

Margaret Sanger (1883-1966) Feminist, women's rights activist, member of Socialist Party with fellow Progressives John Reed, Upton Sinclair, Eugene Debs, Norman Thomas, et al. Founded American Birth-Control League, co-founder of Workers Birth Control Group. Advocate of eugenics. [123]

Upton Sinclair (1878-1968) American novelist, described by TR as "muckraking journalist." Ardent reader of socialist classics and read the socialist weekly *Appeal to Reason*. Member of socialist party and board member of ACLU. Published novel *The Jungle* in 1906, which chronicled the life of an immigrant who is exploited by Chicago stockyard owners. TR received 100 letters per day demanding reforms.

Subsequent legislation, Pure Food and Drug Act 1906, was direct result of Sinclair's novel. Sinclair established the socialist commune Helicon Home Colony in New Jersey which served as a commune for left wing writers. Published novel *Boston* in 1928, which was sympathetic to anarchists Sacco and Vanzetti. Ran unsuccessfully as socialist for governor of California in 1934. Ardent believer in socialism until his death in 1968. [124]

Joseph Stalin (1879-1953) As a young man was sent to a seminary in Tbilisi by mother, to study to become a priest. Stalin dropped out of seminary study and chose revolutionary circles instead. Stalin was a hands on revolutionary unlike Lenin and Trotsky who were the intellectual leaders, often living abroad. Stalin held a life long distrust of educated intellectuals. Appointed to General Secretary of the Communists Party Central Committee in 1922. Following Lenin's death in 1924, Stalin became de facto leader as a result of his purging as General Secretary. Stalin continued to "purge" the Soviet Union of its founding fathers (i.e. Trotsky) and labeled them enemies of the people. Anyone with higher education suspected of being a threat to the revolution. Forced collectivized agriculture which reduced millions to serfs once again. Part of "Big Three" coalition during WWII which included Churchill, FDR and later Truman. Attended Tehran Conference in 1943 and Yalta in 1945 with FDR and Churchill. Met with, among others, Stuart Chase and Rex Tugwell in 1927. Chase and Tugwell were part of FDR's brain trust and both sympathetic towards Stalin and his agenda. *NY Times* wrote glowingly of the Stalin experiment in Russia. NRA under FDR was in part emulating Stalin's model in Russia. [125]

Norman Thomas (1884-1968) Politician, social reformer, joined Socialist Party 1915, co-founder of ACLU, served as co-director for League for Industrial Democracy (founded as ISS) from 1922-1937. Socialist candidate for mayoral race of New York 1925, for governor

1924 and U.S. president in 1928-1948. Studied political science at Princeton during Woodrow Wilson's tenure as professor. Contributor to the Nation and World Tomorrow. Remained influential voice for socialism during FDR's tenure as president. [126]

Rexford Guy Tugwell (1891-1979) Attended University of Pennsylvania later taught at Columbia. Introduced to FDR by Raymond Moley. Part of advisory group for FDR during his term as Governor of New York. Formed original "brain trust" of FDR which included Moley and Berle in 1932. Economist and ardent supporter of New Deal agenda including the production quotas of the AAA. Stated. "Fundamental changes of attitude, new disciplines, revised structures, unaccustomed limitations on activity, are all necessary if we are to plan. This amounts, in fact, to the abandonment, finally, of laissez-faire." [127]

Henry Agard Wallace (1888-1965) Served as Secretary of Agriculture under Presidents Harding and Coolidge. Advocate of government intervention in agriculture, supporter of LaFollete and Progressive Party during 1924 presidential campaign. Supported FDR during 1932 campaign. Appointed Secretary of Agriculture for FDR in 1933, primary architect of AAA. Became running mate of FDR during 1940 campaign. Opposed Winston Churchill in post WWII reconstruction. Promoted cooperation with Soviet Union post WWII, became editor of New Republic and ran as Progressive candidate during 1948 presidential campaign. [128]

Wendell Willkie (1892-1944) Opposed FDR in 1940 presidential campaign. Later became supporter of FDR and joined Roosevelt as a representative in travels to Britain, China, USSR and the Middle East. Ran against FDR once again in 1944 presidential campaign. [129]

CHAPTER 4
BARACK HUSSEIN OBAMA
44TH PRESIDENT 2008-PRESENT

"Associate with men of good quality if you esteem your own reputation; for it is better to be alone than in bad company." [1]

George Washington

President Obama would have been wise to heed these words. Nefarious associations throughout his life, yet the so called media chose to ordain him instead of vetting him. Associations with any one of the following, Ayers, Dorn, Rezko, ACORN, SEIU, Marxist professors, Rev. Wright, Emmanuel, Blago, Axelrod, etc. may be sold as a coincidence. Associations with all of the aforementioned are a PATTERN!!! No executive experience, no private sector experience, a legislative voting record where the majority of his votes cast were "present." Nothing on his resume that would suggest he's capable of handling foreign policy, domestic policy, healthcare or immigration. Nothing on his resume suggests he has the necessary skill set that the Oval Office requires. Aside from his eloquent style when reading from a teleprompter, the man is an empty vessel. Albert Einstein's nickname as a child was "der Depperte" or the "dopey one" because of a speech pattern exhibited early in his life. [2] The ability to speak in public is not a reflection of anyone's intelligence or leadership skills, to wit…Obama. He is the epitome of someone born on 3rd and thinking they hit a triple. He has governed with the statist mindset described by F.A. Hayek in *The Road to Serfdom* as "intellectual hubris." He has governed through the prism of collectivism, whereby we as individuals have no rights, only duties.

President Bush, to his credit, never once blamed President Clinton for the mess he inherited. The last three years of Clinton's presidency saw a rise in the misery index each year. During Clinton's final year in office the Dow fell 2000 points which left Bush with an economy in recession. Clinton's HUD secretaries, Cisneros and Cuomo, pushed for Fannie & Freddie to increase loans to sub prime candidates. Clinton signed a law in 1999 than repealed the Glass-Steagall Act of 1933. The act that separated investment banks from commercial banks was now defunct which put commercial banks at the same risk as investment banks. The September 11, 2001 attacks on the World Trade Center, The Pentagon and Pennsylvania were planned in this country under Clinton's nose. In addition to this, America's interests were attacked six times during Clinton's presidency and his response was to erect a firewall between intelligence agencies which could have thwarted 9/11. Despite all this and whether you hate him or love him, Bush displayed class and never pointed a finger at Clinton.

> *"It is better to offer no excuse than a bad one if at any time you should fall into error."* [3]
>
> ### George Washington

Juxtapose this to the lack of class displayed by President Obama during his first 36 months in office. His incessant blaming of Bush and the Republicans for all problems domestic and foreign speaks volume to his character. Obama reminds me of the little neighborhood dog that yaps at every car and pedestrian that passes by. One day, the little dog gets loose finally catches the car and has no idea what to do with it. Obama campaigned for this job. To insist after the fact that everything is worse than anticipated is disingenuous at the very least. He is nothing more than an academic, a community organizer, a legislator who votes present, and a utopian dreamer who is in a position that far, far exceeds his pay grade. He promised hope and change, an end to bipartisanship, an end to racial divisiveness, and end to DC politics as usual, an end to earmarks, fiscal responsibility, etc…

As of this writing, the country is more polarized than ever across lines of class, religion, politics, race, economics, and policy both foreign and domestic. Obama has displayed an attitude that is arrogant, condescending, dismissive, elitist and one of moral superiority. He is constantly at odds with the will of the people with regard to illegal immigration, healthcare, bailouts, Ground Zero Mosque, Khalid Sheik Mohammed, Arizona Law, border enforcement, Fort Hood Massacre, Christmas Day bomber, Time Square bomber, Cambridge police, deficit spending, national debt, etc…He has taken a stance in direct opposition to a majority of Americans on each and every issue. In true progressive/statist/elitist fashion, Obama continues on with his utopian pipedreams of radically transforming this country. We as a people are far too ignorant to appreciate his intelligence and leadership, or so he believes. His lies, of course, are noble lies.

Since he took office the U.S. workforce has contracted by 2million jobs, gas prices have increased 95%, national debt 44%, deficit spending 150%. He has appeased foreign powers such as Iran, Russia, North Korea, Egypt, Venezuela, G20, Islam, etc…He has treated the following with utter disdain: Israel, England, Christianity, the military, capitalism, Rule of Law, Americans in general, etc…Never in our history has a president done so much harm, in so little time to so many people. From George Washington to George W. Bush, a period of 220 years, the country accumulated $10 trillion plus of debt. Obama is on pace to accumulate $5 trillion plus during his first term, a period of four years. The following quotes by Thomas Jefferson remain pertinent to this day: ⁴

> *"Never buy anything which you have not money in your pocket to pay for. Be assured that it gives much more pain to the mind to be in debt than to do without any article whatever which we may seem to want."*

> *"I know nothing more important to inculcate into the minds of young people than the wisdom, the honor, and the blessed comfort of living within their income; to calculate in good time how much less pain will cost them the plainest style of living, which keeps them out of debt; than after a few years of splendor above their income to have their property taken away for debt, when they have a family growing up to maintain and provide for."*

> *"The question, whether one generation of men has a right to bind another...If one generation could charge another with a debt, then the earth would belong to the dead and not to the living generation. Then, no generation can contract debts greater than may be paid during the course of its own existence."*

> *"The principle of spending money to be paid by posterity, under the name of funding, is but swindling futurity on a large scale."*

> *"...We must make our election between economy and liberty or profusion and servitude...And the forehorse of this frightful team is public debt. Taxation follows that and in its train wretchedness and oppression."*

Jefferson was not alone in his sentiments towards public debt. Washington, Franklin, Madison, et al spoke out against debt in similar fashion. Jefferson, while president cut the public debt in half during his eight years while cutting as many taxes as possible. Andrew Jackson during his presidency sold public land to pay off the national debt and in fact left off with a surplus whereby $28 million was refunded to state coffers. Fast forward to 2012 and we see a president hell bent on leaving not only the next generation but generations with massive debt. As of this writing the national debt is $15 trillion and counting. This figure stood at just $10 trillion 36 months ago. The rate at which Obama is accruing debt is unprecedented throughout mankind's history. It's unsustainable and will saddle future generations with a burden that may be too great to bear. Instead of treating thrift and frugality as a virtue, as the Founders did, Obama treats thrift and frugality as a sickness.

"NEW DEAL" VS. "HOPE & CHANGE"

No better segue into "Hope & Change" than the previous chapter regarding the "New Deal." "'Hope & Change" is proving to be what history has confirmed of the "New Deal," an abject failure by any objective measures. The parallels between Progressive Roosevelt and Progressive Obama are eerily similar. Both were charismatic speakers, both blamed their predecessor for inheriting a mess, both surrounded themselves with academics (i.e. intellectuals), both took advantage of their respective mediums (radio for FDR, web for Obama). They both believed in a centrally planned existence governed by elites (i.e. intellectuals). They both chose theory over experience by selecting very few individuals with private sector experience. Each of them trampled the Constitution and treated the document as obsolete. Thomas Jefferson once said, "In questions of power let us hear no more of trust in men, but bind them down from mischief with the chains of the Constitution"... advice that would have been well heeded by both FDR and now Obama. "Hope & Change" like "New

Deal" makes for great campaign slogans but offers little if anything with regard to actual governance. Both are generic promises made by two Progressives looking to get elected. "Hope & Change" like "New Deal" is explicitly generic by design. Both campaign slogans promised their respective supporters everything the individual could read into the non-specific claim. Both "Hope & Change" and "New Deal" are and were disingenuous at the very least, at worst, both are and were pernicious.

FISCAL RESPONSIBILITY (OR LACK THEREOF)

There is no ambiguity, whatsoever, on where the Founding Fathers stood with regard to debt.

> *"To contract new debt is not the way to pay old ones."* [5]
> **George Washington**

> *"...We shall all consider ourselves morally bound to pay them ourselves; and consequently within the life expectancy of the majority..."* [6]
> **Thomas Jefferson**

> *"...Tis hard for an empty bag to stand upright..."* [7]
> **Benjamin Franklin**

Obama, in keeping with the Founders sentiment on debt, was quoted as saying, "I didn't come here to pass our problems on to the next president or the next generation—I'm here to solve them." Obama's action on the deficit and debt are not only antithetical to the Founders' beliefs they are antithetical to his own words. The national debt in January 2009 when Obama took office was $10.6 trillion. On February 23, 2009 Obama promised to cut the national debt in half during his first term. The national debt as of this writing stands at $15.3 trillion, an increase of 44%. At the current rate, Obama is on pace to accumulate an additional $6 trillion of new debt over a four-year period. Putting this into perspective, it took this country 220 years from Washington to Bush to accumulate $10.6 trillion of debt. In true Keynesian fashion (i.e. perpetual experimentation); one of Obama's first orders of business when he took office was to pass the now infamous Stimulus Bill, a total of 1,071 pages of outright pork at a cost to the taxpayers of $787billion. A small sampling of what our tax funded stimulus was spent on: [8]

- $11,672,000,000   Rural housing service
- $19,900,000,000   Food stamp program
- $ 1,651,227,000   Child care low income families
- $ 295,000,000   State admin cost for food stamp program
- $53,600,000,000   State fiscal fund to avoid layoffs
- $ 5,000,000,000   Weatherization Program
- $ 1,600,000,000   DOE science programs
- $ 6,000,000,000   Innovative technology loans
- $ 4,500,000,000   Federal conversion to green buildings
- $ 650,000,000   Digital to analog TV conversion program
- $ 50,000,000   National Endowment for the Arts grants
- $ 198,000,000   Filipino WWII veterans compensation
- $ 4,690,000,000   Broadband tech program
- $ 2,500,000,000   National Science Foundation activates
- $ 165,000,000   Fish and Wildlife habitat restoration

- $ 146,000,000   National Park Service trails
- $ 105,000,000   Highway infrastructure in Puerto Rico
- $ 8,000,000,000   Hi speed rail assistance

A sampling of what Obama's 2009 budget included; keep in mind his pledge to eliminate earmarks during the 2008 campaign. Total cost in this budget for the 9,287 earmarks was $12.8 billion, which included the following largesse: [9]

- $1,049,000   Control of crickets in Utah
- $ 200,000   Tattoo removal clinic
- $ 190,000   Buffalo Bill Historical Site Wyoming
- $2,673,000   Wood education and research center
- $ 300,000   Promotion of women's sports in Boston
- $ 206,000   Promote wool research
- $2,192,000   Center for Grapes Genetics
- $1,791,000   Swine odor and manure research Iowa
- $ 45,000   Weed removal Mass.
- $ 469,000   Fruit fly facility Hawaii
- $ 800,000   Oyster rehab Alabama
- $4,545,000   Wood research Michigan
- $ 75,000   Create "totally teen zone" Georgia
- $ 300,000   Research for loons
- $ 900,000   Chicago Planetarium
- $ 190,000   Trolley system in Puerto Rico
- $ 380,000   Lighthouse renovation Maine

- $7,800,000   Sea turtle research Hawaii
- $2,600,000   Monitor Hawaii monk seals
- $1,500,000   Research pelagic fisheries Hawaii
- $ 650,000   Beaver research Miss. and North Carolina
- $1,700,000   Honey bee factory Rio Grande Valley

Juxtapose this to what our Founders intended in the general welfare clause of the Constitution. Article 1.8.1 of the Constitution states, "The people of the states hereby delegate to the federal Congress the power to collect taxes, duties, imposts, and excises." The theory behind this clause was to keep the federal government within the available revenue coming in. Congress was granted powers to provide for a common defense and general welfare of the Unites States. The clause was intended to limit the power of taxation; it was not a grant of power to spend. Expenditure of funds was intended for the general welfare and not special welfare (i.e. individuals or preferred groups). Article 1.8.1 states, 'The people of the states empower the Congress to expend money (for the enumerated purposes listed in Article 1, section 8), provided it's done in such a way that benefits the general welfare of the whole people.' The aforementioned earmarks do not benefit the general welfare. Congress and the progressive movement has usurped power and advocated social-welfare legislation over the years. A quote from one of our Founders warned… "It is a general maxim that all governments find a use for as much money as they can raise." [10]

President Harding stated in 1921, "Just government is merely the guarantee to the people of the right and opportunity to support themselves. The one outstanding danger of today is the tendency to turn to Washington for the things which are the tasks or the duties of the forty-eight commonwealths." President Cleveland stated, "The unhappy decadence among our people of genuine love and affection for our Government as the embodiment of the highest and best aspirations of humanity and NOT as the giver of gifts." Another example of Congress usurping power regarding expenditures came in the early 19th century. A fire broke out in Georgetown, a DC suburb, and Congress appropriated $20K to assist the victims. Davy Crockett who was a member of Congress at the time stated; "I have as much sympathy as any man in the house, but Congress has no power to appropriate this money as an act of charity. We have the right as individuals to give away as much of our own money as we please in charity; but as members of Congress we have no right so to appropriate a dollar of the public money...I cannot vote for this bill, but will give one week's pay to the object, and if every member of Congress will do the same, it will amount to more than the bill asks." The bill was defeated and not one member of Congress, save for Crockett came forward to donate a week's salary. [11]

Obama was critical of the deficit spending under Bush throughout the 2008 campaign and has continued his attacks on Bush spending during his three-plus years in office. I'm not here to defend the spending of Bush, who accumulated $3.3 trillion of deficits during his eight-year term. However, we were promised change; unfortunately the change has been for the worse. The budget deficit under Bush in 2007 was $162 billion. Obama has accumulated close to $5 trillion in deficits in just three years. Our monthly deficits under Obama are running close to the yearly deficits that we incurred under Bush. I could be wrong, but I do not think the current path is "Hope & Change." If any private business or household ran their financials like the Federal government both would be driven to bankruptcy. If the individual household spends more than it takes in on a monthly basis, deficits accrue. In order to pay down the deficit, the individual borrows money, which creates more deficits. It's only a matter of time before the interest on the debt overwhelms the individual budget, this leads to bankruptcy. The same scenario applies to private business. Alexander Hamilton was an advocate of running a perpetual debt, although the debt must be sustainable. Unless the individual is wealthy most of us run perpetual debts, mortgages, car payments, credit cards, etc...The point is to run debts that are sustainable and never reach the tipping point whereby the interest on the debt overwhelms the ability to pay anything on the principle. America has reached its tipping point.

FDR inherits a financial crisis from Hoover and turns a recession into a depression that lasted a generation. Obama inherits a financial crisis from Bush and takes a page straight from the FDR, Keynesian, Progressive playbook, which is tax and spend our way to prosperity. The only problem is that the Federal government does not add value to the economy. The federal government does not invest, it taxes and spends. The private sector adds value not the government. Unfortunately, Progressives have and I suppose always will have the same instinctive knee-jerk reaction which is to rely on a centrally controlled economy. As Albert Einstein famously said... "doing more of the same and expecting different results is the very definition of insanity." Despite all evidence to the contrary (i.e. New Deal, Great Society), Obama has lead us to the tipping point of insolvency. Our current debt as a percentage of GDP is 102%. In 2010 the Federal government collected approximately $2.2 trillion in taxes, with a budget of approximately $3.5 trillion. To make up the budget shortfall Obama resorted to borrowing, which simply adds to our debt. The core problem Progressives never seem to realize is one of spending not revenues.

As previously mentioned, no individual or private business can sustain this approach indefinitely without bankruptcy being the end result. Why this basic economic principle is beyond the Federal government's ability to comprehend is truly a mystery. Obama's solution of course is no different from FDR, and for that matter,

Woodrow Wilson who gave us the progressive tax system…tax the rich!!! Currently, the top 1% of earners incur 38% of the tax burden. The top 5% of earners absorb 59% of the tax burden. The top 10% of earners pay 70% of our tax burden. Obama's solution, punish the rich. Unfortunately, at current spending levels, the tax rate would have to be raised over 140% on top earners to make an impact on deficit levels. This is to say, tax the top earners more than they make. Another perspective, the accumulated worth of all billionaires in America is approximately $1.3 trillion. If the Federal government seized every penny of these assets it still would not make a dent in our national debt. Again, Obama's solution is Keynesian economics adnauseam. Despite his "I'm here to solve the problem" pledge, Obama's economic policies, if implemented, will add an average of $1 trillion in deficits per year through 2019. George Bush in his worst year ran a deficit of just under $500 billion. [12]

Deficit spending under Bush averaged approximately 3% of GDP during his eight-year term. Deficit spending under Obama is averaging approximately 10% of GDP during his three-plus years in office. The 10% mark by Obama even eclipses the deficit spending under FDR, which was generally around the 6% mark. Put this into perspective, over the past forty years budget deficits have averaged approximately 2.4% of GDP, which means Bush was slightly above average. Under Obama, deficit spending as a percentage of GDP has been quadrupled, with no end in site. Obama will do nothing but fan the flames of debt with his current schemes. He will borrow 42 cents of every federal dollar spent. He will raise taxes on over 3 million upper income families. He will eliminate tax breaks for charity and eliminate tax deductions for mortgage interest. He will advocate PAYGO and sit idly by when Congress waives it repeatedly. He will add approximately $75,000 of additional debt to every American household over 10 years. He will leave us with permanent deficits that average $1 trillion per year by 2020. If the 2008 presidential election has taught us anything, elections do have consequences. In the case of Obama, those consequences are proving to be nothing short of dire.

Despite the abysmal failures of past Progressive administrations, (i.e. Wilson, FDR, LBJ), Obama is hell bent on taking this country down a path of financial ruin. Federal spending as a percentage of GDP is hovering around 40% under Obama. This is dangerously close to the insane spending levels courtesy of The New Deal. Federal spending was approximately 21% of GDP when FDR took office in 1933. In 1945, after 12 years of Progressive stewardship, federal spending as a percentage of GDP was at 53%. [13] By comparison, federal spending under Coolidge never topped 12% as a percentage of GDP. As a result, the economy thrived and unemployment was near 2% by the end of his second term. By the end of FDR's second term, federal spending as a percentage of GDP had doubled and unemployment stood at 15%. Henry Morgenthau, Jr. was one of the New Deal architects and also served as FDR's Treasury Secretary. Morgenthau himself provided probably the best summary of The New Deal in 1940; "...we have tried spending money. We are spending more than we have ever spent before and it does not work...We have never made good on our promises...I say after eight years of this Administration we have just as much unemployment as when we started...and enormous debt to boot!" [14] Substitute Obama for FDR, Geithner for Morgenthau, and the quote is as pertinent today as it was in 1940.

The call to raise taxes and soak the rich is the same rallying cry Progressives have utilized for decades. Despite the calls for redistribution in the name of fairness, raising taxes does not improve revenues long-term. In fact, tax revenues dating back to 1950 have averaged approximately 18-20% of GDP. Over the same time period, marginal tax rates went from a high of 91% to a low of just under 30%. Higher tax rates may give a slight bump to revenues short-term; however, higher tax rates eventually cause economic activity to slow, thereby lowering revenues. [15] The hallmarks of Keynesian economics are deficit spending (i.e. prime the pump) and perpetual experimentation. FDR policies where based upon this philosophy. The result, private capital was frozen as investors held on to their gains due to the instability of New Deal policies. The Constitution was designed to provide and protect freedom, not redistribution under the guise of fairness. Government's role in a free market should be limited to determining the rules, interpret and enforce. Once government intrudes upon the market and imposes central authority, the coercive power acts to impede freedom. Central planning (i.e. The New Deal) and prohibitive taxation are examples of coercive power. Economic activity controlled by a central authority is not a free market. The only way a free market can act as a check on political power is to remain separate from central authority. [16] Economic polices of Wilson, FDR, LBJ and now Obama lead us nowhere expect down *The Road to Serfdom* as F. A. Hayek aptly described.

"Hope & Change" is nothing more than the iterative process of Progressivism. Spend enough money, pass enough legislation and hope something works. This is the epitome of Progressivism, perpetual experimentation and theory over experience. Can anyone with a straight face claim to have confidence in those currently in charge of our financial future: Obama, Geithner, Bernanke, Dodd, Frank, et al…Can anyone with a straight face claim the economy has improved or will improve courtesy of QE 1, QE 2 or H.R. 4173? Quantitative easing was the brainchild of Ben Bernanke, which is a program designed to stimulate the economy by easing access to cash. In essence, The Fed printed money to buy bonds. Unfortunately, the cash never circulated, the banks simply held onto to the cash influx. QE 1 was introduce by the Fed in late fall 2008 and the program ran through March 2010. QE 2 was introduced by the Fed in November 2010 and was set to expire in June 2011. The inherent problem with

Keynesianism or priming the pump is the eventual outcome, which is inflation. It's not a coincidence that since QE 1 and QE 2 have been implemented the dollar has lost value and is in jeopardy of being removed as the world's reserve currency.

The person responsible for QE 1 and QE 2, in effect, the person in charge of monetary policy for the United States is Ben Bernanke. The current Chairman of the Federal Reserve took over from Alan Greenspan in 2006. His credentials for running The Federal Reserve (i.e. U.S. financial policy): he was a student of economics at Princeton and later taught economics at Princeton. In other words, someone totally devoid of private sector experience, like Obama, Geithner, et al... Bernanke based his decisions on theory over experience, on abstract policies, on the hypothetical born of classroom discussion and his studies of the Great Depression. The Fed was asleep at the wheel under Greenspan regarding the pending financial disaster and is now under the control of Bernanke, a career academic who also failed to recognize the dire financial straits of our economy and worse, how to correct the freefall. [17] In light of his actions, Bernanke's own words in 2008 underscore the fact that he was/is in over his head, "If no countervailing actions are taken, what would be perceived as an implicit expansion of the safety net could exacerbate the problem of "too big to fail," possibly resulting in excessive risk taking and yet greater systemic risk in the future." [18] Bernanke based his policy decisions during the financial meltdown starting in 2006 on what he thought could work based on theory, not what he knew would work based upon experience. His gambles (i.e. QE 1, QE 2) are once again based upon theory and not private sector experience.

H.R. 4173 – Dodd-Frank Wall Street Reform and Consumer Protection Act. The Act was introduced in December 2009 and signed into law July 2010, promises: "To provide for financial regulatory reform, to protect consumers and investors, to enhance Federal understanding of insurance issues to regulate the over-the-counter derivatives markets, and for other purposes." The Act was co-authored by Congressman Barney Frank and Senator Chris Dodd. There is not one person you can point a finger at and place blame for the financial meltdown in 2008. There are scores of individuals who could be and should be held accountable. However, if you put together a top 5 list of the most culpable, Frank and Dodd would rank at or near the top. Frank and Dodd were champions of subprime mortgages dating back to the early days of the Clinton administration. Frank and Dodd, among others, latched onto the home ownership for minority's bandwagon following a 1992 study by the Federal Reserve Bank of Boston. The study concluded that credit scores and loan-to-value ratios were discriminatory in nature. In other words, denying loans to those who cannot afford to repay them is discriminatory. Denying loans to those who are bad credits risks are discriminatory. Frank and Dodd acted as facilitators and coerced the housing market into the risky subprime lending market. The Clinton administration, HUD Secretaries Cisneros and Cuomo, FHA, FDIC, Fannie Mae, Freddie Mac, et al, were all too happy to acquiescence. [19] By the year 2000, Fannie Mae had guaranteed $1.6 trillion of mortgages, many of which were in the subprime category...courtesy of Frank and Dodd. [20]

Frank eventually became the Chairman of the House Financial Services Committee and Dodd eventually became Chairman of the Senate Banking Committee. Both sat idly by for years while Fannie and Freddie became insolvent. Frank repeatedly defended subprime lending and dismissed critique as "overblown." [21] As late as August of 2008, Frank described Fannie and Freddie as being "well capitalized." [22] Dodd, as well as members of both Fannie and Freddie, received sweet heart deals from Countrywide. Angelo Mozilo, CEO of Countrywide Financial, supported both Frank and Dodd and was at the center of the subprime meltdown. Dodd, among others, would become part of the nefarious group known as "Friends of

Angelo." Frank and Dodd sat idly by while Countrywide aggressively lent to risky borrowers and off-loaded these loans to both Fannie and Freddie. [23] In turn, Frank and Dodd encouraged both Fannie and Freddie to participate in the risky ventures. As Chairman of the Senate Banking Committee, Dodd also approved $100 million in bonuses paid to AIG executives, the bonuses were courtesy of taxpayers via the federal bailout. Dodd later said that he "reluctantly" agreed to the bonuses. [24] The top contributor to Dodd during the 2008 elections, AIG of course, at $281,038.00. [25]

Whether Frank and Dodd were complicit in the financial meltdown by design or shear ignorance, they were complicit nevertheless. Frank and Dodd advocating subprime lending was nothing more than political correctness and expedience. Neither has been held accountable for their actions by their respective ethics committees. Neither has been held accountable by the courts. Despite their complicit actions dating back to the early 1990's, Frank and Dodd are now authoring legislation to reform the financial mess they were responsible for creating. Bernanke took over as Fed Chariman in 2006; Geithner was serving as the Chair for the New York Fed during the financial crisis. Like Frank and Dodd, Bernanke and Geithner have been largely devoid of any private experience. Their actions are based first and foremost upon political expedience, ideology, theory, political correctness, identity politics, and classroom abstract thinking. This current edition of "Braintrusters" are as clueless as the original group under FDR. Frank, Dodd, Geithner and Bernanke were all at the center of the financial storm. They were either asleep at the wheel, did not recognize what was coming, saw what was coming and froze like a deer in the headlights, or the financial collapse was by design. Whatever the reason do we really want this current version of "Braintrusters" in charge of our economy, especially given their track record?

H.R.4173 in 2000 plus pages of legislation fails once to address the "too big to fail" maxim. H.R. 4173 does not address "bailouts," in fact, insures that up to $4 trillion in emergency funding be allocated to Wall Street should another crash occur, so much for moral hazard. The future bailouts will be under the prevue of the Fed and Treasury Secretary, as well as a group of regulators, which is the same group of enlightened thinkers who missed the crash the first time around. H.R. 4173 keeps bonuses in play, retains a toothless watchdog via the Office of the Comptroller of the Currency, and creates a position called the Director of Minority and Women Inclusion, and never once address either Fannie Mae or Freddie Mac. [26] Can anyone with a straight face be comfortable with knowing that Obama, Bernanke, Geithner, Frank, Dodd, et al...are responsible for our financial well being. These are the enlightened few responsible for the central planning of our economy. The same group of enlightened despots who brought us to our knees is now promising to rescue us. This current edition of 'Braintrusters' advocated Fannie and Freddie, QE 1, QE 2, raising the debt ceiling, deficit spending, priming the pump, devaluing the dollar, etc...Keep in mind, the U.S.A. lost its AAA credit rating in 2011. This is cause for great concern, not "Hope & Change."

NATIONAL SECURITY (OR LACK THEREOF)

Despite September 11, 2001 the Obama administration has decided it is politically incorrect to refer to terrorists as terrorists. The new PC euphuism for Islamic Terror is dubbed 'man-made disasters.' Despite the threat that Islamic Terror still poses to this country, Homeland Security Secretary Janet Napolitano refused to use the word terrorism during her first appearance in front of Congress in 2009. Napolitano described her "man-made disaster" reference as simply a "nuance." She also spoke of the need "to move away from the politics of fear" in defending her politically correct speech. [27] Since Obama has taken office, we've experienced five domestic terrorist attacks in the United States. Little Rock, AK June 2009, an American Muslim fires upon a U.S. Military recruiting office killing one and wounding another. New York City September 2009, a member of al-Qaeda fails in his attempt to detonate a bomb in the NYC subway system. Fort Hood, TX November 2009, U.S. Military Officer Nadal Malik Hassan kills 13 and wounds an additional 32 at Fort Hood. Detroit, MI December 2009, Nigerian citizen Umar Farouk Abdulmutallab fails to detonate bomb while flying into Detroit. New York City May 2010, car bomb discovered in Times Square before it is detonated.

June 2009, Abdulhakim Mujahid Muhammad kills one soldier and wounds another during a *"man-made disaster"* in Little Rock, Arkansas. Muhammad, formerly known as Carlos Bledsoe, was a U.S. citizen who converted to Islam. Muhammad (a.k.a., Bledsoe) spent time in Yemen where he studied jihad under an Islamic scholar. Subsequent interviews indicate the attack was motivated by political and religious beliefs. Upon arrest, police seize weapons in Muhammad's car which includes an assault rifle. [28] *September 2009,* three residents from Queens are arrested in connection with a plot to detonate bombs in three New York City subways. Subsequent investigation connects the failed *"man-made disaster"* to Al Qaeda leaders in Pakistan. The three suspects from Queens met with Al Qaeda leaders Saleh al-Somali and Rashid Rauf in September 2008 to plan the attempted suicide bombings. The trio from Queens, Najibullah Zazi, Zarein Ahmedzay and Adis Medunjanin, traveled to Pakistan in August of 2008. The original intent was to join the fight in Afghanistan against American soldiers. The Queens threesome was convinced by Al Qaeda leaders to bring the jihad to New York City. [29]

November 2009, Major Nidal Malik Hasan kills 13 people and wounds 32 others in a *"man-made disaster"* at Fort Hood Army base in Texas. Major Hasan, an Army psychiatrist, commits the shooting while shouting, "Allahu Akbar" or "God is greatest." Subsequent investigation indicates Hasan had ties to Anwar al-Awlaki, who serves as a senior Al Qaeda official in Yemen. Investigation points to numerous e-mails exchanged between Hasan and al-Awlaki. [30] *December 2009,* Abdul Farouk Umar Abdulmutallab is arrested following his failed attempt at a *"man-made disaster"* aboard a Northwest flight bound for Detroit, Michigan. Abdulmutallab, a Nigerian student, was trained in Yemen by Al-Qaeda operatives. Despite being on a 'terror watch' list, the State Department issues a visa to Abdulmutallab. A warning had also been issued to the U.S. Embassy 6 months prior to the thwarted suicide bombing by Abdulmutallab's own father. [31]

May 2010, New York's Time Square was evacuated after the discovery of a car bomb. The failed *"man-made disaster"* was perpetrated by U.S. citizen Faisal Shahzad who was trained and funded by the Pakistani Taliban. During his trial, a defiant Shahzad states, "Consider me the first droplet of the flood that will follow," "...we are proud terrorists and we will continue terrorizing you," "His desire is not to defend the United States and Americans but to kill them," and regarding his U.S. citizenship he states he "falsely swore allegiance to his country." Upon being sentenced to life in prison Shahzad states, "I am happy with the deal God has given to me." [32] Rewind to March 2009, newly appointed Homeland Security Secretary Janet Napolitano grants an interview to Spiegel and discusses her first testimony to Congress. During her testimony, Napolitano never mentions the word "terrorism" once and refers to such actions as *"man-made disasters."* Napolitano calls for us to move away from the "politics of fear" with a new emphasis on "authoritative information." Napolitano went on to boast of our improved ability to "...keep track of travelers coming into the U.S." In light of the aforementioned *"man-made disasters,"* the statements by Napolitano would be laughable if the consequences were not so dire.

Fast forward to February 2011, Congressman Peter King initiates hearings on the potential Muslim radicalization in America. Despite the *"man-made disasters"* previously discussed, despite evidence that suggest three-quarters of mosques in the United States actively teach Shariah Law, King is accused of "McCarthy-ite" tactics and "guilt by association." In light of the *"man-made disasters"* listed, Congressman King serves our interests well by raising concerns over the threat of home-grown terrorists. Despite a clear and present danger, Obama, Napolitano, Holder, et al, put us at risk by treating this threat as civilian/criminal in nature. Despite being attacked at home and abroad 6 times during the 1990's, despite having 09/11 planned and executed on our soil, Clinton refused to accept facts and treated each of the 1990's *"man-made disasters"* as isolated incidents and viewed them as criminal in nature as opposed to acts of war. We adopt this politically correct and inherently naïve mindset at our own peril. We will politically correct ourselves into oblivion given the current state of mind within the Obama Administration with regard to terrorism. Philosopher George Santayana said it best, "Those who cannot remember the past are condemned to repeat it." Taking out Usama bin Laden on May 2, 2011, notwithstanding, national security policy under this President is based more upon appeasement than the acknowledgment and defeat of an enemy dedicated to our total destruction. Tracking down bin Laden had more to do with Bush policy (i.e. enhanced interrogation) than anything Obama has implemented during his three-plus years in office.

ENERGY POLICY (OR LACK THEREOF)

The average price for a gallon of gas in January 2009 when Obama took office was $1.79. The average price per gallon of gas as of this writing is $3.50, a 95% increase. The price of a barrel of oil in January 2009 was $38, today it hovers around $110 per barrel. President Bush was excoriated by the press for the slightest increase in gas prices. The implication being that Bush and Cheney were acting in collusion with the oil companies to increase prices (i.e. revenues). Yet, despite the doubling of gas prices under Obama the press remains eerily silent. As of this writing gas prices are expected to hit $3.75-$4.25 per gallon for an extended period. Parts of California have already eclipsed the $5.00 per gallon mark. In 1981 we imported roughly a third of our oil, today we import close to 70%. Canada and Mexico combined account for approximately 30-35% of our oil; we import approximately 30-35% from the Middle East and use approximately 30% from domestic sources. Make no mistake; we are an economy based upon petroleum. Breaking down our energy consumption, oil accounts for approximately 40%, natural gas is 23%, coal is 22%, nuclear is 8%, biomass is 4%, hydroelectric is 2%, geothermal is 0.35%, wind is 0.31% and solar accounts for approximately 0.08%. Oil is number one and represents close to what natural gas and coal provide combined. Alternative sources of energy abound, wind, wave solar, geothermal, hydrogen, ethanol, nuclear, biodiesel, etc...the underlying problem with these alternatives are cost to produce and efficiency. [33]

None of the alternatives mentioned are as cost effective to produce as petroleum products. If not for tax subsides many of the energy alternatives would not exist. Ethanol for one relies upon billions of taxpayer funded subsides, if left to market forces, ethanol would be DOA. The irony in ethanol production is that it consumes oil as part of the process. It takes approximately 1.29 gallons of gasoline to produce 1 gallon of ethanol. Hardly cost effective, even by Progressive standards. In fact, if we were to rely totally upon ethanol to fuel our vehicles, 97% of the United States would need to be converted into farmland...utopia indeed. We are no closer today than we were 30 years ago in having an efficient and cost effective replacement for oil. Market forces bear this out, tax subsides for ethanol are the perfect example. Despite the hard facts, Obama and fellow Progressives continue to live in a world where theory trumps experience. [34]

We have approximately 150-200 years worth of coal reserves, [35] we have billions of barrels of oil reserves in ANWR, [36] we have billions of barrels of oil reserves off our coasts and in the Gulf and we have trillions of cubic feet of natural gas reserves within our borders. Despite our ability to be energy independent, we remain hostage to Progressives and their "green" agenda, which again is based upon theory and not pragmatism. The favorite argument of the left is that it takes years for new drilling to produce oil at the pump. President Clinton vetoed a bill in 1996 that would have opened up production in ANWR. Obama vetoed plans to open up hundreds of millions of acres to offshore drilling that was proposed by President Bush. Both Clinton and Obama acted to appease their green base (i.e. enviro-statists) at the expense of our energy independence, once again, the ill-advised consequences of well intended Progressive ideology. Obama's answer to our energy woes is Cap and Trade, a policy which does nothing to produce efficient energy or create jobs. What it does, is appease the "green" movement at the expense of energy independence and job creation. By levying excess taxes on oil companies, essentially selling permits to pollute, the increased taxes will simly be passed along to the consumer. Cap and Trade will increase the price per gallon at the pump, punish the consumer, and reduce manufacturing jobs. This is not a viable energy policy, it is simply another attempt by Progressives to punish success (i.e. Big Oil) and redistribute wealth (i.e. carbon taxes).

At the heart of Obama's energy policy, or lack thereof, is cap and trade. Cap and trade is nothing more than a euphemism for cap and tax. The entire legislation is beholden to the IPCC, the UN, the enviro-left and the entire myth of global warming. The IPCC is the Intergovernmental Panel on Climate Control and was established in 1988 by the United Nations Framework Convention on Climate Change. These were the same 'climate warriors' that promoted "global cooling" during the 1970's and when empirical data did not prove their deductive approach, "global cooling" became "global warming." [37] What cap and trade does is essentially level a sin tax on carbon emitting companies. [38] Utility companies, such as coal fired plants have a choice between cutting emissions or paying the sin tax. The sin tax is nothing more than buying an expensive permit to pollute. End result, utility companies pay more and simply pass the cost along to the consumer. Cap and trade will also have an effect on jobs specifically manufacturing. According to the Heritage Foundation, some 400,000 manufacturing jobs will be lost as a result of cap and trade due to the inordinate cost of doing business. Cap and trade is sold as a means to stem carbon emissions, however, it is nothing more than a covert means by which to nationalize the utilities and manufacturing industries in this country. [39] Cap and trade will do for the utility industry what TARP has done to the banking and financial industry. In essence, both cap and trade and TARP were sold to the American public under the guise of altruism. The government has to legislate in order to prevent global warming, financial insolvency, etc…Legislation such as cap and trade and TARP are nothing more that Progressive measure towards nationalization. [40]

Candidate Obama gave a clue as to his energy policy (i.e. ideology) in 2008 when he said, "So if somebody wants to build a coal-powered plant, they can; its just that it will bankrupt them because they're going to be charged a huge sum for all that greenhouse gas that's being emitted."[41] America is considered the Saudi Arabia of coal and has approximately 150-200 years worth of coal reserves, coal that generates electricity as well as coal being converted to synthetic oil. With a barrel of oil hovering around $110, the $45 to produce a barrel of synthetic oil from coal is quite reasonable. We should, at the very least, leverage our coal reserves against the current price of oil. Unfortunately, Obama is voting present on this issue. The energy policy of candidate Obama, and now President Obama, is to bankrupt an industry via punitive legislation. Bankrupt an industry that provides energy and thousands of jobs, this is not progress nor is it hope & change. Obama used the Deepwater Horizon spill in the Gulf of Mexico to further his agenda against big oil. Despite his pledge to reduce our dependence on foreign oil, Obama's actions and intent are completely antithetical to his promises. Following the British Petroleum spill, moratoriums were issued on drilling in the Gulf. We now have huge oil reserves in the Gulf being untapped. To make matters worse, Obama allows China, Russia, Cuba and Venezuela to drill a few short miles off the Florida Keys. [42]

Obama's energy plan to date includes: cripple the coal industry via punitive taxes, demonize big oil, blanket moratoriums on Gulf drilling, ignoring oil reserves off both coats, ignoring oil reserves in ANWR and ignoring natural gas reserves throughout the U.S. Obama's energy plan to date also includes: $2 billion in subsidies to Brazilian Petrobras for deep water drilling, millions in subsidies to GE green jobs creation, millions in subsidies to Solyndra Solar, millions in subsidies to Evergreen Solar, millions in subsidies to promote green jobs throughout the economy. General Electric earned $14.2 billion in profits, $5.1 billion within the United States yet paid zero federal taxes. GE continued to receive subsidies for green jobs and saw Chairman Jeffrey Immelt promoted to jobs czar by Obama. Obama continues his crony capitalism approach to energy with companies like Solyndra of Freemont, California, "The true engine of economic growth will always be companies like Solyndra."

Solyndra promised to create thousands of jobs through construction and production of solar panels. As of this writing, Solyndra has yet to turn a profit and has cancelled further construction. [43] Evergreen Solar of Massachusetts has laid off hundreds of workers and moved manufacturing operations to China due to labor costs. Throughout Europe, particularly Spain, the creation of one green job has cost 2.2 in the general economy. Despite all evidence to the contrary, the facts have not deterred Obama from his green economy advocacy. Green jobs cannot survive if left to the free markets, green jobs rely on federal subsidies and mandates for their very existence. This is not an energy policy, its Progressive ideology at its worse. [44]

The prevailing wisdom, or lack thereof, by Progressives is the reliance on theory over experience. Obama and his sycophants continue to vilify big oil at the expense of job creation and energy independence. Obscene profits are the mantra from Progressives, big oil is an easy target. The irony here is that oil as an industry makes less revenue on its product than the federal government. Oil as an industry has profit margins that average between 7-9% of revenues; federal, state and local governments make three times this amount off oil via taxes. The profit margin for oil is far below companies such as Microsoft, eBay, Google, McDonalds, Coca Cola, Apple, etc...In fact, oil as an industry ranks 56th with regard to their profit margin when compared to the aforementioned companies. Microsoft for example nets approximately 30 cents for every dollar of revenue generated, far better than the 7-9 cents that big oil nets. Yet, no other industry is demonized by Progressives like oil. Exxon for example in 2008 paid a total of $116 billion in taxes, more than twice what their net profit was. What is also lost, beyond the federal government earning more from oil than the oil industry itself, profits from the oil industry are distributed throughout 401K plans, pensions and individual investors. [45]

Obama has no objections to subsidizing green jobs via GE, Solyndra and Evergreen Solar. He has no objections to GE paying zero federal taxes on $5 billion in revenues. He has no objections to subsidizing deep water drilling off the coast of Brazil. However, he issues moratoriums on American deep water drilling, advocates an end to oil subsidies and proposes to increase taxes on both domestic oil and gas industries. Raising taxes on these industries could reduce production by as much as 10% by the year 2017 according to the American Petroleum Institute and Woods Mackenzie.[46] If the current legislation to increase taxes on oil and gas are imposed by Congress and Obama, Woods Mackenzie estimates that $15 billion in investments are in jeopardy for the year 2011. Extended over a period of ten years, Woods Mackenzie estimates that $130 billion in investment dollars would be put in jeopardy. The areas impacted include the Gulf of Mexico, the Rocky Mountains, the Northeast, mid-continent, Alaska, and Gulf Coast. Obama's energy policy would put billions of investment dollars in jeopardy, millions of jobs in jeopardy, energy independence in jeopardy, all to appease a Progressive green ideology. What also seems to be lost on Obama and the green agenda is oil and natural gas produce more than simply heat and power. These industries account for approximately 800,000 American jobs and over 5 million American jobs in related industries. Oil and gas are raw material for approximately 96% of American manufactured goods. [47]

Other industries (i.e. GE, Solyndra, and Evergreen Solar) receive subsidies and tax breaks similar to those of oil and gas. In fact, oil and gas combined already pay an effective tax rate that is 70% higher than most S&P Industrials. [48] Unfortunately for oil, gas, coal, synthetic oil, etc…they are on the wrong side of political correctness, which makes for easy targets. The green jobs fantasy has proved to be an abject failure in Spain and throughout Europe. Electricity from solar power is twice per kilowatt hour compared to electricity from natural gas. Solar companies relying on tax subsidies are now shipping jobs to China due to labor costs and their failure to turn a profit in America. Ethanol requires tax subsidies and uses 1.29 gallons of gas to produce one gallon of ethanol. To produce enough ethanol to run all American vehicles, 97% of U. S. land mass would need to be converted to corn fields. Wind power is not consistent, suitable for all locations or cost effective. Wind farms produce only 25-30% of their theoretical capacity due to fluctuations in the wind, too high or too low. Wind farms must rely on traditional power plants as backups. Tax credits to promote hybrid vehicles (i.e. clash for clunkers) failed miserably. Hybrids as an industry, GM, Nissan, Toyota, Honda, Ford, et al, are awash in red ink. [49] North Dakota has an unemployment rate of 3.8% because it tripled oil and gas production. Oil as an industry enriches the federal government far more than it enriches the oil industry. Oil and gas employ approximately 5 million Americans directly or via industry related products. We have the natural recourses to provide energy and jobs in this country for close to 200 years. Common sense should dictate what is blatantly obvious regarding our energy policy. Unfortunately, Progressives live in a world based upon theory, which does not bode well for U.S. energy policy under this administration.

JOB CREATION (OR LACK THEREOF)

"…I guess the shovel ready jobs were not as shovel ready as we thought…"

Obama June 2011

Unemployment under Bush averaged 5.25% during his eight-year term in office and was hovering close to 7% in January 2009. Despite his pledge to cap unemployment at 8% by passing the $787 billion stimulus, unemployment has been near 10% for almost three years.

As of this writing and according to the US debt clock, the US workforce is listed at 141,011,429 which is a contraction of 2 million jobs since 2009. The official unemployment number is listed at 12,974,810 or 8.5%. However, if you account for the underemployed and those unemployed for over two years the actual number is listed as 23,114,806 or 16.3%. The rate currently listed by Obama at 8.5% is misleading as millions are no longer counted due to the length of their unemployment. The current rate is disingenuous as Obama simply changed the denominator in the equation to reflect a lower number. With the exception of some fuzzy math, Obama has done nothing to curb unemployment. Obama has demonstrated an utter lack of coherence with regard to the unemployment issue. His advocacy for unions (i.e. Employee Free Choice Act), green jobs, wind power, solar power, nuclear power (i.e. GE), cap and trade (i.e. carbon emission tax), bailouts, stimulus, etc...is born of political expedience and ideology and has accomplished zero with regard to job creation. His vilification of big oil, natural gas and coal comes at the expense of energy independence and hundreds of thousands of American jobs. Of course it does play to his progressive base, which is the real priority for this political opportunist and chief.

The state with the lowest unemployment number is North Dakota at 3.8%. The reason is they have tripled their oil and gas production leading to thousands of jobs created. [50] Despite having an abundance of natural resources available to us via coal, natural gas and oil, Obama has made a concerted effort to thwart efforts on behalf of these industries to provide energy and create thousands of jobs. Instead of promoting industries (i.e. oil, gas, coal) that are capable of producing clean, efficient energy and creating jobs, Obama continues to appease his green base at the expense of energy and jobs. We have 150-200 years worth of coal; we have billions of barrels of oil within our borders, off both coasts as well as the Gulf of Mexico. We have trillions of cubic feet of natural gas reserves. In other words, we have the capabilities of being energy independent and creating thousands of jobs for Americans. Instead, Obama vilifies these industries while promoting green jobs, subsidizing companies like GE, Evergreen Solar and Solyndra. The state of Massachusetts provided $43 million in subsidies to Evergreen Solar in Devens, Mass. Only to have the company relocate to China and layoff its 800 workers...money well spent according to "Hope & Change" doctrine. Solyndra Inc. of Fremont, California was provided $535 million in subsidies has part of the stimulus package to manufacture solar panels. The company to date has never created the 1000 jobs promised and has yet to generate a profit. According to the California Energy Commission, the cost to generate solar electricity is 26 cents per kilowatt hour. The cost to generate electricity via natural gas is 13 cents. [51]

Obama is basing job creation policies on political ideology, shear incompetence or of malicious intent. Regardless of his intentions or motivation, he refuses to recognize what is so blatantly clear. We have within our means the ability to be energy independence and create jobs, yet Obama consistently advocates for policies that are completely antithetical to both. Political ideology, incompetence, or malicious intent, the case can be made for all three with regard to Obama and his intentions/motivation on employment. The American Enterprise Institute points to Europe as an example of the "green job" alleged utopia. For every green job created in Spain, 2.2 jobs were destroyed in the general economy. The capital needed to create one green job in Italy would create 5 jobs in the general economy. As Europeans realize the green job fantasy is unsustainable and cost prohibitive, the Obama administration continues to advocate for "investment" in green technology despite all evidence to the contrary. As Milton Friedman said, "governments do not add value to the economy." Efficient use of capital resources, free trade markets, models based on supply and demand create jobs and motivate entrepreneurship. Employment markets should be driven by consumer preferences, in other words, consent and free exchange. Government imposing green job fantasies on the market is nothing more than force and taxation. [52] Economist Ludwig von Mises once wrote, "It was learned that in the social realm too there is something operative which power and force are unable to alter and to which they must adjust themselves if the hope to achieve success..." Unfortunately, Obama like all progressives fail to heed what history teaches as he continues to substitute theory over experience.

Teddy Roosevelt, Woodrow Wilson and FDR all utilized executive orders to implement their progressive policies. Obama follows suit with his proposed executive orders on both carbon taxes and secret ballot union elections. Neither issue has majority support within the general electorate or in either house of Congress. Despite this and because of this, Obama plans to issue executive orders that will be enforced as law by the EPA and NLRB. The carbon tax will effectively kill manufacturing jobs in many communities, most notably the oil industries of both Texas and Louisiana. Eliminating secret ballots on unionization essentially forces unionization upon those who would have probably voted against in a secret ballot. The head of the NLRB, Craig Becker, is former chief counsel to SEIU. The Service Employees International Union donated tens of millions of union dues to the election campaign of Obama in 2008. No small coincidence...If the forced unionization measure is signed into law by executive order it will decrease jobs within the US as companies will replace high labor costs with machinery. Since 1990, unionized manufacturing jobs have declined by 75%, whereas non-unionized manufacturing jobs have increased by 15%. [53]

The myth about unions creating jobs is just that, a myth. Unions act in the best interest of unions not in the best interest of the rank and file. To invoke Milton Friedman once again, wages should be a product of supply and demand, and free markets. Initiatives like the "Employee Free Choice Act" are noting more than force and coercion courtesy of the federal government. If wages are not a product of consent and free exchange, there is no free market. Government intrusion under the guise of such polices as the "Employee Free Choice Act" does not add value to the economy nor does it create wealth. Legendary union leader John L. Lewis advocated for the United Mine Workers from 1920-1960. As a product of his numerous strikes that interrupted coal supplies, he was able to secure wages that otherwise would not have been supported via supply and demand. In the long run, John L. Lewis did more for the oil industry than he ever accomplished for the United Mine Workers. Due to the prohibitive costs of labor for mine workers, the price of coal increased. As the price of coal increased the energy market transitioned to oil. Unions did the same to the auto, textile and steel industries. Prohibitive labor costs, courtesy of the unions, drove up the price of both domestic automobiles and domestic steel. As a result, jobs were lost in these industries as steel, textiles and cars were cheaper to buy from oversees competitors. [54]

Unions have outlived their usefulness and serve as nothing more than a Democratic fundraising organization. This is particularly true of public sector unions, who have bankrupted numerous municipalities courtesy of their massive pensions, which are unfunded liabilities. Unions in the steel, textile, auto and airline industries have crippled their respective industries with prohibitive wages and unfunded pensions. The result, millions of jobs lost to oversees companies. Whether it's public or private sector, unions have the same entitlement, free lunch mentality. They want wages and pensions to be based simply on joining a union with no regard to merit or productivity, the teachers unions are the perfect example. Incompetent teachers are not only protected but promoted. Excellent teachers are forced to drag this unproductive "baggage" along. Private schools offer a competitive advantage with regard to education, of course the unions are adamantly opposed to these schools. Despite the Department of Education and the billions of dollars spent over the past decades, teachers unions use the same old mantra, we haven't spent enough. Well, I say, we have spent enough. It is time to abandon teachers unions for free market, supply and demand models. The worst offender of course are the public sector, specifically, the government worker. By the year 2013, retirement money promised to 87,000 state, county and local governments and school districts will exceed the cash on hand by more than $1 trillion. Even the staunchest of union supporters will have to admit the math simply does not add up. [55]

Private sector unions account for approximately 7.2% of the workforce down from 33.9% during the 1940's. The reason, collective bargaining in the private sector is driven by market forces, bailouts to GM and Chrysler, notwithstanding. A better example of market forces and collective bargaining in the private sector is John L. Lewis and the United Mine Workers. Public sector unions, however, are on the rise from 9.8% during the 1940's to 36.8% of the current workforce. Increasing public sector union employees does not add value to the economy; it's a drain on the economy. According to the U.S. Bureau of Economic Analysis, the average salary for a federal employee is $123,409 or twice that of the average private sector employee. Approximately 8 million jobs have evaporated during the current recession; however, the number of federal workers on the taxpayer's dime is at an all time high of 2.15 million. Although the taxpayer does not have a seat at the table for private sector collective bargaining, they can speak with their consumer choices. Unfortunately, the taxpayer does not have a seat at the table for public sector collective bargaining either but has no recourse. Taxpayers serve only to provide and endless stream of entitlements to the public sector courtesy of politicians who are elected to protect the best interest of taxpayers. [56]

California, New York, Illinois, Ohio and New Jersey are on the verge of bankruptcy. Los Angeles, Chicago, New York, Washington, D.C., Newark and Detroit are insolvent as well. The primary reason for this is salaries to public sector unions that far exceed what market forces would bear, as well as billions of dollars in unfunded liabilities (i.e. pensions). [57] Even supporters of big government and public sector unions are seeing the writing on the wall. David Crane is a Democrat and serves on the California Board of Regents, he is quoted, "Collective bargaining in the public sector serves to reduce benefits for citizens and to raise costs for taxpayers." [58] Unions generally secure higher wages, which actually distorts the labor force. Higher wages typically means less can be employed. It's the identical principle of any product, the higher the price the less is bought. Once again, we can use John L. Lewis and the United Mine Workers as an example. Lewis fought for higher wages, which meant fewer miners could be employed. The higher wages were passed along to customers who purchased coal. These customers eventually traded coal for oil because of higher prices which crippled the coal industry. [59]

Fantasy green jobs, Solyndra, Evergreen Solar, the NLRB, the Employee Free Choice Act, unionization, moratoriums on drilling, moratoriums on fracking, etc. will not create jobs. Back to the example of North Dakota, they have a 3.8% unemployment rate. They have tapped into their state's natural resources (i.e. oil and gas) and provided thousands of jobs for their citizens. ANWR, waters of both east and west coasts, the Gulf of Mexico, the Rocky Mountains, etc. represent decades of energy from coal, oil and natural gas. Not only does this represent energy independence, it represents hundreds of thousands of jobs. Obama would serve this country well to put aside progressive ideology and crony capitalism. Let experience trump theory and remove the chains from the free market and entrepreneurship. Appeasing the green agenda, appeasing unions, crony capitalism, vilifying oil, gas and coal industries may result in a second term for Obama but his tactics have done little if anything nor will they to provide job creation and reduce unemployment. Jack Gerard, President of the American Petroleum Industry, summed up Obama perfectly, "If the president were really serious about job creation, he would be working with us to develop American oil and gas by American workers for American consumers." [60] Obama's record on job creation can best be summed by examining the U.S. workforce. In 2009 the total workforce stood at 143 million, today it stands at 141 million, a contraction of 2 million jobs. This is not "Hope & Change" it is America in decline.

TAX CHEATS, INCOMPETENCE, MALFEASANCE & CORRUPTION ADNAUSEAM

Nancy Killefer nominated for Chief Performance Officer withdraws due to unpaid taxes. *Ron Kirk* nominated for U.S. Trade Representative despite owing back taxes exceeding $10K. *Tom Daschle* nominated for DHS Secretary withdraws due to unpaid taxes in excess of $120K. *Kathleen Sebelius* nominated and approved for DHS Secretary despite unpaid tax burdens. *Hilda Solis* nominated and approved for Labor Secretary despite disclosure violations and tax liens against her husband. *Timothy Geithner* nominated and approved for Treasury Secretary despite unpaid taxes and being reimbursed for taxes he did not pay. *Caroline Atkinson* nominated for Undersecretary for International Affairs withdraws due to tax irregularities. [61]

In addition to the aforementioned tax scofflaws, the vetting expertise of the Obama inner circle continued to shine with the following nominations: *Bill Richardson* withdraws from Commerce Secretary Nomination due to pending corruption charges. *Gary Locke* nominated and confirmed for Commerce Secretary despite being involved in campaign finance scandals. *Annette Nazareth* withdraws name from Chief Deputy under Geithner due to allegations of incompetence for her work at SEC.[62] ***H. Rodgin Cohen*** withdraws name from Chief Deputy Position due to conflicts of interest. ***Frank Brosens*** withdraws name from Treasury position, citing personal reasons. ***Scott Polakoff*** was put on leave from his Treasury position due to allegations of fraud. ***Jon Cannon*** nominated for Deputy U.S EPA Administrator, withdraws due to financial irregularities while he served on board overseeing the Clean Water Foundation. Despite his anti-Semitism, ***Charles Freeman*** is nominated for director of National Intelligence Council. Freeman later withdraws from nomination due to numerous improprieties.[63] Irony at its best, Federal government workers currently owe a collective $3 billion in back taxes. Page 129 of Obama's FY12 budget includes his intent on cracking down those delinquent in paying taxes. [64] The 'wise and intelligent few' indeed.

Eric Holder, gatekeeper for presidential pardons under Clinton, incompetent attorney general under Obama. Proponent of civilian trials for terrorstis, opponent of Arizona immigration law despite not having read it, fails to prosecute Black Panthers for voter intimidation despite having it on tape. ***Anita Dunn,*** former white house communications director and Mao enthusiast. ***Rham Emanuel,*** "...you never want a serious crisis to go to waste...". ***John Holdren,*** Science and Technology Czar, as well as global warming fanatic, advocate for wealth redistribution and fervent anti-capitalist. ***Jeffrey Immelt,*** sits on Economic Recovery Board, GE stock has lost 46% of its value under Immelt's tenure. ***Valerie Jarrett,*** chief political advisor to Obama and former Chicago slum lord. ***Van Jones,*** former Green Jobs Czar and full time communist. ***Elena Kagan,*** Supreme Court Justice under Obama despite never having tried a case in court on any level. Advocate for socialism, social justice and views Constitution as defective. ***Samantha Powers,*** Senior Director for Multinational Affairs, married to Cass Sustein, anti-

Semite, globalist, communist sympathizer, advocate for redistributive policies, opposes American exceptionalism. ***Sonia Sotomayer,*** Supreme Court Justice nominated by Obama. Advocate of legal realism, views Constitution as obsolete and should be subservient to international law, believes judges should allow their race, gender, etc… to influence their decision. Advocate for affirmative action and entitlements to illegal aliens. ***Cass Sustein,*** Regulatory Czar and husband of Samantha Powers. Believes Constitution is obsolete and contains no fixed principles or truths.

LIES, DAMN LIES & OBAMACARE

Universal healthcare/socialized medicine is the holy grail of progressive entitlements, or as Vice President Joe Biden described it, "a big f - - - ing deal." The Patient Protection and Affordable Care Act was sold to the American public as a panacea, it would provide affordable healthcare to all, create jobs, control costs and decrease the national debt. According to former Speaker of the House, Nancy Pelosi, the bill would create four million new jobs. According to Obama the bill would be deficit neutral. ObamaCare is government directed health care based upon European welfare states such as Britain, France, Sweden and Germany. Winston Churchill once said that Democracy is the worst form of government, except for all the rest. The same can be said for the healthcare system in the United States; it is the worst except for all the rest. Our constitutional republic was founded upon the principle of government that does the best for the most. It was not based upon a paternalistic government that grants universal entitlements to all. Health care is a privilege, not a right. Healthcare is a business; we have no more right to health care than we do any other goods and/or service. The inherent problem with welfare states (i.e. paternalism) is the slippery slope it creates. As Thomas Jefferson once said, "A government big enough to give you everything you want, is big enough to take everything you have." Somehow, Progressives and their universal entitlement mentality never seem to grasp this. Or perhaps they do, which suggests motives that are more pernicious in nature than altruistic.

Despite the pledge of transparency, "hope & change" gave us ObamaCare which was passed by the Senate on Christmas Eve 2009. Senators had less than 72 hours to digest over 2000 pages of healthcare legislation. Included in the healthcare bill was a separate budget reconciliation bill that included $105 billion worth of pre-funding. [65] Essentially, Democrats led by Pelosi and Reid circumvented normal appropriations procedure and snuck in a provision that pre-funded the bill upon passage. Former Speaker Nancy Pelosi was indeed prophetic when she said, "We have to pass the bill so that you can find out what is in it." The $105 billion of pre-authorized spending is set in motion by automatic triggers through 2019, transparency indeed! The Patient Protection and Affordable Care Act was signed into law on March 23, 2010 and will soon celebrate its two year anniversary. After the signing, Democrats promised the American public that support for the bill would grow over time as the specifics were disseminated. At best, public support for the bill never was above 50%. Since the bill was signed into law in March 2010, Rasmussen has conducted over 50 polls regarding support/opposition to healthcare legislation. In 53 consecutive Rasmussen pools, the majority of those polled supported the repeal of ObamaCare. The bill has become more unpopular with time and continues to do so. [66]

Two years after the health care panacea was passed, polls continue to show the American public's disdain and support for repeal. Twenty-six states have filed suits alleging the bill is unconstitutional. Judge Roger Vinson, U.S. District Court in Florida, ruled against the bill in his decision in Florida v. Health and Human Services. At the heart of his decision, Judge Vinson invokes the original intent of the Commerce Clause. In his opinion, Judge Vinson states, "If it

(Congress) has the power to compel an otherwise passive individual into a commercial transaction with a third party merely by asserting, as was done in the Act, that compelling the actual transaction is itself commercial and economic in nature, and substantially affects interstate commerce, it is not hyperbolizing to suggest that Congress could do almost anything it wants." Vinson went on to state "It is difficult to imagine that a nation which began, at least in part, as the result of opposition to a British mandate giving the East India Company a monopoly and imposing a nominal tax on all tea sold in America would have set out to create a government with the power to force people to buy tea in the first place. If Congress can penalize a passive individual for failing to engage in commerce, the enumeration of powers in the Constitution would have been in vain for it would be difficult to perceive any limitation on federal power, and we would have a Constitution in name only. Surely this is not what the Founding Fathers could have intended." [67]

The decision strikes at the heart of ObamaCare, which is the individual mandate. The mandate imposes a tax on individuals to purchase healthcare. ObamaCare invokes both the general welfare clause and commerce clause of the Constitution. The enumerated powers of Congress are described in Article 1 Section 8 of the Constitution. Article 1.8.1 states, The Congress shall have the power to lay and collect taxes, duties, imposts and excises, to pay the debts and provide for the common defense and general welfare of the Unites States; but all duties, imposts, and excises shall be uniform throughout the United States. Article 1.8.3 states, To regulate commerce with foreign nations, and among the several States, and with Indian Tribes. [68] The enumerated powers granted to the Congress in Article 1, Section 8 was intended to create/monitor free trade between the states. This provision was designed to mitigate local (i.e. State) prosperity at the expense of the general welfare of the nation. In other words, Congress serves as a proponent to the free flow of commerce, which contributes to national prosperity (i.e. general welfare). Article 1 Section 8 does not grant Congress the power to impose commerce. In other words, the federal government cannot force a passive individual into a commercial transaction (i.e. health care mandates). [69] Taken to its logical conclusion, ObamaCare claims health care is under the jurisdiction of interstate commerce even though health care cannot be sold across state lines. ObamaCare also claims that by not buying a product, in this case health insurance, a passive individual is engaging in commerce. [70]

Rising premiums, rationing, socialized medicine, funding for abortion, death panels, amortization of health care, additional debt, etc., were reasons given by opponents of ObamaCare to defeat the bill. The aforementioned reasons were also used by proponents of ObamaCare and they claim the arguments against ObamaCare are nothing more than fear tactics. In fact, proponents of ObamaCare claim the very use of the word is inflammatory in nature and may actually be racially motivated. Proponents, i.e. Progressives, i.e. Liberals, i.e. Democrats claim the term ObamaCare is meant as a disparaging remark. Representative Debbie Wasserman Schultz (D) Florida, actually suggest that using the term ObamaCare is analogous to using the "n" word. The obvious conclusion here is that if one is opposed to the government takeover of approximately 17-20% of our entire economy, one must indeed be a racist. [71] A favorite tactic of Progressives, when they cannot win arguments based upon merit, is to attempt to marginalize their opposition by false claims. In the case of ObamaCare, if you're opposed you're racist. If not so insulting, the claim would be laughable. Arguments for or against ObamaCare should be based on nothing more than evidence and logic. This seems to be lost on proponents such as Wasserman Schultz.

Columnist Larry Elder describes what ObamaCare actually is "an expensive, unpopular, legally dubious piece of legislation that most voters oppose." [72] As previously mentioned, Rasmussen polls confirm that every poll they've taken since the bill was passed in March of 2010 show a majority in favor of repeal. Apparently 50 plus percent of the American electorate are ill-informed, illogical racists. Upon further review, ObamaCare has given us the following panacea. Taxpayer money under ObamaCare would indeed be used to fund abortions. In an attempt to reduce health care costs, the FDA is currently preparing to de-label a breast cancer fighting drug called Avastin. The de-labeling eliminates reimbursements from commercial payers and Medicare and forces the individual to pay excessive out-of-pocket costs.

Again, paternalism is a slippery slope, today its rationing for Avastin, tomorrow it is medications for blood pressure, cholesterol, heart disease, etc...no rationing indeed! [73] As of 01/11/2011, ObamaCare also prevents patients from using tax-sheltered vehicles such as flexible savings accounts (FSA) and health savings accounts (HSA) to purchase over the counter drugs. The FSA and HSA are designed as a consumer driven plan. In other words, the consumer/patient takes responsibility for their health care purchases by shopping around (i.e. consumer driven). Diligence on the part of the consumer/patient is rewarded and reduces the long-term cost of healthcare. New regulations due to ObamaCare undermine the very existence of these consumer/patient vehicles. [74]

The most accurate way to judge the intent of ObamaCare is through Pelosi's own words, "We have to pass the bill so that you can find out what is in it." The chief actuary for Medicare is on record as saying that the claim by ObamaCare to reduce healthcare costs are "false, more so than true." The actuary also said that ObamaCare claims to allow patients to retain their current health insurance are "not true in all cases." [75] The deficit neutral claim is also disingenuous at best. ObamaCare pays for itself with the individual mandate as well as other tax hikes which extend for 10 years. However, the benefits of ObamaCare are limited to six years of provisions.

Whether ObamaCare was well intended but ill advised, or simply a pernicious and covert means by which to take control of 17-20% of our economy, Progressives continue to equate good intentions with good policy. [76] As a result of ObamaCare, and according to Mitch McConnell, "federal health spending is estimated to increase by $450 billion over the next decade." In addition, "taxes will go up more than $550 billion." [77] The $550 billion in additional taxes are due to the numerous tax hikes that were hidden in the 2000 plus page legislation. According to the House Budget Committee, ObamaCare will also add some $700 billion to our deficit over the next decade… deficit neutral indeed! [78]

Most of the arguments given here against ObamaCare will be seen as partisan in nature and marginalized by Progressives. However, the most accurate referendum on ObamaCare is provided by the very people who advocated for its passage. Henry Morgenthau served as FDR's Treasury Secretary and was instrumental in developing and implementing the "New Deal." Morgenthau made the following statement with regard to the "New Deal,""…we have tried spending money. We are spending more than we have ever spent before and it does not work…We have never made good on our promises…I say after eight years of the Administration we have just as much unemployment as when we started…and an enormous debt to boot." Again good intentions do not equate to good policy. Many of those who advocated for ObamaCare are speaking out against it via words and actions. CEO of Starbucks, Howard Schultz, was a vocal proponent for ObamaCare. Shultz is now on record as saying "I think as the bill is currently written and if it was going to land in 2014 under the current guidelines, the pressure on small businesses, because of the mandate, is too great." [79] Also, over 1000 entities have applied for and received waives with regard to ObamaCare. The majority of these waivers have been granted to organizations such as SEIU and other labor organizations that contributed tens of millions of dollars in campaign finances to Obama and were also vocal advocates for ObamaCare. Again, the best referendum on ObamaCare is not from those who oppose it but ironically comes from those who advocate for it.

November 2010, the mid-term elections were a referendum on Obama, Pelosi and Reid. More specifically, it was a referendum on ObamaCare. The Republicans picked up 63 seats in the House and 6 seats in the Senate, the largest Congressional victory for Republicans since 1938.[80] The majority of Republicans ran on a platform whereby repealing ObamaCare was first and foremost. Democrats on the other hand ran away from ObamaCare and avoided at all costs broaching the subject as a campaign issue. The bill becomes less popular with each passing day and will certainly be a major campaign issue in 2012. Sarah Palin was chastised for her references of "death panels." Upon further review, ObamaCare will include guidelines whereby life and death decisions are based upon cost analysis. Essentially, healthcare will be amortized based through a provision called quality adjusted life years (QALY's). Treatment will depend upon a patient's age, cost of the procedure and whether the patient will live long enough to justify the cost. Obviously, QALY's is not referred to as "death panels" in ObamaCare. Semantics aside, the new health care law will ration care based upon bureaucratic guidelines. [81]

As previously mentioned, ObamaCare is based on the European welfare states: Germany, UK, France, Spain, etc…The best way to preface a comparison between the U.S. and others is to invoke Churchill's view on Democracy and relate it to healthcare. The United States system of healthcare is the worst except for all the rest. Progressives and advocates of universal care, socialized medicine, and single payer systems invoke selective statistics to make their case. Unfortunately, the operative word in the comparative statistics is selective. Taking the following numbers at face value and using them to impose universal care is not only naïve and disingenuous, it's dangerous and nefarious.

	%GDP	Per Capita$	Life Exp	Infant Mortality
USA	16%	$6102	77.5	6. 9
Switzerland	11.6%	$4077	81.2	4.2
Canada	9.9%	$3165	79.9	5. 3
France	10.5%	$3159	80.3	3.9
Germany	10.6%	$3043	78.6	4. 1
Sweden	9.1%	$2825	80.6	3. 1
UK	8.1%	$2508	78.5	5. 1
Japan	8%	$2249	82.1	2. 8
Spain	8%	$2094	80.5	3. 5
Average	8.9%	$2560	78.3	4. 0

The United States is unique due to its size (3.7 million square miles), population (309 million) and heterogenic society. Europe as a whole comprises 3.8 million square miles and the combined populations of Germany, France, UK, Spain, Canada, Sweden and Switzerland are 305 million. America is a heterogeneous society, a mix of religions, ethnicities, races, languages, etc…The individual countries of Europe as well as Canada, Japan, Mexico, et al are homogenous societies by comparison. The point here relates to the maxim on statistics; there are lies, damn lies and statistics. If taken at face value, the aforementioned comparative statistics regarding healthcare would lead any objective person into believing America is not getting what she pays for with regard to health care. The statistics bear this out and show other developed countries spending far less with equal or better outcomes. However, the health care comparative statistics are misleading as they compare apples to oranges. Each country utilizes different methodologies to calculate their respective statistics (i.e. life expectancy, infant mortality). Money spent on health care is a factor in health care statistics; however, it is one of many. Cultural and societal aspects, individual freedoms, diet, job, activities, etc...all contribute to life expectancies and infant mortality rates. Unfortunately, those who advocate universal health, i.e. socialized medicine, i.e. ObamaCare fail to mention this when using these statistics to make their case. It's disingenuous at best...destructive at its worst.

Advocates of ObamaCare, (i.e. socialized medicine, i.e. universal health, i.e. government control) use the comparative statistics to claim that their version of healthcare will provide unlimited care to all, with no premiums, no co-payments, no deductibles, no rationing, no waiting times and the physician of their choice. In other words, Progressives try to sell their utopian version of a "free lunch." Once again, proof positive that Progressives in general live in a world whereby theory trumps reality, there is no free lunch. The fact is, health care is a business. The most effective way to run a business is based upon market–oriented features such as competition and consumer choice. The irony with regard to the healthcare argument is that the European models advocated for by Progressives are actually moving towards a market-oriented system. In other words, as the American system strives to be more European, the European system strives to be more American. [83] Progressives and advocates of universal care want the best of both worlds, high quality of care, low costs, zero rationing, etc...You can't have your cake and eat it to! Under systems such as Canada and the United Kingdom, healthcare costs are controlled by rationing care. Under the American system, healthcare is not rationed to the extent we see in Canada or England; hence, costs are guaranteed to be higher. No system can provide the best of both worlds. It's impossible and not the least bit practical to suggest we would improve American health care by adopting a system from any country. Healthcare systems throughout the world adopt a system that is unique to their character based upon politics, history, national identity, etc...[84]

The point here, using comparative and selective statistics to compare healthcare in America vs. Canada vs. Japan vs. Germany vs. France vs. the UK, et al, is subjective. Cultural and societal aspects of any country are as much a factor in healthcare statistics as that of costs. Unfortunately, the comparative and selective statistics used by Progressives conveniently ignore cultural/societal differences in lieu of political expediency. What the subjective and selective numbers fail to mention, universal/single payer systems utilized in the UK, Canada, Portugal and Greece have many things in common. Most notably these national healthcare systems are characterized by limited access to hi-tech equipment (i.e. CT, MRI), extremely long waiting times for both primary care and specialists, limited access to drugs, surgery, rationing, etc...As a trade off, healthcare costs in these countries as a percentage of GDP are substantially lower than the that of the U.S. On the flip side, countries that employ a market-based approach (i.e. U.S.) to health care such as France, Switzerland, Norway and Germany have higher costs as a percentage of GDP but have better access to hi-tech equipment, shorter wait times for both primary and specialty care, better access to drugs, surgery, etc...The lesson here, and contrary to Progressive hyperbole, you can't have your cake and eat it to! [85]

Competition, cost sharing, consumer choice, market prices, decentralization, etc...are the hallmarks of any successful business model looking to balance, supply, demand, price, efficiency and quality. The United States has approximately 1300 private health insurers nationwide. Unfortunately, government regulations prohibit these companies from competing across state lines. The commerce clause within the Constitution was designed to allow the free flow of business across state lines in the interest of the general welfare. The very opposite happens with regard to healthcare. The prohibition of competition across state lines simply drives up costs, limits care and decreases quality by artificially imposing upon supply and demand. The same would happen with any goods and service. Consider this, what would happen if every state restricted its residents from crossing county lines to purchase any goods or service? What if we were forced to buy a car, TV or food item within the boundaries of our county of residence? The answer, costs go up, quality goes down because supply and demand (i.e. market-oriented) are artificially manipulated. This is the inherent problem with centralized control over any aspect of our economy, most notably healthcare.

Again, the problem with comparative data in healthcare is its subjectivity. Organizations such as the World Health Organization (WHO) consistently rank the United States as one of the worst when compared to Organisation for Economic Co-operation and Development (OECD) countries. The WHO looks at costs, life expectancy and infant mortality rates as the Holy Grail by which to measure a healthcare system. The WHO does not factor in exogenous measures such as wealth, national identity, lifestyles, crime, accidental deaths, homicides, tobacco, alcohol and drug use, etc... [86] Again each country is unique in its national identity and cultural behavior. Each country adopts a healthcare system that fits within the boundaries of exogenous factors. When you factor in methodology, it's near impossible to rank countries objectively. Americans are quite wealthy compared to the rest of the world. We spend more because we make more. Health, as a goods and service, is not immune from this fact. Our affluence allows us choices with regard to lifestyle that effect measures such as life expectancy and infant mortality. A twenty year old rock climber that dies from the activity is factored into to our overall life expectancy. A teenage driver killed as a result of alcohol is factored into our overall life expectancy. Many countries do not include military deaths in their life expectancy numbers, the United

States does. Methodology matters and is not reflected in selective statistics.

Another misleading measurement is infant mortality rate. [87] If you look strictly at the numbers, the United States statistics for infant mortality is abysmal when compared to what we spend. Again, methodology matters and there is more than meets the eye when looking at comparative numbers. Due to the high level of prenatal care and hi-tech resources available in this country, many fetuses survive the pregnancy that would otherwise die in other countries. Unfortunately, many fetuses who survive prenatal conditions in the United States will succumb to their conditions post childbirth. This artificially raises the infant mortality rate in this country. By comparison, countries such as Cuba simply abort fetuses with health care problems that would lead to early death. [88] Cuba does not count these abortions, which artificially lowers their infant mortality rate. Again, methodology matters. Another problem with taking the comparative numbers at face value, they do not reflect the cost of capital investment and the priority that each country places on its value. We in the United States give high priority to technology. Hence, capital investment within the United States is high which is reflected in our cost as a percentage of GDP. The Unites States ranks second to Japan in their respective priorities on capital investment. A look at capital investments of OECD countries, numbers of scanners are per million populations: [89]

CT scanners	CT scanners	MRI scanners
Japan	92.6	35. 3
USA	32.2	26. 6
Switzerland	17.9	14. 3
Greece	17.1	2. 3
Germany	15.4	6. 8
Spain	13.3	7. 7

Portugal	12.8	3. 9
Canada	10.8	4. 9
France	7.5	3. 2
UK	7	5
Average	18.8	8. 8

Again, methodology matters. The United States places a higher priority on capital investment (i.e. high technology) and the costs as a percentage of GDP reflect this. Countries such as the UK and Canada, who Progressives want us to emulate, spend far less on capital investment. What the numbers fail to show is how the emphasis on capital investment, or lack there of, effects outcomes for specific diseases. The United States outperforms the entire world with respect to cancer, heart disease and pneumonia. The five-year survival rates in the United States for cancer in men are 62.9%, for women 66.3%. By comparison, Italy has a 59.7% rate for men and 49.8% rate for women. In Spain, the rate for men is 59%, for women 49.5%. In the UK, the rate for men is 44.8% and 52.7% for women. If you look at one specific disease, colon cancer, the rates in Canada are 6.7 per 100,000 compared to 4.8 per 100,000 in the United States. In Canada the fatality rate for colon cancer is 41%; in the United States that rate is 34%. Canada pays the price, more precisely, its citizens pay the price for the lack of capital investment. [90] Once again, single payer/universal health/socialized medicine systems come at a price. There is no healthcare panacea/utopia that provides unlimited free care. Perhaps the best referendum against universal care is once again provided by those who advocate universal care. Three hospitals in the United States combine to treat 18,200 foreign patients. Many of these are foreign dignitaries who chose The Mayo Clinic, The Johns Hopkins Hospital and the Cleveland Clinic over their respective universal care systems. Amongst these are the former Italian Prime Minister Silvio Berlusconi, who chose the Cleveland Clinic for heart surgery and Canadian Member of Parliament, Belinda Stronach who sought treatment in California for breast cancer. [91] Our emphasis on capital investment is reflected in the numbers below. Based on these values I suggest America is getting what she pays for with regard to healthcare. Five-year survival rates for cancer types.

Type of Cancer	United States	Europe
Prostate	99.3%	77.5%
Skin Melanoma	92.3%	86.1%
Breast	90.1%	79.0%
Corpus Uteri	82.3%	78.0%
Colorectum	62.5%	56.2%
Non-Hodgkin's Lymphoma	62.0%	54.6%
Stomach	25.0%	24.9%
Lung	15.7%	10.9%
Total Malignancies (Men)	**66.3%**	**47.3%**
Total Malignancies (Women)	**62.9%**	**55.8%**

Progressives are selective with their use of statistics. The numbers above reflect the emphasis on capital investment in the United States and demonstrate we are indeed getting what we pay for. When looking at cancer as a whole, a man in the United States is 40% more likely to survive past 5 years when compared to his European counterpart. Selective amnesia on the part of Progressives as this is never pointed out when advocates for universal care are making their ideological case. [93] When compared to individual countries the United States once again comes out on top. When comparing breast cancer in the United States vs. Germany, women in Germany have a 52% higher mortality rate. When comparing the United States vs. the UK, British women have an 88% higher mortally rate for breast cancer. When comparing colorectal between the United States and the UK, British men have a mortality rate that is 40% higher than their American counterpart. When comparing the United States to Canada, mortality rates for breast cancer are 9% higher for Canadian women. The mortality rate for prostate is 184% higher in Canada and colorectal has a mortality rate 10% higher. If we compare the availability of certain drugs (i.e. statins) that prevent heart disease, the United States has much better access to those in need of life saving drugs. Approximately 56% of Americans in need of statin drugs have access, only 23% of Germans have access and only 17% of Britons have access. [94]

When you compare preventive screening in America vs. other countries we also fair much better than our universal care counterparts. Approximately 89% of women in America have had a mammogram compared to 72% of Canadian women. Approximately 54% of American men have had a PSA test vs. 16% for their Canadian counterpart. Approximately 30% of Americans have had a colonoscopy compared with only 5% of Canadians. On average, patients in Canada and the UK wait twice as long as their American counterpart to see a specialist. At any given time there are approximately 900,000 Britons on a waiting list for any given procedure. This number is even worse in Canada where approximately 1.8 million wait for some type of treatment or hospitalization. Statistics Progressives fail to mention in their ideological zeal to push universal care/socialized medicine down our collective throats. Another category Progressives conveniently omit from their comparative analysis is again our emphasis on capital investment. The United States, alone or in conjunction with another country, is responsible for medical innovations such as MRI, CT, ACE inhibitors, statin drugs, CABG surgery, proton pump inhibitors, selective serotonin inhibitors, cataract extraction and lens implants, hip replacement, knee replacement, etc...Research and development comes at a price, America incurs much if not all of the costs, the benefits are felt worldwide. [95]

Another key area the Progressives and their politically correct allies refuse to mention or even discuss is healthcare costs as it relates to illegal immigrants. Most estimates put the number of illegal aliens in this country at approximately 13 million. No other country in the world incurs such a cost with their respective healthcare system. Many countries that Progressives want us to emulate with regard to heathcare refuse to treat illegal aliens. The United States does not; in fact it is a crime for any hospital to refuse treatment regardless of the status (i.e. illegal vs. legal) of the individual. The cost of illegal immigration to the United States is estimated to be approximately $113 billion. Of the $113 billion spent, approximately $17 billion goes toward healthcare for illegal aliens. The federal government picks up approximately $6 billion while the states and local government incur the remaining $11 billion. [96] Putting ideology aside, the system is not viable, there is no free lunch, except of course if you are in the United States illegally. We ignore this issue at our own peril.

Unfortunately, much of the Progressives argument for universal healthcare is based upon emotion and theory, facts are generally ignored. Progressives advocate for a universal healthcare system run by government bureaucrats. Do we really want our healthcare rationed by the same people who brought us Fannie Mae and Freddie Mac, the DOT, the post office, Amtrak, the Department of Education, etc...? Probably not! Progressives also invoke the term 'free' when referring to universal care, healthcare is not free in this country or any other. Healthcare comes at a price and is generally subsidized through some type of tax, i.e. employer, employee, VAT, excises, etc...It is by no means free. Progressives invoke the argument that universal care provides health benefits to 100% of the population. Advocates of socialized medicine point at the 47 million in the United States that have no insurance. The figure given is disingenuous as it fails to breakdown the 47 million. Millions are here illegally, millions choose not to purchase insurance and millions who are eligible for Medicaid have not applied. The fact is hospitals in America are required by law to provide emergency treatment regardless of status. The true number of uninsured in this country is closer to 5% which compare favorably to the European and Canadian models. [97]

Philosopher George Santayana warned, "Those who do not remember the past are doomed to repeat it." FDR experimented with price and wage controls during the 1930's as part of the 'New Deal'. Government control of price and wages within any part of our economy is doomed to failure. FDR proved this, yet we head down the same path with ObamaCare. Government's intrusion with regard to wage and price controls simply de-incentivize private business from capital investment. The end result, private companies hold on to their capital, investment dries up and medical advances come to a screeching halt. The private sector is based upon merit, profit motives, competition and ingenuity, market-oriented features that promote cost control, efficiency and quality. Government jobs are based upon mandated salaries and have very little to do with merit, hence, there is no motive to be efficient. Again, do we want a civil servant being responsible for decisions related to our health care? I think not! Once you remove the market-oriented features that should drive any goods and service and leave it to central government to control, costs eventually will sky rocket followed soon thereafter by rationing. [98]

Healthcare is not perfect in the United States, or anywhere else for that matter. Some minor reforms are necessary, however, fundamentally transforming 16% of our economy to appease approximately 5% of the population is totally absurd. ObamaCare being passed on Christmas Eve was no accident. Asking Congress to read 2000 plus pages in 72 hours and vote on Christmas Eve should say volumes about the bill's intention. Ironically, the major portions of our healthcare system in America that require attention were not even addressed in the bill. If we are truly interested in reforming healthcare in this country, let's start with eliminating healthcare to illegal aliens, allowing private insurance to compete across states lines and address tort reform. Addressing those three areas alone would decrease overall costs, increase competition and increase quality. Unfortunately the political will in this country is absent with regard to true healthcare reform. ObamaCare is nothing more than the fruition of a decades-long dream on the part of Progressives and part of the overall entitlement mindset that is rampant throughout the left. Teddy Roosevelt would have been wise to kill the baby in the bath water a century ago. Unfortunately he did not; the legacy of course was the "New Deal," the "Great Society" and now ObamaCare. When will politicians in this country heed the words of Albert Einstein, "…thinking that doing more of the same will lead to a different outcome is a sign of insanity." [99]

LEADERSHIP & TRANSPARENCY (OR LACK THEREOF)

Winston Churchill's description of the British government during the 1930's, "So they go in strange paradox, decided to be undecided, resolved to be irresolute, adamant for drift, solid for fluidity, all-powerful to be impotent." [100] Churchill's quote in describing the British government is the perfect summation of the Obama administration. Obama and his sycophants have been devoid of both leadership and transparency. As a state Senator within the Illinois legislature, Obama voted present no less than 129 times, which is antithetical to any claim of leadership qualities. Obama has had ample opportunity to demonstrate both leadership and transparency, yet he has failed miserably by any objective measures. He promised to roll up his sleeves upon taking office and has done nothing but point fingers since. He left Obamacare to the incapable hands of Reid, Pelosi and fellow Democrats. He dithered as Iranian students protested the election of Mahmoud Ahmadinejad in the summer of 2009 and missed the opportunity to fan the flames of democracy in a country begging to be free. Obama voted present.

Obama and the Democrats controlled the White House and both Houses of Congress in the fall of 2010, yet failed to pass a budget, than blame Republicans. Obama lectures us on fiscal responsibility yet proposes an FY12 budget that exceeds tax revenues by $1.5 trillion. The country has been sustained on 2-3 week continuing resolutions since January of 2011 and Obama has demonstrated nothing but passivity and timidity. Obama sits on the sidelines hoping the House and Senate will resolve the budget issue on their own. The most accurate referendum on Obama and his utter lack of leadership comes form one of his most ardent supporters. Ruth Marcus of the Washington Post admits to, "generally sharing the president's ideological perspective." Marcus describes Obama as follows, "For a man who won office talking about change we can believe in, Barack Obama can be a strangely passive president. There are a startling number of occasions in which the president has been missing in action – unwilling, reluctant or late to weigh in on the issue of the moment. He is too often, more reactive than inspirational, more cautious than forceful." [101] A look at Obama's track record on Iran, the budget, healthcare, British Petroleum, Petrobras, energy independence, Egypt, Libya, Syria, Israel, labor unrest, Fort Hood, NYC Times Square bomb plot, NYC subway bomb plot, etc…it's hard to argue with the summation of Marcus.

Obama has had ample opportunity to display both leadership and transparency on a multitude of issues. Instead of leadership, he has opted for cronyism. In the wake of the BP oil disaster in 2010, Obama was quick to issue drilling moratoriums in the Gulf of Mexico, costing the US a vital supply of oil as well as thousands of jobs for the Gulf Cost region. Obama claimed that deep water drilling was dangerous to the environment than sends $2 billion to the Brazilian government to subsidize Petrobras and their deep water drilling for oil. This is not leadership it is simply crony capitalism. Obama calls for the rich to pay their fair share than promotes GE CEO Jeffrey Immelt to chair his committee on job creation. GE by the way had $14 billion in profits last year, $5 billion in the US and paid zero taxes. GE is also the principal contractor of nuclear power plants in the US, which Obama is now championing. This is not leadership; it is quid-pro-quo crony capitalism. Obama defended a $535 million subsidy to Solyndra Inc of California, which is a solar panel manufacturing company in Fremont, CA. The company promised to create 1000 green jobs with the subsidy, and to date as yet to show a profit. Solyndras majority owner, George Kaiser was also the top fundraiser for Obama during the 2008 election. Leadership indeed…[102]

Obama bailed out private auto companies GM, Chrysler and their union counterparts the UAW. Obama completely usurped the bankruptcy laws of the US by putting the unsecured claims of the union membership over the contractual claims of secured bondholders. In addition, Obama's Transportation Secretary Ray LaHood told the American public to boycott Toyota in light of a politically motivated investigation that proved to be nothing more than a witch-hunt. The Health and Human Services Department has issued over 1000 waivers for ObamaCare, many of the waivers issued to labor unions and businesses that supported Obama in the 2008 election cycle. [103] There has been zero demonstration of either leadership or transparency on the part of Obama. What Obama has demonstrated is political expedience, quid-pro-quo legislation and crony capitalism. A centrally planned, socially engineered society is not leadership, it is not transparent, and it is nothing more than progressivism at its very worse. [104]

UNITED WE STAND...

"whose asses to kick"... "hand to hand combat"... "If they bring a knife to the fight, we bring a gun"...[105]

Obama

The great unifier, or so we were told, Obama was packaged as the "Hope & Change" candidate, someone who would rise above the dynamics within D.C. and identity politics in general. Obama would move this country past the divisive politics based upon race, gender, age, class, ethnicity, religion, etc...The country would galvanize around his leadership and transformative cult personality. Obama would restore our place as world leader...or as John Winthrop described in 1630, "We shall be as a city upon on a hill. The eyes of the world are upon is."[106] Obama was, we were told, the "One" we've been waiting for. Based upon the climate in this country after three-plus years of "Hope & Change," we are more polarized than ever with regard to race, age, class, gender, ethnicity, religion, etc... "Hope & Change" has turned out to be nothing more than political hyperbole no less than "The New Deal" was. "Hope & Change"... more like bait and switch. Obama was billed as "Hope & Change," someone who would galvanize the country, someone who called for a return to civility. However, those who oppose Obama policies based upon merit are labeled as divisive, tea-baggers, misogynistic, homophobic, racist, anti-Semitic, bitter clingers, typical white people, etc...Obama, Reid, Pelosi, Weiner, Dean, *NY Times*, *LA Times*, et al...have done their progressive best to balkanize this country and have the unmitigated gall to label it "Hope & Change."

Rhetorical gems that have galvanized our country: "... representative of the extraordinary work that our men and women in uniform do all around the world-Navy Corpsman (pronounced corpse-man) -Christian Brossard" *02/05/2010*... "The Cambridge police acted stupidly" *07/22/2009*... "I bowled a 129, it was like

Special Olympics or something" ***03/19/2009***... "I think when you spread the wealth around, it's good for everybody" ***10/12/2008***... "Its not surprising, then, they get bitter, they cling to guns or religion or antipathy to people who aren't like them or anti-immigrant sentiment or anti-trade sentiment as a way to explain their frustrations." ***04/11/2008***..."But she is a typical white person." ***03/20/2008***. "I won...I'm the President." ***01/23/2009***... "We don't mind the Republicans joining us. They can come for the ride, but they gotta sit in the back." ***October 2010***... "We're going to punish our enemies and we're going to reward our friends who stand with us on issues that are important to us" ***October 2010***... "That helped to create the tea-baggers and empowered that whole wing of the Republican Party to where it now controls the agenda for the Republicans." ***11/30/2009***... "The golden age of an objective press was a pretty narrow span of time in our history. Before that, you had folks like Heart who used their newspapers very intentionally to promote their viewpoints. I think FOX is part of that tradition...It's a point of view that I think is ultimately destructive..." ***September 2010***.

The following passages are excerpts from Obama's book, *Dreams of My Father*, "I ceased to advertise my mother's race at the age of 12 or 13, when I began to suspect that by doing so I was ingratiating myself to whites"... "There was something about him that made me wary; a little too sure of himself, maybe. And white."... "I never emulate white men"... "It remained necessary to prove which side you were on, to show your loyalty to the black masses, to strike out and name names."... "As I imagined myself following Malcolm X's call, one line in his book stayed with me. He spoke of his wish that the white blood that ran through him, there by an act of violence, might somehow be expunged."... "In Indonesia, I'd spent 2 years at a Muslim school, 2 years at a Catholic school. In the Muslim school, the teacher wrote to tell mother I made faces during Koran studies. In the Catholic school, when it came time to pray, I'd pretend to close

my eyes, then peek around the room. Nothing happened. No angels descended. Just a parched old nun and 30 brown children"…"Black politicians discovered what white politicians had known for a very long time: that race-baiting could make up for a host of limitations."
107

The following passages are excerpts from Obama's book, *The Audacity of Hope*," "The Republican Party has been able to win elections not by expanding its base but by vilifying Democrats, driving wedges into the electorate, energizing its right wing, and disciplining those who stray."… "I have to side with Justice Breyer's view of the Constitution—that it is not a static but rather a living document and must be read in the context of an ever-changing world." … "For most politicians, money is not about maintaining status and power. It is about scaring off challengers and fighting off fear…When I decided to run for Senate, I found myself spending time with people of means…I became more like the wealthy donors I met, in the sense that I spent more time above the fray, outside the world of hardship of the people that I had entered into public life to serve."… "So I owe those unions. When their leaders call, I do my best to call them back right away. I do not consider this corrupting in any way"…"We cannot drill our way out of the problem. Instead of subsidizing the oil industry, we should end every single tax break the industry currently receives and demands that 1% of the revenues from oil companies with over $1 billion in quarterly profits go toward financing alternative energy research and infrastructure."… "We can eliminate tax credits that have outlived their usefulness and close loopholes that let cooperations get away without paying taxes." 108

Whether its referring to Navy Corpsman as corpse-man, pointing the finger at Cambridge police or his attempted humor at the expense of Special Olympics, Obama is not the great unifier we were promised. His arrogance is on full display by claiming "I won" and telling Republicans to sit in the back of the bus. He is dismissive toward whites by referring to his own grandmother as a "typical white person" and wishing he could expunge his own white blood. He condescendingly refers to tea party members as "tea-baggers" and dismisses their conservative held beliefs as "clinging to guns and religion." He verbal attacks on whites, conservatives, FOX News, religion, capitalism, et al, is neither hope or change. It is simply politics (i.e. identity politics, i.e. Progressive politics) as usual.

Obama refers to the Constitution as dynamic, which is antithetical to what the Founders believed. Obama endears himself to wealthy donors at the expense of those he claims to protect all in the name of political expedience. He fosters a quid pro quo relationship with unions yet denies any corrupting factor. He vilifies big oil and their tax subsidies, yet remains eerily silent on Jeffery Immelt and GE, who paid zero taxes on revenues of $15 billion. Obama refers to opposing voices during the 2010 mid-terms as enemies that must be punished...this is 'Hope & Change?' This is what we've been waiting for? This is the great unifier? This is the platform of reconciliation? The questions of course are rhetorical. The country is more polarized today than it was in January of 2009, and more so than we've been in decades. Not in spite of Obama but because of Obama. Taking an overview of Obama's own words and past relationships (i.e. Rev. Wright, Bill Ayers), puts into perspective what his true intentions were when he promised to fundamentally transform this country.

ON "THE ROAD TO SERFDOM"...

"When authority presents itself in the guise of organization, it develops charms fascinating enough to convert communities of free people into totalitarian States."

The Time (London) February 24, 1937

This quote was taken from *The Road to Serfdom* by F. A. Hayek. It is in reference to the collective mindset that was pervasive during the 1930's in Nazi Germany, Fascist Italy and Communist Russia. It can easily be applied to 2012.Three years into "Hope & Change" and I like many Americans are now looking to November and hoping for change. Whether you supported Obama in 2008 and plan to in 2012, an objective look at his abysmal record must leave even the most ardent supporter feeling a bit queasy. "Hope & Change" now has a record, which includes a contraction of the U.S workforce of 2 million jobs. The record also includes gas prices that are 95% higher than three years prior, a real unemployment rate of 16.5%, a debt to GDP ratio of 102%, a 44% increase in our national debt, deficit spending that has averaged $1.5 trillion/year, loss of our AAA credit rating, 46 million now on food stamps, ObamaCare, clash for clunkers, bailouts, etc...Social programs will run close to 60% of our budget for FY12, federal expenditures as a percentage of GDP is now 45%. Federal loan guarantees to green energy giants First Solar, Solyndra and Evergreen, all of which are now insolvent, GDP growth in 2011 that was under 2% for the year. This record is not "Hope & Change," it is America in decline.

After three years of Obama the President now has a record by which we can judge him on and by any objective standard he has been an abject failure. As we head to November and perhaps the most important election in a generation, a few questions come to mind. Has Obama governed under the guise of social justice (i.e. collectivism) and coercive legislation? Or, has he governed with 'We the People' as a backdrop, where the individual is allowed freedom of choice? Has Obama governed through the prism of a planned economy? Or, has he governed under the founding principle of entrepreneurship? Has Obama favored arbitrary government? Or the Rule of Law? Has Obama been a skillful demagogue by pandering to the docile and gullible (i.e. classicism)? Or, has he united us as a nation as "Hope

& Change" promised? Has Obama espoused the principles of social justice, wealth redistribution, dependence, reliance, et al...? Or has he espoused the principles of independence, self-reliance, personal responsibility, initiative, et al...? Has Obama governed under the guise of collective duties? Or individual rights? The questions of course are all rhetorical, as the answers are all self-evident.

THE "WISE & KNOWLEDGEABLE FEW"

The chapter on Obama began with the following quote:

> *"Associate with men of good quality if you esteem your own reputation; for it is better to be alone than in bad company."*
>
> **George Washington**

The individuals listed below collectively represent everything that is antithetical to our Founding Fathers, The Declaration of Independence, the Constitution and the principle of original intent. An incestuous relationship exists between these pernicious souls whose belief system permeates throughout The White House. Obama promised a fundamental transformation of this country via "Hope & Change." Benjamin Franklin warned against losing our Republic due to apathy...Obama surrounds himself with these individuals not by accident but as a matter of ideology. It's time this country wakes up and heeds the words of Benjamin Franklin. These enlightened despots share a common belief in anti-Semitism, anti-American exceptionalism, anti-free trade capitalism, anti-Constitution, anti-individual, anti-self reliance, anti-religion, etc...Collectively they advocate for global governance, subservience to world courts, secularism, collective rights, socialism, statism, Communism, labor movements, abortion on demand, cradle to grave entitlements, in other words a Progressive Utopia.

AFL-CIO (1881 – present) The Federation of Organized Trades and Labor Unions formed in 1881, reorganized as the American Federation of Labor (AFofL) in 1886. Membership of 150,000 in 1886, grew to three plus million by 1924. Samuel Gompers was president of AFL from 1886-1924 and tried to distance his union from the socialist labor movements (i.e. IWW). John L. Lewis organized the Committee for Industrial Organization (CIO) within the AFL in 1935. Lewis withdraws from AFL in 1938 and forms the Congress of Industrial Organizations. The AFL and CIO merge in 1955 to from the AFL-CIO, the largest labor organization in the world. [109]

David Axelrod (1955 – Present) Served as senior advisor to Obama. Founded political/PR firms AKP&D Message & Media and ASK Public Strategies. Led senate campaign of 2004 and presidential campaign in 2008 for Obama. AKP&D ran ads in 2009 promoting Obama's healthcare disaster at a cost of $12 million. Ads were placed by SEIU and PhRMA. Both SEIU and PhRMA deny using AKP&D because of Axelrod connection. The industry pays for Axelrod's $2 million severance as well as his son's wages. Axelrod also in charge of fear-mongering ads that supported huge utility hikes. Axelrod's firm also handled the patient dumping scheme at The University of Chicago Medical Center. The scheme was spearheaded by Michelle Obama and outsourced low-income patients to other facilities. Axelord's firm handled the PR campaign to re-brand the University of Chicago Medical Center.[110]

William Ayers (1944 – Present) Leader of Weather Underground group in late 1960's. Weather Underground group an offshoot of the Students for a Democratic Society (SDS). Ayers' summary of the Weather Underground ideology, "Kill all the rich people. Break up their cars and apartments. Bring the revolution home, Kill your parents." Ayers, by the way, raised in affluent suburb in Chicago. Active participant in 1969 "Days of Rage," New York City bombings in 1970, Capitol bombings in 1971 and Pentagon bombing in 1972. Days of Rage included 300 Weatherman rioting in Chicago. Authored *Fugitive Days* in 2001 where he boasted with pride of the bombings. Ayers is quoted in 2001, "I don't regret setting bombs," and with regard to America, "What a country...It makes me want to puke." Ayers' girlfriend killed in 1970 when bomb she was working on with fellow Weatherman exploded. Bomb was intended for dance at Fort Dix. Ayers' finger prints found throughout bomb making facility, which included C-4, weapons and Marxist-Lenin literature. Ayers co-authored *Prairie Fire: The Politics of Revolutionary Anti-Imperialism* in 1974. *Prairie Fire* was in reference to Mao Zedong quote, "a single spark can start a prairie fire." The 1974 book describes the movement as guerrilla and communist. The book calls for a socialist revolution, a communist party and the end of capitalism/imperialism. It calls for the end of white supremacy and the white bourgeoisie. *Prairie Fire* dedicated to Sirhan-Sirhan. Ayers and girlfriend Dohrn surrender to FBI in 1980, case against them thrown out on a technicality. Ayers' comment, "Guilty as sin, free as a bird, America is a great country."

Ayers and Dohrn host meetings during mid 1990's to introduce and kick off Obama's political career. Ayers founded the Chicago Annenberg Challenge in 1995, stated goal was to teach against the oppressive nature of American society. Ayers and Obama sat on Woods Fund of Chicago from 1999-2002. During 2007 reunion of the Weather Underground and SDS, Ayers states that America stands for oppression and authoritarianism. Served as professor of education at University of Illinois from 1987-2010. Pictures of Malcolm X, Mumia Abu-Jamal and Che Guevara on office door. As of 2008, Ayers elected as VP for curriculum studies at the American Educational Research Association. Group exerts great influence regarding what is taught in America's public schools. Ayers also sits on board of Miranda International Center, group dedicated to Cuba style government in Venezuela. Of the three children between Ayers and Dohrn, one is named Zayd after a Black Liberation Army revolutionary. Weatherman and Black Liberation Army were co-conspirators in 1981 Brinks murder. [111]

Carol Browner (1955 – Present) Former White House energy and climate advisor to Obama. Served as EPA administrator from 1993-2000 under Clinton. Browner listed as one of 14 leaders of Commission for a Sustainable World Society, a socialist group which advocates global governance. Served on Board of Directors for progressive Center for American Progress. Member of Socialist International group, a global initiative that is critical of U.S. policies. Socialist International advocates global governance, global warming, open borders, global economy, cap and trade, etc...Prior to leaving office in 2000, Browner instructed staff to erase all hard drives for top EPA officials. Browner and husband part of lobbying effort in 2006 to have Dubai Ports World assume operations of six major U.S. ports. [112]

Cloward & Piven (1966) Strategy proposed by Columbia sociologists ***Richard Andrew Cloward (1926-2001)*** and ***Frances Fox Piven (1932 – Present).*** Designed to overload the system with impossible demands, leads to chaos, economic collapse and eventually the fall of capitalism. Cloward and Piven based their crisis strategy and were inspired by the 1965 riots in Watts's district of Los Angeles. Cloward and Piven were advocates of the sabotage and destruction of the welfare system. By overloading the system, financial chaos and political unrest ensues, thereby empowering the poor. The end goal here was to replace capitalism with socialism. The strategy used fear, turmoil, violence, etc...to create the perfect storm that would lead to collapse and the end goal of income redistribution.

Cloward and Piven coordinated efforts with George Wiley a black militant and founder of the National Welfare Rights Organization. The orchestrated demonstrations, pickets, riots, demands, violence, destruction, etc...proved successful. Welfare roles in New York City alone went from 4.3 million to 10.8 million from 1965-1974. New York City declared bankruptcy in 1975, New York state was on the brink. Cloward and Piven were guests of Clinton in 1996 during signing of Personal Responsibility and Work Opportunity Reconciliation Act. Organizations such as ACORN, Project Vote, and Human SERVE continue to utilize the Cloward and Piven strategy techniques of bullying, violence, protests, fear, etc...and receive financial support from George Soros and the Open Society Institute. The 2008 financial meltdown was characteristic of the Cloward and Piven strategy. Community organizers demanded banks engage in high risk loans by picketing outside the homes of bank executives. Bully, harass, threaten, undermine, demand, intimidate, etc...[113]

Steven Chu (1948 – Present) Serves as Secretary of Energy within Obama Administration. Advocate of global warming, green jobs, elimination of coal industry, increasing the cost of gas, cap and trade, revolution to solve global warming, punitive carbon taxation, electric cars, global climate councils, UN global warming projects, etc...In other words, the quintessential enlightened despot. [114]

Bernadine Dorn (1942 – Present) Wife of William Ayers, leader of Weatherman group, leader of SDS, active participant in New York City bombings, 1970, Capitol bombings 1971 and Pentagon bombings 1972. Established "fork salute" in 1969 for Weatherman as tribute to Charles Manson's murder of pregnant actress Sharon Tate. Tate and others were murdered by repeated fork stabbings. Active participant in 1969 Days of Rage riots in Chicago which left district attorney Richard Elrod paralyzed for life. Dohrn celebrates Elrod's paralysis by singing a parody of Bob Dylan's song… "Lay, Elrod, Lay." Co-authored 1974 book *Prairie Fire* with husband William Ayers. Dohrn and Ayers lived underground for years until surrendering to FBI in 1980. Charges eventually dropped on technicality. Hosted and kicked off political career of Obama with husband Ayers during mid-1990 at their Chicago home. Spoke at 2007 reunion of Weatherman and SDS, praised the continued efforts to overthrow capitalism and shed the white skin privilege. Participated with Ayers, Code Pink and pro-Palestinian in anti-Israel demonstration. [115]

Anita Dunn (1958 – Present) Played integral role in starting 2008 presidential run for Obama and served as White House communications director. Proudly states that their campaign made experience a negative trait during 2008. Calls Mao Zedong one of her favorite political philosophers. Married to Robert Bauer, personal attorney to Obama. Calls news organizations critical of Obama, "opinion journalism masquerading as news." [116]

Rham Emanuel (1959 – Present) Major Democratic fundraiser, drafted by Clinton in 1991 to spearhead fundraising for presidential run. Also served on Board of Directors for Freddie Mac during subprime loan fiasco…Emanuel walked away with millions in compensation. Served as Obama's Chief of Staff prior to mayoral run in Chicago. Infamous for his temper, threatens two Democratic supporters with steak knife at 1992 dinner, sends another a decomposing fish. Central figure in the "Citizenship USA" movement designed to exploit immigration as potential pool for Democratic voters. INS was pressured into naturalizing as many immigrants as possible as fast as possible. Fingerprints and criminal records were ignored in many cases, during one ceremony in Chicago, 11,000 sworn in en masse. Emanuel facilitates more than 1 million applicants by year's end 1996. Many of these immigrants were granted citizenship without proper vetting. As the economy tanked in late 2008, Emanuel states, "You never want a serious crisis to go to waste--and what I mean by that is it's an opportunity to do things that you think you could not do before." Emanuel fails to disclose his rent free arrangement while serving under Obama in DC, despite the ethics rules that oblige him to do so. [117]

Richard Falk (1930 – Present) Law professor at Princeton, despite Jewish ancestry, he is sympathetic to Muslim cause. Participate in Socialist Scholars Conference and is board member of The Nation. Claims US warnings of terror are political tool used by USA to frighten its citizens. Claims use of terror warnings is nothing but scare tactics. Called the Ayatollah Khomeini a liberator in 1979. Compares Israel, in its treatment of Palestine, to the Nazis and their treatment of the Jews. Calls suicide bombings a "valid method of struggle." [118]

Robert Gibbs (1971 – Present) Served as communications director for Senator Obama and White House Press Secretary for President Obama. Played integral role in Obama's political career from state Senator to President. Part of the Axelrod, Plouffe triumvirate that molded Obama and the Hope & Change strategy. [119]

Eric Holder (1951 – Present) Replaced Jamie Gorelick as Deputy Attorney General under Janet Reno in 1997. Described as "the gatekeeper for presidential pardons" under Clinton. Holder was central figure in the 176 last minute pardons granted by Clinton in January of 2001 prior to leaving office. Last minute pardons facilitated by Holder included Weather Underground members Susan Rosenberg and Linda Evans. Marc Rich, fled country to avoid prosecution on tax fraud, tax evasion racketeering, etc...Rich, through his ex-wife, contributed $1.5 million to Clinton interests.

Holder played integral role in Clinton's 1996 pardon of 16 members of Puerto Rican terrorist groups known as FALN. The terrorist group, with Marxist beliefs, responsible for 130 bombings from 1974-1983, which killed six and left 80 others wounded. Holder was central figure in leading clemency campaign for FALN members despite the members themselves never filing for clemency or showing any signs of contrition. Family members of those victimized by FALN never notified of the clemency procedure by Holder and the Justice Department. Despite his actions, Holder accuses conservatives of making a mockery of the rule of law. Holder calls for a "progressive future," calls the US a "nation of cowards," files brief on behalf of terror suspect and al Qaeda member Jose Padilla. Holder suggests Islamic terrorists have right to be treated as criminal defendants as opposed to enemy combatants. Holder accuses Arizona Governor Jan Brewer of racial profiling in April 2010 for new Arizona immigration law despite never having read the law. Holder refuses to admit to House Judiciary Committee that radical Islam played a role in 2009 Fort Hood terror attack or 2010 Times Square Bombing incident. Holder refuses to prosecute Black Panther members for obvious voter intimidation in Philadelphia during 2008 presidential campaign.[120]

John Holdren (1944 – Present) Harvard professor, Science and Technology Czar under Obama. Peace activist, anti-capitalist, advocate for global government, advocate for wealth redistribution, advocate for population control, advocate of global warming, served on editorial board of the Bulletin of Atomic Scientists. Bulletin members were later accused of providing secrets to Soviet Union. Breaks down his anti-capitalist viewpoint to mathematical equation I=PAT. I represents negative environmental impact, P stands for population growth, A represent affluence and T technology. Holdren

is the poster boy for progressive ideology, theory over experience.
121

Jeffrey Immelt (1956 – Present) Chairman of the Board and CEO of General Electric since 2000. Since replacing Jack Welch, GE stock has dropped close to 60% since 2000. Serves on Obama's Economic Recovery Advisory board, chairman of Obama's panel of economic advisors, and Chairman on the Council on Jobs and Competitiveness. Despite the horrendous performance of GE with Immelt at the helm, he has earned over $30 million in compensation over the past three years. During the same time period, GE stock has lost 46% of its value. From 2001-2009, GE cut some 24,000 jobs and is the chief outsourcer of jobs to China and India. Immelt played critical role in developing policy that allowed GE to pay zero taxes on $5 billion earned in USA. GE was largest beneficiary of TARP despite not being eligible, GE Capital was beneficiary of $120 billion in loans from FDIC, and benefited from billions in subsidies from TLGP fund. Immelt has been an abject failure at GE by any objective measures yet is in charge of our economic recovery...this is the epitome of the "Hope & Change" scam. [122]

Valerie Jarrett (1956 – Present) Chicago lawyer and political insider. Hired Michelle Robinson, fiancée of Barack Obama, in 1991 while working for Mayor Richard Daley. Responsible for connecting Obama to the wealthy and politically powerful in Chicago. Serves as Obama's chief political adviser in White House. Jarrett served as President of Habitat Company, which oversaw low-income housing in Chicago. During her 12 year reign, the 1960's housing projects that her company oversaw is in ruins and virtually uninhabitable. While serving as State Senator, Obama sponsored numerous bills that allocated millions at housing projects that benefited real estate moguls like Jarrett. Jarrett was a slum lord who ran the units into he ground and was paid millions as a real estate developer to restore the properties…another "Hope & Change" whitewash. [123]

Van Jones (1968 – Present) Self-proclaimed communist, angry black separatist, anarchist, revolutionist and political activist. Served as Obama's Green Job Czar until 2009. A committed Marxist and anti-capitalist, who claims the free-market exploits the nonwhite minorities, Central figure in support movement for cop killer Mumia Abu Jamal. Jones models his tactics for revolution on the writings of Saul Alinsky, author of *Rules for Radicals*. Signed the 9/11 Truth Statement accusing Bush having knowledge of the 9/11 attack. Leading member of STORM, a bay area Marxist-Maoist revolutionary movement. STORM has ties to Workers World Party and the South African Communist Party. Jones founded Green for All, funded by George Soros via his Open Society Institute. Jones founder of Color of Change, accuses America of being overly racist, calls for a transformation of the US into a socialist society. Why is this man allowed anywhere near a position within the White House? The vetting by the White House staff is either totally inept, or people such as Van Jones are specific targets to implement their agenda. It's either or…[124]

Elena Kagan (1950 - Present) Nominated by Obama in 2010 as Supreme Court Justice replacing Justice John Paul Stevens. Princeton grad whose senior thesis was titled, "To the Final Conflict: Socialism in New York City, 1900-1933." Kagan expresses disappointment that socialism's greatness never challenges capitalism and the established parties. Met Obama in 1991 while serving as assistant law professor at University of Chicago. Advocate for social justice, affirmative action, abortion, gay rights, constitutional rights for terrorists, international law, views Constitution as a living document that was defective as originally conceived. Appointed to Supreme Court by Obama and confirmed by the Senate despite never having argued a case in court on any level. [125]

Rashid Khalidi (1950 – Present) Friend of Obamas (Michelle and Barack) since early 1990's. Khalidi organized fundraiser for Obama during 2000 election for Congress. Obama sat on board of directors for Woods Foundation with Ayers that donated $75,000 to Khalidi's Arab American Action Network. Khalidi is former professor at University of Chicago, currently professor at Columbia for Middle East Studies. Refers to killing Israelis as resistance and opposes two-state solution. Virulent anti-Semitic, dedicated his 1986 book, "*Under Siege: P.L.O. Decision-Making During the 1982 War,*" to Yasser Arafat. Served as former operative of P.L.O. and founded the Arab American Action Network in 1995. AAAN views Israel as racist and calls the 1948 creation of Israel a catastrophe. Referred to terror attacks after 9/11 as "hysteria about suicide bombers." [126]

Stephen Lerner (1958 – Present) Union organizer, member of SEIU, advocates a "strategy for forcing political change through orchestrated crisis." Bases his philosophy on the Cloward & Piven approach to overwhelming the system. Advocates mass civil disobedience that would put banks on the edge of insolvency. Calls for millions to stop paying their mortgages that would in effect collapse the baking system and capitalism in general. Advocates for the redistribution of wealth, a common theme amongst those that surround Obama. [127]

Open Society Institute (Founded 1993) Founded and financed by George Soros as a mechanism for social justice (i.e. socialism). Advocates global governance, wealth redistribution, abortion, open borders, legalized drugs, affirmative action, gay rights, high taxes, government spending, anti-capitalism, legal rights for terrorists, Constitutional rights for illegal immigrants, gun control, etc... Supports progressive organizations: Tides Foundation, Tides

Center, ACLU, NARAL, Amnesty International, ACORN, Planned Parenthood, Moveon.org, Centers for American Progress, Malcolm X Grassroots Movement, AFSCME, SEIU, United Steel Workers, AFL-CIO, etc...Donates to the following progressive organizations that share the same political ideology: We Interrupt This Message, The Independent Media, Community Rights Counsel, Equal Justice Works, National Council of La Raza, Mexican American Legal Defense and Education Fund, Population Services International, Western States Center, Esperanza Center, Institute on Taxation and Economic Policy, Network for Progressive Texas, Center for Law and Social Policy, Center for Policy Alternatives, DEMOS, etc...[128]

David Plouffe (1967 – Present) Advisor to Obama, also served as campaign manager. Runs consultant firm Plouffe Strategies, runs AKPD Message and Media with Axelrod. A central figure in the incestuous relationship between the White House and GE. Paid millions by GE as consultant prior to joining White House staff. NBC and MSNBC major cheerleaders for Obama in 2008 and continue to act as pro-Obama media. GE owns both networks, Plouffe in the middle as both consultant and advisor. GE benefits as it receives millions from federal government via TARP, tax breaks, etc...So much for Hope & Change ridding DC of lobbyists. [129]

John Podesta (1949 – Present) Former Clinton Chief of Staff, member of Advisory Council for ACORN, CEO of Center for American Progress (founded by George Soros). Key figure in whitewashing the numerous Clinton scandals. Key figure in assisting Clinton with executive orders that bypassed the Congress and American people. Famously quipped, "Stroke of the Pen. Law of the land. Kind of cool" when referring to Clinton's abuse of executive orders. Served as advisor to Obama following 2008 election. [130]

Samantha Powers (1970 – Present) Serves as Special Assistant/ Senior Director for Multinational Affairs to Obama. Authored *A Problem from Hell*, and *Chasing the Flame*, both are nothing more than a referendum on US foreign policy. Married to Cass Sustein. Given credit as principle architect of current policy in Libya. Referred to as fellow traveler by 1960's leftist Tom Hayden. Advocate of redistributive policies, advocate of global governance, which would force America to subordinate her national sovereignty. Advocate of a post-America, which would take away in piecemeal fashion America's power and sovereignty in favor of international law. Her foreign policy beliefs are completely antithetical to American exceptionalism. Chasing the Flame paints former UN diplomat Sergio Vieira de Mello as hero. When in fact, Sergio Vieira de Mello was a committed Marxists, anti-capitalist, anti-American who advocated for redistributive policies and international governance. [131]

Wade Rathke (1948 – Present) Founder of ACORN, former member of Students for a Democratic Society, ties to George Soros' Shadow Party, activist in the National Welfare Reform Organization, co-founder of Tides Foundation, founded locals of SEIU, ties to AFL-CIO. Advocate of social justice, workers rights, peoples rule, socialism, Cloward & Piven strategy, Saul Alinsky tactics, etc... Central figure within ACORN and the massive voter fraud schemes in 12 separate states. Primary goal was to elect Democrats at any cost, including by fraudulent means. Facilitated Maximum Eligible Participation strategy that promotes entitlements (i.e. welfare). Basically a takeoff of the Cloward & Piven strategy that looks to overwhelm the system and eventually collapse it. [132]

Tony Rezko (1955 – Present) Financial backer of Obama dating back to early 1990's. Owned Rezmar Corporation in Chicago which oversaw multiple low-income housing projects. Obama would later serve as State Senator in a district that included numerous Rezko properties. Rezko served as chair of Obama's campaign finance committee in Illinois. Involved with Obama on shady real estate deal in Kenwood neighborhood of Chicago. Numerous lawsuits filed against Rezko by creditors who were seeking to recover millions. Involved with kickback schemes with former Illinois Governor Rod Blagojevich. Indicted in 2006 on extortion charges and jailed in 2008. [133]

Ken Salazar (1955 – Present) Interior Secretary for Obama, central figure in the moratorium on deep water drilling in the Gulf of Mexico. Committed eco-activist, low balled drilling application figures. Salazar reported that less than 50 applications were pending, when in fact close to 300 were pending. The feet dragging on the part of Salazar has cost the Gulf Coast thousands of jobs, while supporting deep water drilling in Brazil, again at the cost of American jobs. [134]

SEIU Socialist labor organization within the AFL-CIO with approximately 2 million members. Largest union of healthcare workers in the U.S. Largest union of long-term workers in U.S. Second largest union of public service employees and largest security union in U.S. SEIU plays major role in George Soros' Shadow Party, a pro-Democrat organization involved with voter fraud. Supports the Employee Free Choice Act, which would abolish the secret union election. Incestuous ties to ACORN, both jointly manage a number of locals throughout the country. SEIU director of financial reform calls for plan to collapse the American economy. Lerner proposed a plan to target JP Morgan with financial terrorism. Goal was to take down Morgan and collapse the American economy in the name of wealth redistribution. SEIU involved with the beating of conservative activist in St. Louis, involved with extortion in Seattle. Patrick Gaspard served in SEIU union for nine years, later served as political director for Obama during 2008 campaign. Gaspard worked for SEIU and Obama simultaneously. Obama promised to "paint the nation purple" following his election, suggested that SEIU serve as a civilian national security force. [135]

George Soros (1930 – Present) Billionaire currency manipulator, socialist, atheist, anti-Semitic, anti-American, etc...Finances progressive foundations; Open Society Institute, Center for American Progress, Tides Foundation, Tides Center, Amnesty International, Malcolm X Grassroots Movement, Moveon.org, Planned Parenthood, National Council of La Raza, NARAL, Mexican American Legal Defense Fund, ACLU, etc...Born in Hungary and assisted the Nazis when they stole from fellow Hungarian Jews. In his own words, Soros views himself as "some kind of god"... "exaggerated view of self-importance"... "I carried some rather potent messianic fantasies"... "Some kind of god, the creator of everything"... "Benevolent"... "All seeing"... "conscience of world." Used wealth to facilitate coups in Croatia, Georgia, Slovakia and Yugoslavia. Used speculative power to destroy the British Pound and collapse the Malaysian markets. Major campaign donor to Obama in 2008 and against Bush in 2004. Anti-capitalist despite making billions in the free market. Advocate for more government regulation, socialism, global governance, open borders, legalized drugs, expand social entitlements, amnesty for illegal aliens, socialized medicine, affirmative action, U.S. disarmament, radical environmentalist, etc...Anti-free market and Republican, yet owns 1.9 million shares of Halliburton. Advocate for higher taxes yet shelters his own wealth by headquartering in Curacao. Despite his Jewish heritage, speaks out against Israel and America. Blames anti-Semitism on American foreign policy. Works to lessen the influence of pro-Israeli lobby AIPAC. [136]

Sonia Sotomayor (1954 – Present) Nominated by Obama in 2009 as Supreme Court Justice replacing Justice David Souter. Views America as racist nation. Advocate for legal realism, affirmative action, entitlements to illegal aliens, supports quotas on the federal bench based upon race, gender, ethnicity, sexual orientation, supports subservience of American law to international law, etc…In her own words "I am a product of affirmative action, I am the perfect affirmative action baby"… "I would hope that a wise Latina woman with the richness of her experiences would more often than not reach a better conclusion than a white male"… "I wonder whether by ignoring our differences as women or men of color we do a disservice both to the law and society"… "our gender and national origins may and will make a difference in our judging"… "there is no objective stance but only a series of perspective"… "learn from foreign law and the international community when interpreting our Constitution"… "the law changes along with the circumstances"… "judges should do more than interpret the law or look to the original intent of the writers of the law or the Constitution"… "Judges should bring in outside influences from social sciences, psychology and politics, plus their own views to craft the law"… "court of appeals is where policy is made." [137]

Andy Stern (1950 – Present) Served as president of SEIU, trained at Midwest Academy which was created by Students for a Democratic Society. Midwest Academy a breeding ground for radical union techniques and community organization. Also served on America Coming Together, funded by Soros. Forces members into political action in support of Democratic Party. Forces companies to unionize under SEIU using boycotts, pickets and demonstrations. Stern's philosophy, "We prefer to use the power of persuasion, but if that doesn't work we use the persuasion of power." Serves as central figure in Soros' Shadow Party, which is far left union activist. Advocate for taxing the rich, social justice, wealth redistribution, socialized medicine, global governance, economy led by government and not by private sector, etc…SEIU donates over $60 million to 2008 Obama campaign, Stern a frequent visitor to White House. [138]

Cass Sustein (1954 – Present) Met Obama in 1990's while both were at University of Chicago. Harvard law professor currently serves as head of the White House Office of Information and Regulatory Affairs. Advocate for a second bill of rights, animal rights, collective rights, higher taxes to support more entitlements, believes Social Security, Medicare, food stamps, et al are rights granted by the government. Believes Constitution is a living document with no fixed principles or truths. Believes the Constitution is outdated and argues against the doctrine of original intent. Believes Justices should be free to read whatever they want into the words of the Constitution. Believes that rights exist only to the extent that government grants them. Believes that federal law should be interpreted by the sitting president and not by judges. Believes that liberty is a function of dependency. Married to Samantha Power. [139]

Tides Foundation (Founded 1976) & Tides Center (Founded 1976) Founded by activist Drummond Pike. Originally established as a public charity. Wealthy donors give money, Tides distributes the money to various progressive movements. Essentially it acts to launder money. A wealthy progressive can donate to Tides and claim plausible deniability as Tides distributes money to activist causes. The wealthy donor remains anonymous. Tides Center serves as a buffer for Tides Foundation insulating it against potential litigation. Wade Rathke serves on board for Tides Foundation and Tides Center. Tides financially supports and advocates for gay rights, collective rights, labor movements, radical environmentalism, abortion, secular rights, anti-war, anti-free trade, anti-firearms, etc…Incestuous relationship with

George Soros, the Shadow Party, and Open Society Institute. Soros has contributed over $7 million to Tides. Recipient of Tides money include the following progressive organization: ACLU, ACORN, Amnesty International, Center for American Progress, Borders Action Network, CAIR, Global Exchange, NARAL, NOW, NWF, PETA, NAACP, Sierra Club, WWF, etc...Notable donors to Tides activities include Barbara Streisand, John Kerry, Ben & Jerry's, AT&T, Bill Gates, Fannie Mae, etc...Tides Foundation and Tides Center also receives millions in grants from the federal government. [140]

Richard Trumka (1949 – Present) President of AFL-CIO, former head of United Mine Workers, involved with Teamsters money-laundering scheme to support Democrats, frequent visitor to White House. His legacy at United Mine Workers was one of violence. Advocate of strikes as bargaining tool and specifically violent strikes. Quoted as saying, "kick the shit out of every last one" in reference to those who opposed his union members. Violence includes beatings, gunshots, vandalizing homes, etc...and were organized, orchestrated and encouraged by Trumka. Honored in 1994 at the annual Eugene Debs Award, Debs was former socialist candidate for president in early 20th century. Central figure in founding the Campaign for America's Future in 1996, co-founders included Tom Hayden, Andy Stern, Frances Fox Piven, Richard Cloward, Jesse Jackson, etc... Advocate of Marxist principles of anti-capitalism, class warfare, anti-free market, etc...Trumka quoted in 2010 with regard to his involvement with labor, "...I saw it as a vehicle to do massive social change to include lots of people." Openly welcomes Communist Party USA members to join AFL-CIO. Serves on Obama's Economic Recovery Advisory Board. [141]

Woods Foundation (Founded 1941) Founded by Frank Woods and Woods Charitable Fund. Essentially the fund promotes the expansion of the welfare state. Former board members include William Ayers, Bernadine Dohrn and Obama. Woods Foundation grants funds to numerous Progressive organizations including ACORN, Tides, AAAN, Trinity United Church, etc...[142]

Reverend Jeremiah Wright (1941 – Present) Anti-American, anti-Semite, anti-white...advocate of Black Liberation Theology, which has Marxist tenets. Black Liberation Theology seeks to overthrow capitalism in favor of a social utopia. Wright in his own words regarding America; "land of the greed and home of the slave"... "Racism is alive and well, racism is how this country was founded"... "America is the number one killer in the world"... "We support Zionism shamelessly"... "We started the AIDS virus"... "We are selfish, arrogant, ignorant self-centered egoists"... "Americans chickens are coming home to roost"... "God damn America"... Advocates a Black Value System, whereby blacks patronize black only businesses. Describes blacks who do not support his beliefs as "darkies," "colored leaders," "Oreos," "Uncle Tomisim", etc...Served as Obama's pastor and spiritual advisor for 20 years, performed marriage ceremony and baptized both Obama's children. [143]

CHAPTER 5
PERSONAL BEST...

GEORGE WASHINGTON

1ST PRESIDENT 1789-1797

"I was summoned by my country, whose voice I can never hear but with veneration and love." [1]

George Washington

Perhaps no quote epitomizes George Washington better than the one above. Whether it was destiny, divine intervention, or interposition of Providence, George Washington was the right man at the right time in American history. His influence was apparent early on and continued throughout his life, which included serving as the first President of the United States. A brief look at Washington's biography included: born in Virginia 1732...served as surveyor for Culpepper County 1749...served with British during French-Indian War 1754-1758...commander of Virginia forces 1755-1758...member of Virginia House of Burgess 1759-1774...attended first Continental Congress 1774...attended second Continental Congress 1775... elected Commander in Chief Continental Army June 16, 1775... does not accept his $500/month stipend as Commander in Chief, requests for expenses only...appoints chaplain to each Army unit as one of his first orders of business as Commander in Chief...chaplains paid on par with officers…calls for religious services each Sunday… forced British from Boston March 1776…leads American troops across Delaware River and defeats British/Hessian troops in Trenton December 1776…holds desperate troops together during the winter of 1777-1778 at Valley Forge…holds desperate troops together during winter of 1779-1780 at Morristown…defeats British at Yorktown October 1781…leadership prevents Army coup March 1783… resigns commission December 1783…presided over Constitutional Convention May –September 1787…signed Constitution September 17, 1787…unanimously elected first President of the United States and served first term 1789-1793…added the phrase "so help me God" during first inaugural April 30, 1789…Every president since Washington ends their oath with "so help me God"…served second term as President of the United States 1793-1797…declined annual salary of $25,000/year as President…calls religion and morality the great pillars of mankind, proclaims that national morality cannot exist without religious principles during Farewell Address September 17, 1796…passes away on December 14, 1799. [2]

George Washington was the quintessential patriot. A man who epitomized the colors of our flag, red (bravery), white (purity) and blue (perseverance). A devout Christian who was the very summation of American exceptionalism. When viewed in context with our history and through the prism of any generation, Washington stood above all in terms of what he meant to our founding and growth. Is there a politician alive today that we could imagine forfeiting their salary? Is there a politician alive today that we could imagine serving their country as a matter of duty and honor as opposed to motives based upon ambition and avarice? Both questions are rhetorical as the answers to both are self-evident. Washington was an ardent supporter of education, particularly that of religion. He strongly opposed the party system for reasons that are blatantly obvious in the 21st century. He viewed an uncontrolled party system in terms of a fire, all consuming. He warned against party factions subverting the will of the people. He was an advocate of friends to all and allies to none regarding foreign policy. He viewed debt as immoral, as did all of our Founding Fathers. He understood the underlying power of the Constitution, that government derives its power from the consent of the people. Maintained that our Constitution was for a moral, virtuous and religious citizenship. Was an ardent supporter of a currency backed by either gold or silver. Advocate for the Rule of Law and warned against minority rule usurping our Republican government. Ardent supporter of the separation of powers and self-government. Advocate of family and marriage; like most Founding Fathers viewed the union between man and woman as the making of the complete human being. Spoke often of the "invisible hand," "providential agency," "divine intervention" and "Supreme Being" in expressing his gratitude to God for his intervention on behalf of our independence.

On April 30, 1789, Washington took the oath of office and finished it with an impromptu, "So help me God." [3] During his First Inaugural Address Washington spoke of his "fervent supplication to that Almighty Being." [4] In his Farewell Address Washington spoke of religion and morality as great pillars of human happiness, [5] he spoke of national morality being tied to religion. Washington's words and actions echo the beliefs that our country was founded upon. His career as military and political leader run parallel to the principles espoused within The Declaration of Independence; of "self-evident truths," of rights being endowed by a "Creator," a belief in "Natures God," in "Divine Providence" and a "Supreme Being." Washington actually turned down the annual salary of $25,000 as he did when appointed commander in chief in 1775. Congress did decline his offer and voted him the salary. Could anyone imagine a politician today declining his salary...rhetorical of course as the answer is self-evident. [6]Washington would not recognize what our

Constitutional Republic has morphed into as everything he stood for and represented is completely antithetical to what we are as a nation today. Something our politicians are lacking today, particularly our president, is accountability. Washington once said, "I shall never attempt to palliate my own faults by exposing those of another." [7] Advice our current president would do well to heed.

ABRAHAM LINCOLN
16TH PRESIDENT 1861-1865

"Don't interfere with anything in the Constitution. That must be maintained for it is the only safeguard of our liberties."

Abraham Lincoln

Whether Divine Intervention or not, Abraham Lincoln was the right man at the right time in a critical moment in our nation's history. Without George Washington the United States of America may never have gained a foothold as a sovereign nation. Without Abraham Lincoln the United States of America may have ceased to exist as a sovereign nation. America had struggled with the paradox of liberty and slavery since its inception of 1776. The three-fifths compromise, the Northwest Ordinance of 1787, etc…all lay testament to a conflicted nation. Thomas Jefferson said of slavery, "We have a wolf by the ears, and we can neither hold him, nor safely let him go." [8] Lincoln spoke to this paradox in his "House Divided" speech in 1858. During this speech Lincoln invoked the Bible and the words of Jesus Christ, "And if a house is divided against itself, that house cannot stand." (Mark 3:25). Lincoln threw down the gauntlet and challenged us a nation to aspire to the words of The Declaration of Independence, "We hold these truths to be self-evident, that all men are created equal, that they are endowed by their Creator with certain unalienable Rights, which among these are Life, Liberty and the pursuit of Happiness."

Lincoln began what would become a successful and lucrative law career in Illinois in 1837. As for politics Lincoln was a Whig, the forerunner to the Republican Party. He served four consecutive terms in the Illinois Legislature starting in 1834 and was elected to the Congress in 1846 and chose not to run for re-election in 1848. If not for the Kansas-Nebraska Act of 1854, Lincoln may have simply plied his trade as a successful lawyer and never returned to politics. The Missouri Compromise of 1820 established the boundary for free states and those of slavery. The dividing line would be established at latitude 36-30'. Slavery would be allowed south of the dividing line, would not be allowed north of the line. The union existed in relative peace and blissful ignorance until the Kansas-Nebraska Act of 1854. Sponsored by Stephen A. Douglas, it essentially repealed the Missouri Compromise. The Kansas-Nebraska Act called for popular sovereignty, each state would be allowed to support or ban slavery through the will of the electorate. This was the sentinel moment for Lincoln, the country as a whole and the survival of the union. Lincoln engaged in politics once again, helped found the Illinois Republican Party and began a campaign giving nearly 200 speeches over the next six years against slavery. The speeches included his "House Divided" as well as several debates in 1858 against Stephen A. Douglas for Senate.

Although Lincoln lost to Douglas in 1858 it set the stage for his campaign and eventual victory in 1860. The country at this time was leading a factious existence. Mostly along lines of free vs. slave, numerous party factions formed: Whigs, Conscience Whigs, Cotton Whigs, Democrats, Fire-eaters, barn burners, American Party, Know-nothings, Republicans, Black Republicans, Jefferson Republicans, Constitutional Union Party, Copperheads, Northern Democrats, Southern Democrats, etc...[9, 10] The irony of Lincoln being elected as our 16th President, he was sworn in on March 4, 1861 by Chief Justice Roger B Taney. Taney presided over The Supreme Court in 1857 during Dred Scott v. John F. A. Sandford. Taney read his 50 page opinion which stated Dred Scott was not an American citizen and was indeed considered property. By the time Lincoln was sworn into office in March of 1861, seven southern states had already seceded led by South Carolina. [11] The southern states met in February of 1861, established the Confederate States of America and elected Jefferson Davis president who gave his inaugural address on February 18, 1861. [12]

On April 12, 1861, a relief squadron dispatched by President Lincoln to Fort Sumter in Charleston harbor was fired upon. The attack and subsequent surrender of Fort Sumter to the Confederacy began the Civil War. Lincoln issued his Emancipation Proclamation on January 1, 1863. In so doing, Lincoln proclaimed all slaves in Confederate territory are "forever free." Although it did not actually free any slaves, the Emancipation Proclamation served as a rallying cry for abolitionist and set the stage for the XIII Amendment, which officially abolished slavery in December 1865. The Proclamation also served to galvanize the Union effort against the Confederacy and abolition of slavery. [13] Lincoln gave his Gettysburg Address on November 19, 1863. As a dedication to those who perished a few months earlier Lincoln evoked the words of our Founders. He spoke of liberty, freedom, God and a government of the people, by the people and for the people. [14] Lincoln's resolve and sense of purpose held the Union together. Despite the utter lack of success with his military leadership, Lincoln finally settled on General Grant as his commander over all union armies. Lincoln and the Union armies had suffered through the likes of McDowell, McClellan, Pope, Burnside, Hooker and Meade. [15] Grant's promotion turned the tide and eventually led to the Confederate armies defeat.

Lincoln won re-election in 1864. Richmond fell on April 2, 1865 and Lee surrender to Grant at Appomattox on April 9, 1865. [16] Five days later, on April 14, 1865, John Wilkes Booth shot Lincoln yelled "Sic simper tyrannis" (Thus ever to tyrants), fled the Ford Theater, was later captured and shot on April 26, 1865. [17] Lincoln, like many Americans, recognized slavery for what it was a moral evil. He also recognized, like Jefferson, that the country was holding a wolf "by the ears." As such, he hoped slavery would be marginalized by limiting its practice to the South. If this were the case, slavery would die a gradual death. However, the Kansas-Nebraska and Dred Scott decision forever changed the landscape. Destiny took over and essentially Lincoln's hand was forced. His legacy: liberty, union, the belief that we are created equal, the belief that we are endowed with unalienable rights granted by God. The belief that these rights include life, liberty and the pursuit of Happiness. The belief that government is of the people, by the people and for the people. Lincoln's war on slavery led to the XIII Amendment, which outlawed slavery in 1865. The XIV Amendment which granted slaves citizenship in 1866. The XV Amendment granting blacks the right to vote in 1870. Amendments XIII, XIV and XV can be attributed to Lincoln's belief in our Founding documents, which represent the very essence of liberty and freedom, rights granted by God. [18]

THOMAS JEFFERSON
3ᴿᴰ PRESIDENT 1801-1809

"When the people fear the government its tyranny, when government fears the people its liberty." [19]

Thomas Jefferson

"We hold these truths to be self-evident, that all men are created equal, that they are endowed by their Creator

with certain unalienable Rights, that among these are
Life, Liberty and the pursuit of Happiness – That to
secure these rights, governments are instituted among
Men, deriving their just powers from the consent of the
governed..." [20]

Thomas Jefferson authored The Declaration of Independence at 33 years of age in 1776. This document, especially the aforementioned passage, set the tone for our founding and very existence. One can argue that our founding document penned by Jefferson surpasses all others for its brevity, sense of purpose and perpetual inspiration. The Declaration of Independence is 1337 words. It serves as an indictment against the British throne, but more importantly proclaims the core principles with regard to broad political guidance. These principles, which the Founders were of a common mind, include equal rights and the consent of the governed. [21] Beyond the broad political guidance, The Declaration invokes the concept of lex aeterna, or the law of nature. Jefferson invokes the Laws of Nature and of Natures God within the first paragraph of The Declaration. This is a reference to the time of creation when God infused a moral law into the hearts of man. [22] This passage alone makes The Declaration a transcendent document as it can apply to any time in mankind's history because the truths are self-evident. [23]

Jefferson referenced Natures God, Creator, Supreme Being and Divine Providence within The Declaration. These references are not arbitrary but invoke a belief that there is a greater design or purpose regarding our existence. These references invoke the Founder's belief in man's capacity for liberty, of self-governance and self-reliance. [24] The Founders to a man overwhelmingly believed that faith and freedom is mutually dependant upon each other. Jefferson himself is quoted, "The God who gave us life, gave us liberty at the same time...The hand of force may destroy, but cannot disjoin them." [25]

Jefferson authored and signed The Declaration along with 55 of our Founding Fathers, which concludes with…a firm reliance on the protection of divine Providence, we mutually pledge to each other our Lives, our Fortunes and our sacred Honor. [26] The Declaration stands as our founding document, but could have easily served as a death warrant for all who signed, including Thomas Jefferson. The Declaration stands today in stark contrast to legislative documents. As previously stated, The Declaration contains a mere 1337 ***words***. By contrast, Obamacare contains approximately 2000 ***pages***; the financial reform bill contains approximately 2300 ***pages***. I doubt very much that future generations will celebrate either bill for its brevity, sense of purpose or view these documents as transcendent.

Prior to being elected the country's third president, Jefferson served in the Virginia legislature, served in Congress, served as minister to France, as our first Secretary of State and our second vice president. Jefferson authored The Declaration of Independence as well as Virginia's Statute for Religious Freedom. Jefferson was a devout Christian and believer in the teachings of Jesus Christ. His personal motto was "Rebellion to Tyrants is Obedience to God." [27] Upon taking office, Jefferson discontinued the policy of paying off Barbary rulers. Both Washington and Adams felt it was cheaper to pay than to engage in war. Jefferson took a different tact and fought the Barbary rulers until 1805. Essentially, Jefferson fought the first war on terror in American history. Although negotiations for the Louisiana Purchase began with President Adams, Jefferson oversaw the completion and announced the purchase on July 4, 1803. The Louisiana Purchase doubled the size of The United States at a cost of $12 million or roughly 12 cents an acre. [28] Jefferson is also responsible for the Lewis & Clark expedition, which Jefferson referred to as the "Corps of Discovery." The planning actually began in the early 1790's and was implemented in 1804. The Lewis & Clark expedition opened up the northwest to the remainder of the country. [29] At Jefferson's request, Congress bans importation of slaves in 1808. [30]

Jefferson was an anti-Federalist, an advocate of limited and frugal federal government, sat on the committee that designed our nation's seal, advocated for an enlightened electorate, spoke out against deficit spending and accumulation of debt, spoke out in favor of religious freedoms, spoke out in favor of religious education, he spoke out against fractional banking, fiat currency and central banks. Jefferson reduced our national debt by 26% during his term as president. He spoke out in favor of strong local governments and was an advocate of decentralization, he also authored The Declaration of Independence and spoke of self-evident truths. Jefferson believed the basic principles upon which the country was founded, religion, morality and knowledge. He was a proponent of the Northwest Ordinance passed in 1787 particularly with Article 3, "Religion, morality and knowledge being necessary to good government and the happiness of mankind, schools and the means of education shall be forever encouraged," Jefferson referred to these basic principles, "in which God has united us all" Jefferson was also a strong advocate of binding our political leaders to "the chains of The Constitution." [31]

The legacy of Thomas Jefferson reaches far beyond his tenure as President. John Adams description of Jefferson was he could "calculate an eclipse, survey an estate, tie an artery, plan an edifice, try a cause, break a horse, dance a minuet, and play the violin." [32] Jefferson became head of his family in 1757 following the death of his father. [33] Jefferson found himself head of the family estate at age fourteen and graduated from the College of William & Mary at age nineteen after being accepted as an advanced student at the age of sixteen. Jefferson furthered his education, particularly law, under George Wythe who was a signer of The Declaration of Independence and participant at the Constitutional Convention. Under Wythe, Jefferson studies were not limited to the law but included religion, physics, language, math, philosophy, chemistry, anatomy, politics, history, etc...Jefferson was admitted to the bar in 1767, a year later was elected to represent his county in the House of Burgesses. [34] Jefferson made a name for himself internationally in 1774 when he wrote a paper titled, "A Summary View of the Rights of British America." The paper essentially pronounced American colonists as British citizens and should be afforded certain unalienable rights.

Jefferson attended the Second Continental Congress in Philadelphia in 1775. In June of 1776, Jefferson joined with Benjamin Franklin, John Adams, Roger Sherman and Robert Livingston to form a committee to write a declaration. Jefferson was tabbed, despite his young age, to draft The Declaration which was adopted on July 2, 1776...which concludes with, "And for the support of this declaration, with a firm reliance on the protection of Divine Providence, we mutually pledge to each other our lives, our fortunes, and our sacred honor." Jefferson actually left Congress shortly after The Declaration was adopted. By October of 1776, he was back home in Virginia and serving on the state assembly at Williamsburg. During his tenure at the state assembly Jefferson introduced legislation that would serve as the forerunner to the Constitution. Although it took years to pass, legislation introduced by Jefferson included a bill to abolish slavery, revising the civil code, and revising the criminal code. Additional legislation abolished primogeniture and entail, both were remnants of the aristocracy and feudal systems. Jefferson also introduced legislation that would guarantee religious freedom. Jefferson served as Governor of Virginia in 1779 and later served as minister to France in 1784. He also played a critical role during the Constitutional Convention in 1787 via correspondence with James Madison. [35] Again, Jefferson's legacy extends well beyond his presidency. He was one of our Founding Fathers and played a crucial role in the birth of America. Like Washington, he was the right man at the right time in our nation's history.

RONALD REAGAN
40TH PRESIDENT 1981-1989

"...We raise our voices to God who is the author of this most tender music. And may He continue to hold us close as we fill the world with our sound, in unity, affection and love, one people Under God, dedicated to the dream of freedom that He has placed in the human heart, called upon now to pass that dream on to a waiting and hopeful world." [36]

Ronald Reagan

Reagan was conservative, he was religious, and he was a man of principles and ideals. He believed in American Exceptionalism, he believed in government for the people and by the people. Reagan was a man of his word and said what he meant; even the Russians admired him for his leadership claiming that "word and deed are the same." [37] Reagan was pro-life, believed in the free market and American entrepreneurship. His policy towards the Soviet Union and Communism in general was brilliant for its brevity, "We win they lose..." [38] Reagan survived the Republican establishment, an assassination attempt, colon cancer, skin cancer, liberals, Iran-Contra, the October 1987 crash, Tip O'Neill, losing control of Congress, Communism, Beirut, Brezhnev, Andropov, Chernenko, Gorbachev, etc...He survived and conquered due to his resolve, he stayed the course, he did not make any attempt to "run to the middle" [39] for political expedience. Reagan did not backtrack nor apologize for his core beliefs. Core beliefs that were founded in the Constitution. Reagan asked a simple question during the 1980 presidential campaign, "Are you better off than you were four years ago?" [40] The question is as relevant today as it was 30 plus years ago. "Word and deed are the same..." The Russians recognized early on the resolve that Reagan would bring to bear throughout his eight year tenure as President. Excerpts from Reagan's First Inaugural Address on Tuesday, January 20, 1981 would lay the foundation for the American revival under Reagan, who would plant his flag unapologetically.

"You and I as individuals can, by borrowing, live beyond our means, but for only a limited period of time. Why then, should we think that collectively, as a nation, we are not bound by that same limitation."...
"In this present crisis, government is not the solution to our problem."..."But if no one among us is capable of governing himself, then who among us has the capacity to govern someone else?"...Reagan spoke of "We the people...this breed called Americans..." "We are a nation that has a government—not the other way around. And this makes us special among the nations of the Earth. Our government has no power except that granted by the people. It is time to check and reverse the growth of government which shows signs of having grown beyond the consent of the governed."... "Now, so there will be no misunderstanding, it is not my intention to do away with government. It is, rather, to make it work—work with us, not over us, to stand by our side, not ride our back."... "We are a nation under God, and I believe God intended for us to be free."... "And, after all, why shouldn't we believe this? We are Americans, God bless you, and thank you." [41] *Reagan encapsulated the principles and ideals that our country was founded upon. He called, not for a radical transformation, but for a return to the very principles espoused by Washington,*

Jefferson, Adams, Franklin, Madison, et al…And he was unapologetic for doing so.

Reagan did indeed inherit a mess from Carter; however, he never pointed the finger of blame. He took office, took responsibility for the task at hand and acted upon his principles. Reagan inherited the Iran Hostage crisis, a misery index that hovered around 20%, stagflation, high unemployment, high inflation, high interest rates, high gas prices, etc…The same day that Reagan took office in January of 1981, the hostages were released from Iran after being held captive for 444 days. Reagan also abolished price controls on oil and the Council on Wage and Price Stability. [42] Reagan recognized that the socialism espoused by liberals was strangling the life out of the American economy. He believed in supply side economics, that lowering taxes will stimulate economic growth and eventually lead to more revenue. Reagan signed the Economic Recovery Act which served to lower both taxes and spending. Reagan worked with Prime Minister Thatcher, Pope John Paul II and Lech Walesa of Poland to combat the world wide creep of Communism. He held fast in Grenada, supported the Contras in Nicaragua, labeled the Soviet Union the "evil empire" and proposed the Strategic Defense Initiative that would eventually lead to the collapse of the Berlin Wall and defeat of Soviet Communism. Reagan recognized Socialism for what it was and what Churchill once described… "the equal sharing of misery."

Reagan gave his Second Inaugural Address on January 21, 1985 after a successful campaign based upon "Morning in America." [43] Reagan began by stating, "God bless you and welcome back"… Reagan also stated that "…government, the people said, was not our master, it is our servant: its only power that which we the people allow it to have."… "We asked things of government that government was not equipped to give. We yielded authority to the National

193

Government that properly belonged to States or to local government or the people themselves. We allowed taxes and inflation to rob us of our earnings and savings and watched the great industrial machine that had made us the most productive people on Earth slow down and the number of unemployed increase.”…Reagan spoke of our “values of faith, family and work.” He spoke of a troubled world, “when Americans courageously supported the struggle and free enterprise throughout the world, and turned the tide of history away from totalitarian darkness and into the warm sunlight of human freedom.”…He spoke of the struggle for what is most valuable to man, “his right to self-government.”…He proclaimed, “Freedom and incentives unleash the drive and entrepreneurial genius that are the core of human progress.”…He said, “We must simplify our tax system, make it more fair, and bring the rates down for all who work and earn.”…He stated, “My friends, together we can do this, and do it we must, so help me God.”…He asked, “If not us, who? If not now, when?”…He called for a “balanced budget” and reduction in our “national debt.” Reagan spoke out against, “Governments desire to spend its citizen’s money and tax into servitude when bills come due.” “Let us make it unconstitutional for the Federal Government to spend more that the Federal Government takes in.” [44]

Reagan stated that “we are all Americans pledged to carry on this last, best hope of man on Earth.” He invokes images of Washington at Valley Forge, of Lincoln during the Civil War. He speaks of the “American Sound.” “It is hopeful, big-hearted, idealistic, daring, decent and fair.” He credits God as the “Author of this most tender music,” and states we are “one people under God.” He finishes his Address with “God bless you and may God bless America.” [45] Reagan was conservative and proud, American and proud. He was unapologetic for his religious beliefs, his belief in a limited federal government, his belief in the private sector, his belief in supply side economics, and his belief in a strong military. He stayed the course against Communist creep and was victorious. He stayed the course against liberal opposition to Reaganomics and was victorious. He indeed was a man of his words, as the Russians described, "word and deed are the same." Reagan planted his flag and was unapologetic. Hope and change to Reagan was more than just a bumper sticker and campaign slogan. It meant a revitalized America, a return to our Constitutional Republic as designed. Hope and change to Reagan was not a radical transformation but a return to our Founding principles.

Reagan inherited the Carter "malaise," high interest rates, high taxes, high unemployment, gas lines, an energy crisis, the Iranian Hostage Crisis, a demoralized and under funded military, etc…Our GDP when Carter left office was approximately $2.7trillion, after eight years of Reaganomics, it was approximately $5.1trillion…an 89% increase.[46] Unemployment under Carter prior to leaving office was hovering around 7%, under Reagan unemployment stood at 5.3% when Bush took office in 1989, a decrease of 25%. The misery index under Carter went from 12.72 to 19.72 during his four-year tenure, an increase of 55%. Reagan took the misery index down from 19.33 to 9.72 during his eight-year tenure, a decrease of 50%. [47] The day Reagan took office he ended price controls, the Council on Wage and Price Stability and announced the Iranians had released 52 Americans held hostage for 444 days. After eight years of the Reagan Presidency, it was indeed "Morning in America." The following is an excerpt from a speech Reagan gave in 1974…it stands as testament to Reagan's belief in American Exceptionalism: "We cannot escape our destiny, nor should we try to do so. The leadership of the free world was thrust upon us two centuries ago in that little hall of Philadelphia…We are indeed, and we are today, the last best hope of man on earth." [48]

CALVIN COOLIDGE
30ᵀᴴ PRESIDENT 1923-1929

"The wise and correct course to follow in taxation and in all other economic legislation is not to destroy those who have already secured success but to create conditions under which every one will have a better chance of being successful." [49]

Calvin Coolidge

Perhaps the most underrated and underappreciated president in our nation's history. Possibly the president treated most unfairly by history. Coolidge and his predecessor Harding have been blamed unjustly for the greed of the 1920's and eventual collapse leading to the Great Depression. Coolidge took office on August 2, 1923 following the death of President Harding. President Coolidge stayed the course and continued implementation of Harding's plan, a national budget, national debt reduction, tax reduction, etc...Calvin Coolidge was an advocate of The Founders belief; he who governs best governs least. [50] Coolidge believed, governments like individuals, should live within their means. He believed that governments are non productive, unlike the private sector. The national debt in 1921 when Wilson left office was approximately $29 billion. Wilson actually increased our nation's debt by over 700% during his eight-year tenure. Coolidge on the other hand reduced this debt to approximately $16billion when he left office. [51] Unemployment was at 20% when Wilson left office. Unemployment under Coolidge averaged 3.3% during his six-year tenure and even dipped below 2% late in his term as president. [52] The gross domestic product under Coolidge averaged 7% annual growth during his term as president. Although, GDP increased under presidents Wilson and FDR, it came at the expense of our national debt. Coolidge not only decreased debt but increased GDP as well. [53]

Calvin Coolidge was an advocate of laissez-faire economics and American capitalism. [54] Coolidge believed, like The Founders and Adam Smith, in the invisible hand of government. They did not believe in the beneficent (i.e. meddling) hand of government. [55] Coolidge ran his life and the presidency according to one simple principle; first do no harm. Under Coolidge, the federal government was less than 2% of our GDP. By contrast, we are approximately 45% today. Coolidge believed in American business and the private sector. Coolidge said in 1925, "The chief business of the American people is business." [56] The Treasury Secretary under Coolidge was former railroad magnate, Andrew Mellon. Coolidge was in full agreement with his Treasury Secretary and philosophy. Mellon believed, "The way to wealth, if you desire it, is as plain as the way to market. It depends chiefly on two words, industry and frugality. That is, waste neither time nor money but make the best use of both." [57] Advice our current administration would be wise to heed.

Under Coolidge and Mellon excessive taxes were viewed as prohibitive. They did not view taxes as a moral issue but a practical one. The top rate under Wilson was over 70%. Taxes under Coolidge at Mellon's urging were decreased. The resultant effect was an increase in revenues and a budget surplus. Coolidge and Mellon believed that when government taxed too much, revenues actually decreased. Overtaxation simply hurt the federal government by decreasing revenues. Excessive taxes were simply not paid, as the rich found loopholes to avoid the excessive taxation. [58] To quote Coolidge. "...the wise and correct course to follow in taxation and all other economic legislation is not to destroy those who have already secured success but to create conditions under which every one will have a better chance to be successful." [59] Coolidge also did away with the excessive profits tax, saying "it was wrong to say that profits were excessive anyhow, when they created the work." The legacy of Calvin Coolidge is small government, the invisible hand, lower taxes, lower debt, budget surplus, historic lows for unemployment, vibrant GDP growth, belief in the private sector, in hard work and frugality. The standard historical legacy blames Calvin Coolidge for a decade of greed, false growth, low morality and The Great Depression. American capitalism, the October 1929 contraction, Coolidge policy did not create the depression. The contraction in 1929 was a simple self-correction of the market.

The U.S. economy was not alone in dealing with a contraction. Markets in other areas of the world experienced contractions as well, New Zealand, Japan, Romania, Chile, Denmark, Finland and Sweden. All of these markets recovered and saw an increase in industrial production much faster than the U.S.A. The problem in this country was not Coolidge, Mellon, American capitalism, laissez-faire economics, the private sector, etc…The problem in this country was intervention by Hoover and a loss of faith in the free market. FDR threw fuel on the fire and turned a minor recession into a major depression. His blind faith in European style collectivism, Keynesian economics, perpetual experimentation, centrally planned economy, priming the pump, excessive taxation, etc… His reliance on a "Brain Trust" with no private sector experience, a "Brain Trust" who valued theory over experience, is why the U.S. lost an entire decade and did not recover until the 1950's. History has been unkind (i.e. subjective) to Calvin Coolidge, unjustly so.

COMMON DENOMINATOR…

There is a common thread that binds together Washington, Lincoln, Jefferson, Reagan and Coolidge. They do believe that word and deed are the same, they believe in God, and American Exceptionalism. They believe in The Declaration of Independence and the Constitution as originally written, that of fixed truths and principles. They believe in the rights of an individual, rights endowed by our Creator not the federal government. They believe in the invisible hand of government not the beneficent hand (i.e. central planners). They believe in free markets, they believe in the right to pursue happiness and are opposed to any notion that government exists to provide equal results. They believe in State's rights and the underlying principles of checks and balances. They believe in a common defense, a strong military presence. They believe in the notion of friends to all allies to none, of trust but verify. They believe in the notion that man can govern himself, that the American experiment is unique in the history of the world. They believe that we are indeed the last best hope. Each of these presidents served at precisely the right moment in our nation's history. Whether it was Divine Providence or not, they were the right man at the right time. Most importantly, they stayed the course; they did not compromise principles for political expedience. Each of these men planted their own flag and was unapologetic for their core beliefs and belief in America.

CHAPTER 6
PERSONAL WORST...

FRANKLIN DELANO ROOSEVELT
32ND PRESIDENT 1933-1945

"The country needs and...demands bold, persistent experimentation. It is common sense to take a method and try it. If it fails, admit it frankly and try another. But above all, try something." [1]

FDR

Winston Churchill paid the following tribute to the RAF fighter pilots on August 20, 1940... "Never in the field of human conflict was so much owed by so many to so few." [2] One can turn that tribute around, and based upon his record and legacy, one can say of FDR... Never has one man done so much (i.e. damage) to so many, although, Obama is clearly on his way to eclipsing FDR's legacy of destruction and progressive dystopia. Perhaps the most objective summary of FDR and his New Deal policies comes from his own Treasury Secretary. Henry Morgenthau wrote in his personal diary, "...we have tried spending money. We are spending more than we have ever spent before and it does not work...We have never made good on our promises...I say after eight years of the Administration we have just as much unemployment as when we started...and enormous debt to boot." Morgenthau was a long time friend of FDR and served under him from 1929 until 1945. Morgenthau served as Treasury Secretary under FDR from 1933-1945. His admission of FDR's failure came in 1940 after eight years of New Deal policy. During these eight years, unemployment averaged 18.6%.

The national debt when FDR took office in 1933 was approximately $22 billion. When FDR passed away in 1945, the national debt stood at approximately $260 billion...an increase of over 1000 percent. [3] During his First 100 days, FDR experimented with the gold standard, taking the United States on-off-on, etc... His perpetual experimentation made a weak dollar weaker, stymied the economy and turned a recession into a depression.. If in fact, FDR let the market self correct as opposed to government meddling (i.e. Keynesian), the recession would never have reached depression levels. FDR drove us into a depression he did not lead us out of one. FDR issued an executive order in 1933 that forced U.S citizens to sell their gold assets back to the U.S. government. FDR invalidated the gold clause and refused to honor government contracts. FDR said the following upon issuing the executive order with regard to private holdings of gold..."We seldom know, six weeks in advance, what we are going to do."

Among his many failures, FDR's alphabet legislation is perhaps the epitome of the New Deal philosophy, throw enough money around, pass enough legislation and give the illusion of recovery. The CCC, TVA, NRA, AAA, WPA, et al...are perfect examples of this philosophy. The Civilian Conservation Corps put approximately 250,000 to work, but it was nothing but costly make work and did nothing to abate long-term unemployment. The Tennessee Valley Authority was sold to the public as a means to jobs and cheaper electricity. History has demonstrated that the private sector would have created more jobs and produced electricity at cheaper rates. The National Recovery Act was also part of the frantic 100 days.

The NRA was government meddling ran amuck, it produced 700 new codes with 10,000 pages of legislation. The Supreme Court ruled against the NRA in many cases involving constitutionality. The Agricultural Adjustment Administration was also passed during the frantic 100 days. In an attempt to artificially control supply and demand, FDR ordered the elimination of 6 million pigs. The attempt was to artificially lower the supply, thereby artificially raising demand and cost. Unfortunately, all it did was remove 6 million pigs from the market. The ill-advised plan did not have the desired effect.

The Works Progress Administration was another example of money, legislation and creating the illusion of recovery. The WPA spent $11 billion on 1.4 million projects over its eight year existence; it was ripe with confusion, corruption and waste. FDR passed the Social Security Act in 1935. Initially packaged as Old Age Survivors Insurance (OASI), Social Security has morphed into an entitlement behemoth with trillions of unfunded liabilities. Perhaps the largest Ponzi scheme in history, Social Security was an annuity the United States government coerced private citizens to buy. As a reaction to numerous Supreme Court decision against his New Deal policies, FDR announces the Federal Court Reorganization bill. This was FDR's attempt to pack the Supreme Court by increasing the number of justices from nine to fifteen. Of course, FDR would have chosen the additional six. Despite unemployment hovering around 20%, private sector money stagnated due to his perpetual experimentation, FDR passed the Revenue Act in 1935. Revenues of course being euphuism for taxes. The top rate increased from 25% to 79%, corporate taxes increased and FDR implemented an undistributed profits tax. FDR in his infinite wisdom (i.e. or lack thereof) throws gasoline on a fire with his Revenue Act.

Nothing speaks to the arrogant, condescending, paternalistic, statist attitude of FDR and his New Dealers than the use of executive rs. During his twelve-year tenure in the Whitehouse, FDR issued

3522 executive orders. [4] The presidents from Washington to Hoover, 1789-1932, combined issued approximately 4000 during the 143 year span. Probably the most infamous of these executive orders issued by FDR was EO9066. FDR issued EO9066 on February 19, 1942. The order interred 110,000 Japanese-Americans, of which 64% were citizens. Adding to the legacy of FDR is the crash of 1937 where the DOW fell from 190 to 114 from August to December of that year. A contraction to an economy already in the throws of a depression. In 1938, FDR introduced the Federal National Mortgage Association better known as Fannie Mae. FNMA was a vehicle of pushing home ownership as a means of social entitlement. In other words, more social engineering. Fast-forward to 2008, and Fannie Mae's destructive legacy is put into perspective. Although FDR had many faults, he was an equal opportunity politician. Not only did FDR squeeze the life out of the US economy for years, he literally squeezed the life out of Eastern Europe by acquiescing to Stalin's demands. FDR met with Stalin and Churchill in Tehran in December of 1943, the first of three meetings between the allies. During the meeting FDR conceded to Stalin's demand to takeover most of Eastern Europe including Poland. FDR's only request of Stalin was to keep the agreement secret so as not to alienate the Polish vote in America. FDR was up for re-election in 1944.

Based upon his record, it is very difficult to argue that FDR was not the worst president in our nation's history. Certainly there have been worse based upon shear incompetence (i.e. Carter, Obama) or corruption. However, when viewed in terms of malicious behavior (i.e. attempts to pack the Supreme Court), record on unemployment, record on national debt, record on deficit spending, abuses of power (i.e. NRA), legacy of social security (i.e. trillions of unfunded liabilities), legacy of Fannie Mae, ceding Eastern Europe to Communism following WWII, arrogance, condescension, dismissiveness, etc...one would be hard pressed to find a president that was more damaging during his tenure and left behind a legacy that America is still digging out from than FDR.

WOODROW WILSON
28TH PRESIDENT 1913-1921

"...we are not bound to adhere to the doctrines held by the signers of the Declaration of Independence." [5]

Woodrow Wilson

The quote epitomizes the contempt for which Wilson held towards our founding documents. Statist, socialist, racist, Progressive... whatever the label, Wilson was a true believer. Whereas TR and FDR, although narcissist, both were politicians at heart, nothing less nothing more. Both would have trumpeted the virtues of conservatism, free trade markets and the Constitution if it were politically expedient. Wilson on the other hand was an academic, a social engineer. He believed in the Progressive virtues of moving past (i.e. progress) the Constitution. He was an advocate of the top down welfare state implemented by Otto von Bismarck in late 19th century Germany. Wilson believed in the beneficent hand of government, of central control, of consolidation, of theory over experience, he was an advocate for the rights of the collective over the individual. Wilson believed that the Constitution was obsolete; he viewed it as an impediment to his Progressive ideology. The Constitution was viewed as a living document which translates to no fixed truths or principles. The Constitution, in Wilson's view, was to mold to an ever changing society or whims of the current administration. This of course is completely antithetical to what The Founders intended.

Wilson's legacy of Progressive legislation haunts us to this day, to vit...The Federal Reserve Act was passed in 1913. This was nothing ⁃ than a knee jerk reaction to financial panics in 1873, 1884,

1890, 1893 and 1907. The Fed was established to serve as the 'lender of last resort.' To lend financial stability to excessive swings in the free market, to allay fears during times of contraction. The legacy of the Fed is why The Founders were opposed to central banks and fiat currency…inflation! From 1789 to 1913 the value of the U.S. dollar increased by 13%. Since the Fed was established in 1913, the U. S. dollar, even though it serves as the reserve currency for the world, has lost 93% of its value. This is due to fiat currency, or paper money. The XVI Amendment was also passed in 1913 which implemented our current system of progressive taxation. This was nothing more than the Progressive, socialist maxim of redistributing wealth. The federal government was now an active participant in the free market by taxing the rich and redistributing the assets. The XVII Amendment, also passed in 1913, took away states rights to elect U.S. Senators and gave this to the general electorate. This completely usurped the rights of the state to elect their Senator and if necessary to recall. The Founders viewed The House of Representatives as the people's house; the Senate was established to represent states rights. The net effect of the XVII Amendment was simply a further consolidation of power.

The Espionage Act of 1917 and the Sedition Act of 1918 remind us of the true nature of Progressive ideology…it is totalitarian by nature, nothing less nothing more. These Acts, collectively, made it illegal to profess any criticism of the U.S. government. Thousands were imprisoned as a result of this Act which was nothing more than a usurpation of the 1st Amendment. The Founders believed in individual rights and the freedom of speech. The Espionage Act and Sedition Act were diametrically opposed to these ideals. The XVIII Amendment, better known as prohibition, was passed in 1919. This was another product of Progressive legislation based upon the beneficent hand, social engineering and theory over experience. Ratified in 1919 and repealed by the XXI Amendment in 1933, prohibition was an abysmal failure. Instead of leading to temperance, it did nothing but foster an atmosphere of graft and corruption for 14 years. The League of Nations was proposed by Wilson in 1918 as part of his Fourteen Points Plan. The 14th point being to establish a League of Nations. Nothing better epitomizes the arrogance, condescension, elitist attitude of Progressives. Wilson actually viewed himself as one of the "wise and knowledgeable few." His League of Nations proposal was nothing more than a veiled attempt to circumvent the U.S Constitution and cede U.S. sovereignty to global governance.

Wilson's legacy also includes the issuance of 1803 executive orders. [6] Keep in mind, from George Washington to William McKinley, 1789-1901, there were only 1262 executive orders issued combined. Wilson issued an astonishing 1803 executive during his eight-year tenure, 1913-1921. His records and legacy on debt was equally abysmal, the debt when Wilson took office in 1913 was approximately $2.9 billion, after eight years, the debt in 1921 was approximately $24 billion. An increase of over 700%. Wilson was a racist; he was fond of the pro-KKK film, "Birth of a Nation." He was an advocate of eugenics, signing legislation as Governor of New Jersey that provided the state with the power to determine who should procreate.[7] He viewed the Constitution as Darwinian in nature, always evolving, as opposed to the Founders' view of Newtonian, fixed truths. Wilson shared his political DNA with Marx, Engels, Bismarck, communist, statist, Progressives, totalitarian, et al…Everything he believed in ran counter-intuitive to the beliefs of Washington, Jefferson, Adams, Franklin, the Constitution, The Declaration of Independence, free markets, conservatism, et al…

WILLIAM JEFFERSON CLINTON
42ᴺᴰ PRESIDENT 1993-2001

Clinton was/is a true politician in the spirit of TR and FDR, one who acts out of political expedience more so than pure ideology (i.e. Woodrow Wilson). However, regardless of his intentions he was an embarrassment and an abject failure. His legacy includes being impeached by The House of Representatives, being disbarred, perjured himself in front of a Federal Grand Jury, having sex with a 20 year old intern inside the Oval office, could not define the meaning if 'is', engaged in social engineering (i.e. subprime mortgages) and, most damaging to the country, he was asleep at the wheel as Al Queda planned 09/11 in this country on his watch. Make no mistake; if Clinton does his job as Commander and Chief, September 11, 2001 never happens. The financial meltdown during 2008 as a result of subprime lending can be traced back to the social engineering of Clinton and his HUD secretaries as well as Clinton's repeal of the Glass-Steagull Act.

Fannie Mae and Freddie Mac were gifts of FDR and LBJ respectively. These government sponsored entities were designed to increase home ownership and viewed home ownership as a social entitlement instead of something earned. In other words, spreading the wealth around. Fannie and Freddie, implemented years ago, kicked into over-drive during the 1990's under Clinton. This eventually led to the housing bubble, the bubble bursting, collapse of the market and contraction of our economy. All traced to Clinton era, progressive, social entitlement ideology. Upon taking office in 1993, Clinton appointed Henry Cisneros as the Department of Housing and Urban Development Secretary. Cisneros pushed home ownership as an entitlement and was an advocate of subprime lending. A 1992 study issued by the Federal Reserve Bank of Boston suggested that mortgage denials were based more upon race than the ability to repay. Cisneros latched onto this, sold it to Clinton who viewed it as a way to appease the minority vote. The end result, government mandating laws that coerced private banks to engage in sub prime lending. These subprime mortgages were backed by Fannie and Freddie who acted as a guarantee against defaults. [8]

The basis of the 1992 Boston Federal Reserve study suggested that traditional means of deciding creditworthiness was discriminatory. Credit values and loan to value ratios became archaic and racist. Home ownership was a social entitlement, regardless of one's ability to repay a mortgage. Never wanting a good crisis to go to waste, like any true Progressive, Clinton seized on the opportunity and pushed subprime lending via Cisneros, Barney Frank, Christopher Dodd, Maxine Waters and future HUD Secretary Andrew Cuomo. [9] The Clinton administration, via the Community Reinvestment Act, the Federal Housing Authority, the Treasury Department, the FDIC and Cisneros essentially coerced private banks to engage in very risky subprime mortgages. Social engineering at its very worst...the financial collapse we have still not recovered from is proof positive. Subprime lending is social engineering and further evidence that Progressives do indeed view themselves as the "wise and knowledgeable few"...Clinton marched in lock step to this ideology. Wall Street was obviously complicit due to its moral hazard behavior and greed. However, if not coerced into subprime lending, the market would never have engaged in this risky venture. Clinton threw fuel on the fire with the passage of the Gramm-Leach-Biley Act of 1999. This Act repealed the Glass-Steagull Act of 1933, which was designed to restrict commercial banks from engaging in risky investment banking. Clinton's repeal of this Act, via Gramm-Leach-Biley, relaxed restrictions and allowed commercial banks to engage in risky business (i.e. subprime mortgages). [10]

September 11, 2001 was a direct result of Clinton's National Security policy or more appropriately, lack thereof. ***February 26,***

1993, a bomb designed to take down the World Trade Center towers detonated. Fortunately the bomb did not have the desired effect. Unfortunately, six people were killed with over 1000 injured. It took one month to gain control of the damage. [11] Clinton's reaction, he never once visited the site. Although the subsequent arrest, trial and conviction were good news, the bigger picture of global terror was ignored by the Clinton administration. This was treated as a criminal act, not one of terror. *October 3, 1993*, U.S. military Special Forces were poised to break the power hold of a local warlord. What should have been an easy snatch and grab turned into a disaster for U.S forces. Ninety-nine Army Rangers were ambushed by over one thousand Somalis. The end result for the under supplied and outmanned U.S. forces were 18 soldiers killed, 78 wounded. Clinton's reaction, withdraw troops, no reprisal against Somali insurgents. The incident in Somali was the sentinel moment for bin Laden and Al Queda. They declared war; Clinton viewed it as an isolated incident and ignored it. [12]

June 25, 1996, a tanker with thousands of pounds of explosives detonated at the Khobar Towers in Dharan, Saudi Arabia. This apartment complex was used to house U.S. servicemen. End result, 19 U.S. serviceman were killed, close to 400 Americans in total were wounded. The bomb also killed dozens of innocent Saudis. Soon after the attack, bin Laden officially issues his fatwah, or declaration of war, against the United States. Clinton's reaction, tough talk no action. He continued to treat these terror attacks as criminal activity, his only action was to allow law enforcement agencies to investigate. Clinton should have recognized the global terror initiative and brought the full power of the U.S. military to bear. Another example of the 'wise and intelligent few' having zero common sense. [13] *August 7, 1998*, U.S. embassies in Nairobi, Kenya and Dar-es-Salaam, Tanzania were the victims of terror once again. Bombs exploded virtually simultaneously killing 11 U.S. citizens during the attack. In total over 220 were killed and in excess of 5000 were injured. Clinton's reaction, missile strikes at high valued targets in Afghanistan and the Sudan. Unfortunately, due to bad intel, the high value targets were not so high value. The missile strikes took aim at "terrorist facilities and infrastructure," in reality the missile strikes did neither. Instead of striking back at bin Laden and Al Queda, these strikes simply poisoned relationships with Pakistan and the Sudan. [14]

October 17, 2000, while docked for refueling in the Aden Harbor of Yemen, the U.S.S. Cole was the target of another terrorist attack. Suicide bombers attacked the U.S.S. Cole with a speed boat loaded with explosives. [15] The net result, the blast left a hole 40 feet in diameter, killed 17 seamen and injured 39 others. Clinton's response, dispatch the FBI and not the military. More of the same from the Clinton administration, despite years of attacks, terrorism was treated as criminal in nature instead of military. The net result of Clinton's refusal, inability, and naiveté to take military action was September 11, 2001. Each time we were attacked Clinton was reticent with military reprisal. This National Security policy, or lack there of, did nothing but embolden bin Laden and Al Queda. Clinton failed to recognize global terror. He shifted responsibility from the CIA and military to the FBI. The FBI was limited to issuing warrants which are completely useless. Clinton cut military spending by 25% during his tenure. Troops were deployed for longer stints with less and less equipment. Despite the growth of global terror, the numerous attacks on U.S. interest, Clinton granted clemency on August 11, 1999 to 14 members of the Puerto Rican terror group FALN. The pardon was opposed by the U.S. Senate (95-2), The U.S. House of Representatives (311-41), the FBI, Fraternal Order of Police and the U.S. Attorneys Office. [16]

Despite the fatwah issued against the United States, the multiple attacks on U.S. interest during his tenure, Clinton turned down numerous opportunities from the Sudan to take custody of bin

Laden. He took the CIA out of the game and forced the FBI to pursue this as criminal activity. He downgraded the military and created a firewall between intelligence agencies precluding anyone from connecting the dots. The seeds of September 11, 2001 were planted on February 26, 1993 and sown on October 1993, June 1996, August 1998 and October 2000. Terrorists reaped the benefits of their efforts on September 11, 2001. Once again, the fact remains, if Clinton had done his job as Commander and Chief, September 11, 2001 would never have occurred. The Monica Lewinsky fiasco, perjury, subsequent disbarment and impeachment were national disgraces. Clinton's role in the subprime mortgage disaster and the attacks on September 11, 2001 are both criminal and negligent. His legacy also includes, the first president to be impeached for personal malfeasance, the first president to be disbarred from the U.S. Supreme Court and state court. Clinton's friends and associates garnered the most convictions and guilty pleas of any president. First president to be held in contempt of court. Greatest number of domestic and foreign illegal campaign contributions. Clinton without doubt, and based solely upon his record, ranks as one of the worst presidents on our nation's history. [17]

THEODORE ROOSEVELT
26TH PRESIDENT 1901-1909

Chapter one of this book began with the following quotes:

"Personal property…is subject to the general right of the community to regulate its use to whatever degree the public welfare may require it."

Theodore Roosevelt

"The theory of the Communists may be summed up in the single sentence: Abolition of private property."

Karl Marx

The question was posed, why is someone who shares the same ideology as Karl Marx carved into Mount Rushmore as one this country's greatest presidents? Teddy Roosevelt ranks as one of the worst presidents because he ushered in the era of Progressivism in this country. Winston Churchill warned Europe of Communism following WWI and suggested "killing the baby in the bathwater." Unfortunately, Europe did not take heed of his warning. TR had the opportunity to kill Progressivism in its infancy. Instead he latched onto the social justice, social engineering, statist, mindset of the Progressives for reasons of political expedience. I truly believe TR was more politician than true believer. He carried the mantle of social justice to curry favor with a populist movement, nothing more nothing less. He did not bequeath this country billions in debt like Wilson and FDR. He did not turn a blind eye to national security like Clinton did which led to 09/11. He did not leave us legacy costs such as SS, Medicare, and Medicaid that are currently bankrupting this country, thanks to FDR and LBJ. What he did bequeath the United States was Progressivism. The following paragraph taken from chapter one is TR in his own words. No one can determine what is truly in one man's heart, whether TR was a politician pandering to this movement or true ideologue is perhaps lost to history. However, regardless of his intentions, Progressivism was allowed to take roots on his watch.

Roosevelt gave a speech in April 1912 describing "Who is a Progressive?" Included in the speech were the following statements: "...We of today who stand for the Progressive movement here in the United States are not wedded to any particular kind of machinery, save solely as means to the desired ends. Our aim is to secure the real and not the nominal rule of the people...For this purpose we believe in securing for the people the direct election of United States Senators...Every man is to that extent a Progressive if he stands for any form of social justice...The big business concern that is both honest and far-sighted will, I believe, in the end favor our effort to secure thorough-going supervision and control over industrial big business, just as we have now secured it over the business of inter-State transportation and the business of banking under the National law...I stand for the adequate control, real control, of all big business...when I protest against unfair profits..."

Roosevelt was proud of his Progressive ideology, which advocated social expediency over natural rights, redistributing private property in the name of social justice, expansion of national government, state control over numerous aspects of public life, nationalize private business, centralized and bureaucratic state, elastic view of the Constitution and secular in nature. Progressives like TR operate under the guise of altruism, righteousness, social justice and benevolent social control. Their elitist mindset and theoretical goal for some earthly utopia/panacea always decays into coercive legislation, depravity, usurping liberties and subverting the Constitution. The Constitution specifies general welfare, not special welfare. History has painted TR as a man of strength, a "commanding personality," who has a "thirst for activity." He was described as "a steam engine in trousers," a "wonderful little machine," a man with a zest for the "strenuous life." [18] All perhaps true, unfortunately, he was also someone who failed to recognize the nefarious and pernicious nature of Progressivism. He failed to recognize that this movement shared its political DNA with socialist, communist, statist, etc...He failed to recognize this social movement was completely antithetical to the Constitution, The Declaration of Independence and everything The Founders espoused.

TR was an advocate of consolidating power, of centralized control, of a strong bureaucratic government. Prior to TR, executive orders were used sparingly. From Washington to McKinley, 1789-1901, 1262 executive orders were issued. TR himself issued 1081 executive orders during his tenure as president, 1901-1909. TR was also an advocate of usurping state's rights by allowing the general electorate to elect U.S. Senators. This would later come to fruition under Wilson by passing the XVII Amendment. This was nothing more than consolidating power in a centralized bureaucracy. TR viewed The Constitution as Darwinian (i.e. evolving) in nature and not Newtonian (i.e. static). TR viewed the federal government's role as paternalistic and beneficent. TR admired the Bismarckian Welfare state implemented in Germany during the late 19th century. When true grit was required, TR did nothing but appease the likes of Lincoln Steffens, Upton Sinclair, Jane Addams, Herbert Croly, Robert Lafollette, John Dewey, Walter Rauschenbusch, et al...TR had the opportunity to kill the baby in the bath water and instead allowed it to flourish. Instead of recognizing Progressivism for what it was and is, TR stood idly by. Instead of fighting for what the Founders intended, individual rights, TR allowed the collective rights mindset to infect this country. A mindset that is pervasive to this very day.

Thomas Jefferson once said, "All theory yields to experience." TR and fellow progressives espoused the exact opposite. TR was an advocate of central planning as opposed to the free market. TR was an advocate of socialistic principles as opposed to capitalism. TR viewed himself as one of the "wise and knowledgeable few." TR was the first environmental activist, grabbing millions of acres for the federal government as he did not trust the private sector. Under TR, the Interstate Commerce Clause and Hepburn Acts were utilized to their full extent and expanded the coercive measures of the federal government. Prior to the ICC and Hepburn Acts, railroad profits increased and prices decreased, with the coercive measures of the federal government, profits decreased as prices increased. Another example of legislation being well intended but ill advised. If TR did not recognize the destructive nature of Progressivism, if TR did not recognize that the Progressive ideology was counter-intuitive to what our Founders believed he was simply negligent. If TR did recognize the destructive nature and counter-intuitive beliefs system, than his actions were malicious. Either way, he his credited with ushering in the Progressive mindset that still invades our political thought process like a systemic disease. Whether it was negligence and ignorance or maliciousness, TR ranks as one of the worst presidents in U.S. history.

BARACK HUSSEIN OBAMA
44TH PRESIDENT 2008-PRESENT

"Its not surprising, then, they get bitter, they cling to guns or religion or antipathy to people who aren't like them or anti-immigrant sentiment or anti-trade sentiment as a way to explain their frustrations." April 11, 2008
Barack Hussein Obama

If George W. Bush ranks as one of the worst presidents in U.S. history, as liberals suggest, where does that leave "the messiah," Barack Hussein Obama. As of this writing everything in this country is worse today than it was in January 2009. For example: the price of gas, the price of oil, healthcare, national debt, deficit spending, divisive politics, unemployment, GDP growth, debt as a percentage of GDP, deficits as a percentage of GDP, foreign policy, domestic policy, reliance on foreign energy, etc...we have troops in 3 wars instead of 2, we are more divided now in terms of gender, race, ethnicity, politics, religion, etc...than we have been in generations. "Hope & Change" was nothing more than bait and switch. It was style over substance, an empty campaign promise that anyone would read into what they wanted to, a bumper sticker, and nothing more nothing less. A community organizer that is in so far over his head, it begs the question, how did the electorate hand this man the keys to the kingdom? How does a man who allegedly has an IQ of 160 mispronounce corpsman repeatedly? How does a man of such great intelligence claim we have 57 states? How does a man who is part of the "wise and knowledgeable few" think Austrians speak Austrian? How does a man of such superior intellect and articulation require a teleprompter to speak to middle school children? The "mess" Obama inherited from Bush was no less than what Bush inherited from Clinton. Love him or despise him, Bush took office and never once pointed the finger at Clinton for 09/11 or the subprime mortgage disaster that was looming. Since day one, Obama has pointed the finger at everyone but himself. Yes, he inherited a mess, but his actions and his alone have simple made things considerably worse.

Gas was less than $2/gallon in 2009, today it hovers around $4/gallon. Oil was under $38/barrel in 2009, today it hovers at around $100/barrel. Unemployment under Bush averaged 5.25% over his eight-year tenure. Unemployment under Obama has hovered between 9-10% for over 36 months. It took the United States from 1789-2008 to accumulate $10trillion of debt, a period of 219 years. Obama has accumulated more then $5trillion in debt in three-plus years. Bush set a record for deficit spending with $400 billion with his final budget. Obama's current budget proposal includes spending of $3.7trillion on $2.2trillion in revenues. Obama promised to withdraw troops in Iraq and Afghanistan. Today not only are American troops still deployed, we're involved in Libya as well. Obama promised to close Guantanamo Bay, it remains open as of this writing. Obama excoriated Bush for many of his foreign policies and national security measures, yet most if not all remain in place. Obama promised shovel ready jobs via his $800billion Stimulus…yet joked in June of 2011 that the jobs were not as shovel ready as they thought. In fact the U.S. workforce has contracted under Obama by 2 million jobs. Obama excoriates the wealthy for not paying their fair share, yet GE and Jeffery Immelt pay zero taxes on $5billion in revenues. This country has an estimated 200-300 years worth of natural resources between oil, coal, natural gas, shale, etc…despite our dependence on foreign oil and a stagnant economy, Obama will not veer from his green economy panacea which is nothing but a pipe dream. In fact, in January of 2012 Obama vetoed plans for the Keystone Pipeline which would have created an estimated 20,000 jobs.

Our current deficit spending hovers around 10% as a percentage of GDP. Even the socialist style European welfare state tries to cap deficit spending as a percentage of GDP at 3%. Despite our national debt rising to levels that have destroyed the economies of Greece, Spain, Portugal, Ireland and most of Europe, Obama stays the course with his Keynesian style, New Deal approach. Prime the pump at all costs, if spending billions and trillions does not work, spend even more. The 18th century American philosopher George Santayana warned against not learning the lessons of history. Albert Einstein claimed the very definition of insanity is repeating the same activity and expecting different results. Obama refuses to heed the word of either at this country's peril. As a Senator, Obama excoriated Bush for requesting a hike in the debt ceiling, calling Bush irresponsible. Today President Obama excoriates the GOP for resisting a hike in the debt ceiling, calling the GOP irresponsible. Regardless of the label, socialist, communist, Marxist, statist, Progressive, liberal, populist…Obama is an ardent believer in redistributing wealth. He is an ardent believer in the beneficent hand of government. He is an ardent believer in more than the right to pursue happiness, he believes in equal results. He nationalized healthcare, which includes mandates to buy insurance. Nothing in the Constitution empowers the President, Congress or The Supreme Court the power to force Americans into buying anything.

He nationalized the U.S. auto industry and circumvented the contractual rights of secured bond holders. He nationalized the banking industry by signing into law the Financial Reform Act, which did nothing to address the root cause of the meltdown, Fannie and Freddie. He sold Obamacare as a panacea yet provided over one thousand waivers to those who supported his campaign. Millions of jobs have been lost in the private sector since Obama took office; however, the public sector continues to expand under his watch. Obama promotes civility yet castigates those that are in disagreement with him...using references such as "bitter clingers," "tea-baggers," "typical white person" etc...He promotes civility yet asks... "whose asses to kick," told the GOP they can come along for the ride but they must "sit in the back." Professed the Cambridge police "acted stupidly," just after admitting he did not know all the facts. He proclaimed, "If they bring a knife to the fight, we bring a gun." Accuses the GOP of scare tactics, yet claims physicians are amputating feet and performing unnecessary surgeries. Despite having the necessary revenues to pay SS, the military and interest on the debt, he claims payments to the elderly will cease as of August 2, 2011 if the debt ceiling is not raised. He resorts to a pre-09/11 mentality, eliminating the word terror from our lexicon and treating Islamic terror as a criminal activity...eerily similar to Clinton.

He has appointed and presided over an administration rife with tax cheats, corruption, incompetence and malfeasance...Tim Geithner, Van Jones, Valerie Jarrett, Cass Sustien, Elena Kagan, Carol Browner, Samantha Powers, Hilda Solis, Kathleen Sebelius, Jeffery Immelt, Rham Emanuel, Anita Dunn, Eric Holder, John Holdren, Steven Chu, et al...His past and present is rife with associates who at the very least can be described as nefarious...Black Liberation Theology, Jeremiah Wright, Tony Rezko, William Ayers, Bernadine Dorn, Rashid Khalidi, Andy Stern, George Soros, SEIU, Richard Trumpka, Wade Rathke, et al...Despite being in office for less than four years, Obama already qualifies as one of the nation's worst presidents by virtue of his accomplishments or lack there of. He may very well eclipse the damage done by FDR by the end of his first term. God forbid Obama serves a second, if he does, he most assuredly will go down as the worst president in our nation's history based on his current policies/agenda. Our current malaise sits squarely on his shoulders, no one else. The fact remains, if Obama had received a fraction of the criticism leveled at Bush, warranted or not, Obama would have stepped down long ago.

COMMON DENOMINATOR

There is a thread that binds together Teddy Roosevelt, Woodrow Wilson, FDR, Bill Clinton and Barack Obama. More than a simple label...Socialist, liberal, Progressive, Communist, populist, statist... these presidents believe in a common theme completely antithetical to The Declaration of Independence, the Constitution, American Exceptionalism, conservatism, fixed truths and principles (i.e. Newtonian theory), free markets, capitalism, individual rights, etc...The collective ideology of these five presidents advocate for social justice, social welfare, collective rights, a living Constitution (Darwinian theory), redistributing wealth, nationalization of industry, nationalization of healthcare, nationalization of banking, consolidation of power, centrally planned economy, large bureaucratic government, usurping States' rights, usurping individual rights, etc...Based upon their records, words, beliefs, legislation, agendas, et al, these five presidents have more in common with the likes of Marx, Engels, Bismarck, Stalin, Castro and Chavez than they do with Washington, Jefferson, Franklin, Adams, Madison, Monroe, Lincoln and Reagan. The common denominator for TR, Wilson, FDR, Clinton and now Obama is a mind set that is completely inimical to liberty. It is a mindset best described by economist F.A. Hayek in *The Road to Serfdom* as "intellectual hubris." [19]

Conclusion

Thomas Paine once said, "These are the times that try men's soul." Ronald Reagan once said, "If not us, who? If not now, when?" Benjamin Franklin warned, "We have a Republic, if we can keep it." All three are as relevant today as when first spoken. We have a real unemployment rate of 16.5%, our public debt is 102% of our GDP, oil hovers at around $100/barrel, gas remains at around $4/gallon, S&P downgrades our credit rating from AAA to AA+, a first in our nation's history. The current administration is frozen like a deer in the headlights, not knowing what to do or when to do it. Progressivism has been tried in this country and around the world and without exception has been an abject failure. It's time to "plant our flag" and return to the principles that made America exceptional...religion, morality, limited government, free trade markets, competition, self-reliance, individual rights, The Declaration of Independence and the Constitution. We have a choice; liberty or tyranny, a return to our founding principles or a fundamental transformation. This is a zero sum game...Progressivism is a villainous perfidy. The inherent genius behind our founding was simple, Washington, Jefferson, Madison, Sherman, Franklin, Hamilton, et al, understood that we as human beings are not perfect and never will be. Progressivism (i.e. social engineering) is predicated upon the belief that imperfect man can devise a perfect (i.e. utopian) society. As students of history and human nature, our Founding Fathers acknowledged our imperfections, hence the beauty and genius of our Constitution. It's a system based upon checks and balances and more importantly shared powers. Our government derives its powers from the consent of the governed...We the people.

"The summer soldier and the sunshine patriot will, in crisis, shrink from service of their country; but he that stands it now deserves the love and thanks of man and woman. Tyranny, like hell, is not easily conquered; yet we have this consolation with us, that the harder the conflict, the more glorious the triumph...Heaven knows how to put a proper price upon its goods; and it would be strange indeed if so celestial an article as FREEDOM should not be highly rated." [1]

Thomas Paine

References

PREFACE

1. Judge Andrew P. Napolitano, *Lies the Government told you; Myth, Power and Deception in American History,* (Thomas Nelson, Inc. 2010), page 316

2. Perry, Allison, Skousen, *The Real George Washington; The True Story of America's Most Indispensable Man,* (National Center for Constitutional Studies 2009), page 730

3. W. Cleon Skousen, *The Making of America; The Substance and Meaning of the Constitution,* (National Center for Constitutional Studies 2007), page 216

4. W. Cleon Skousen, *The Making of America; The Substance and Meaning of the Constitution,* (National Center for Constitutional Studies, 2007), page 123

5. James M. McPherson, *To The Best of My Ability",* (Agincourt Press 2004), page 120

6. Glenn Beck, *Common Sense, The Case Against an Out-of-Control Government,* (Mercury Radio Arts/ Threshold Editions 2009) page 165

7. David Barton, *Original Intent; The Courts, the Constitution & Religion,* (WallBuilder Press, 2005) page 96

8. William J. Bennett, *America, The Last Best Hope Volume I,* (Thomas Nelson, Inc. 2007), page 368

9. W. Cleon Skousen, *The Five Thousand Year Leap*, (American Documents Publishing, L.L.C., 2009), page 147

10. W. Cleon Skousen, *The Five Thousand Year Leap*, (American Documents Publishing, L.L.C., 2009), page 107

11. W. Cleon Skousen, *The Making of America; The Substance and Meaning of the Constitution*, (National Center for Constitutional Studies, 2007), page 247

12. William J. Bennett, John T.E. Cribb, *The American Patriot's Almanac*, (Thomas Nelson, Inc. 2008), page 502

13. David Barton, *Original Intent; The Courts, the Constitution & Religion*, (WallBuilder Press, 2005), page 77

14. W. Cleon Skousen, *The Five Thousand Year Leap*, (American Documents Publishing, L.L.C., 2009), page 120

15. Perry, Allison, Skousen, *The Real George Washington; The True Story of America's Most Indispensable Man*, (National Center for Constitutional Studies 2009), page 757

16. Milton Friedman, *Capitalism and Freedom*, (The University of Chicago Press 2002), page 3

17. James M. McPherson, *To The Best of My Ability"*, (Agincourt Press 2004), page 451

18. W. Cleon Skousen, *The Five Thousand Year Leap*, (American Documents Publishing, L.L.C. 2009), page 60

19. William J. Federer, *Prayers and Presidents, Inspiring Faith From Leaders of the Past*, (AmeriSource, Inc. 2011), page 88

20. David Barton, *Original Intent; The Courts the Constitution & Religion*, (WallBuilder Press 2005), page 111

21. David Barton, *Original Intent; The Courts the Constitution & Religion*, (WallBuilder Press 2005), page 144

22. William J. Bennett, *America, The Last Best Hope Volume II*, (Thomas Nelson, Inc. 2007), page 528

23. William J. Bennett, John T.E. Cribb, *The American Patriot's Almanac*, (Thomas Nelson, Inc. 2008), page 212

24. Perry, Allison, Skousen, *The Real George Washington; The True Story of America's Most Indispensable Man*, (National Center for Constitutional Studies 2009), page 520

25. William J. Bennett, John T.E. Cribb, *The American Patriot's Almanac*, (Thomas Nelson, Inc. 2008), page 43

26. William J. Bennett, *America, The Last Best Hope Volume II*, (Thomas Nelson, Inc. 2007), page 533

27. W. Cleon Skousen, *The Five Thousand Year Leap*, (American Documents Publishing, L.L.C., 2009), page 47

28. David Barton, *Original Intent; The Courts the Constitution & Religion*, (WallBuilder Press 2005), page 178

29. David Barton, *Original Intent; The Courts the Constitution & Religion,* (WallBuilder Press 2005), page 50

30. W. Cleon Skousen, *The Five Thousand Year Leap,* (American Documents Publishing, L.L.C., 2009), page 46

31. W. Cleon Skousen, *The Five Thousand Year Leap,* (American Documents Publishing, L.L.C., 2009), page 64

32. David Barton, *Original Intent; The Courts the Constitution & Religion,* (WallBuilder Press 2005), page 100

33. Matthew Spalding, *We Still Hold These Truths, Rediscovering Our Principles, Reclaiming Our Future,* (ISI Books 2009), page 64

34. W. Cleon Skousen, *The Five Thousand Year Leap,* (American Documents Publishing, L.L.C., 2009), page 77

35. Perry, Allison, Skousen, *The Real George Washington; The True Story of America's Most Indispensable Man,* (National Center for Constitutional Studies 2009), page 669

36. Perry, Allison, Skousen, *The Real George Washington; The True Story of America's Most Indispensable Man,* (National Center for Constitutional Studies 2009), page 651

37. W. Cleon Skousen, *The Five Thousand Year Leap,* (American Documents Publishing, L.L.C., 2009), page 205

38. W. Cleon Skousen, *The Five Thousand Year Leap,* (American Documents Publishing, L.L.C., 2009), page 208

39. W. Cleon Skousen, *The Making of America; The Substance and Meaning of the Constitution,* (National Center for Constitutional Studies, 2007), page 394

40. James M. McPherson, *To the Best of My Ability,* (Agincourt Press 2004), page 452

41. W. Cleon Skousen, *The Five Thousand Year Leap,* (American Documents Publishing, L.L.C., 2009), page 208

42. Mark R. Levin, *Liberty and Tyranny, A Conservative Manifesto,* (Simon & Schuster, Inc. 2009), page 88

43. W. Cleon Skousen, *The Five Thousand Year Leap,* (American Documents Publishing, L.L.C., 2009), page 207

44. W. Cleon Skousen, *The Five Thousand Year Leap,* (American Documents Publishing, L.L.C., 2009), page 209

45. W. Cleon Skousen, *The Five Thousand Year Leap,* (American Documents Publishing, L.L.C., 2009), page 27

46. Matthew Spalding, *We Still Hold These Truths, Rediscovering Our Principles, Reclaiming Our Future,* (ISI Books 2009), page 159

47. http//thequoteblog.com/benjaminfranklin-on-the-pursuit-of-happiness

48. W. Cleon Skousen, *The Five Thousand Year Leap,* (American Documents Publishing, L.L.C., 2009), page 129

49. Matthew Spalding, *We Still Hold These Truths, Rediscovering Our Principles, Reclaiming Our Future,* (ISI Books 2009), page 140

50. W. Cleon Skousen, *The Five Thousand Year Leap,* (American Documents Publishing, L.L.C., 2009), page 126

51. Amity Shlaes, *The Forgotten Man,* (Harper Collins Publishers 2007), page 37

52. W. Cleon Skousen, *The Making of America; The Substance and Meaning of the Constitution,* (National Center for Constitutional Studies, 2007), page 219

53. W. Cleon Skousen, *The Five Thousand Year Leap,* (American Documents Publishing, L.L.C., 2009), page 27

54. W. Cleon Skousen, *The Five Thousand Year Leap,* (American Documents Publishing, L.L.C., 2009), page 90

55. W. Cleon Skousen, *The Five Thousand Year Leap,* (American Documents Publishing, L.L.C., 2009), page 132

56. W. Cleon Skousen, *The Making of America; The Substance and Meaning of the Constitution,* (National Center for Constitutional Studies, 2007), page 215

57. Milton Friedman, *Capitalism and Freedom,* (The University of Chicago Press 2002), page 166

58. Milton Friedman, *Capitalism and Freedom,* (The University of Chicago Press 2002), page 118

59. Mark R. Levin, *Liberty and Tyranny, A Conservative Manifesto,* (Simon & Schuster, Inc. 2009), page 67

60. Mark R. Levin, *Liberty and Tyranny, A Conservative Manifesto,* (Simon & Schuster, Inc. 2009), page 78

61. William J. Bennett, *America, The Last Best Hope Volume II,* (Thomas Nelson, Inc. 2007), page 462

62. W. Cleon Skousen, *The Five Thousand Year Leap,* (American Documents Publishing, L.L.C., 2009), page 126

63. W. Cleon Skousen, *The Five Thousand Year Leap,* (American Documents Publishing, L.L.C., 2009), page 85

64. F. A. Hayek, *The Road to Serfdom,* (The University of Chicago Press 2007), page 20

65. James M. McPherson, *To the Best of My Ability,* (Agincourt Press 2004), page 452

66. W. Cleon Skousen, *The Five Thousand Year Leap,* (American Documents Publishing, L.L.C., 2009), page 121

67. William J. Bennett, *America, The Last Best Hope Volume II,* (Thomas Nelson, Inc. 2007), page 533

68. Perry, Allison, Skousen, *The Real George Washington; The True Story of America's Most Indispensable Man,* (National Center for Constitutional Studies 2009), page 208

INTRODUCTION

1. W. Cleon Skousen, *The Making of America; The Substance and Meaning of the Constitution,* (National Center for Constitutional Studies, 2007), page 188

2. W. Cleon Skousen, *The Five Thousand Year Leap,* (American Documents Publishing, L.L.C., 2009), page 15

3. Newt Gingrich, *Real Change, From the World That Fails to the World That Works,* (Regnery Publishing 2008), page 82

4. Daniel J. Flynn, *A Conservative History of the American Left,* (Crown Publishing Group 2008), page 19

5. Glenn Beck, *An Inconvenient Book,* (Threshold Editions 2007), page 192

6. Thomas Sowell, "How Smart Are We?", www.realclearpolitics.com/articles/2010/07/27/how_smart_are_we_106479.html

7. Glenn Beck, *Broke, The Plan to Restore our Trust, Truth and Treasure,* (Threshold Editions 2010), page 3

CHAPTER 1

1. http://kenfran.tripod.com/teddy.hym

2. http://marxists.org/archive/marx/works/1848/communist_manifesto

3. Ronald K. Pestritto, William J. Atto, *American Progressivism,* (Lexington Books 2008), pages 35-44

4. W. Cleon Skousen, *The Making of America; The Substance and Meaning of the Constitution,* (National Center for Constitutional Studies, 2007), page 253

5. http://www.presidency.ucsb.edu/data/orders.php

6. W. Cleon Skousen, *The Five Thousand Year Leap,* (American Documents Publishing, L.L.C., 2009), page 107

7. W. Cleon Skousen, *The Five Thousand Year Leap,* (American Documents Publishing, L.L.C., 2009), page 121

8. W. Cleon Skousen, *The Five Thousand Year Leap,* (American Documents Publishing, L.L.C., 2009), page 120

9. W. Cleon Skousen, *The Five Thousand Year Leap,* (American Documents Publishing, L.L.C., 2009), page 119

10. W. Cleon Skousen, *The Five Thousand Year Leap,* (American Documents Publishing, L.L.C., 2009), page 121

11. James M. McPherson, *To the Best of My Ability,* (Agincourt Press 2004), page 186

12. Mark R. Levin, *Liberty and Tyranny, A Conservative Manifesto,* (Simon & Schuster, Inc. 2009), page 4

13. William J. Bennett, *America, The Last Best Hope Volume I,* (Thomas Nelson, Inc. 2007), page 517

14. James M. McPherson, *To the Best of My Ability,* (Agincourt Press 2004), page 186

15. Daniel J. Flynn, *A Conservative History of the American Left,* (Crown Publishing Group 2008), page 137

16. Daniel J. Flynn, *A Conservative History of the American Left,* (Crown Publishing Group 2008), page 138

17. Milton Friedman, *Capitalism and Freedom,* (The University of Chicago Press 2002), page 2

18. Daniel J. Flynn, *A Conservative History of the American Left,* (Crown Publishing Group 2008), page 140

19. Ronald K. Pestritto, William J. Atto, *American Progressivism,* (Lexington Books 2008), page 6

20. Ronald K. Pestritto, William J. Atto, *American Progressivism,* (Lexington Books 2008), page 11

21. Ronald K. Pestritto, William J. Atto, *American Progressivism*, (Lexington Books 2008), page 18

22. W. Cleon Skousen, *The Five Thousand Year Leap*, (American Documents Publishing, L.L.C., 2009), page 132

23. Matthew Spalding, *We Still Hold These Truths, Rediscovering Our Principles, Reclaiming Our Future*, (ISI Books 2009), page 195

24. Matthew Spalding, *We Still Hold These Truths, Rediscovering Our Principles, Reclaiming Our Future*, (ISI Books 2009), page 204-205

25. Ronald K. Pestritto, William J. Atto, *American Progressivism*, (Lexington Books 2008), page 220

26. Ronald K. Pestritto, William J. Atto, *American Progressivism*, (Lexington Books 2008), pages 35-44

27. Jonah Goldberg, *Liberal Fascism, The Secret History of the American Left from Mussolini to the Politics of Meaning*, (Doubleday 2007), page 98

28. Ronald K. Pestritto, William J. Atto, *American Progressivism*, (Lexington Books 2008), pages 42

29. Milton Friedman, *Capitalism and Freedom*, (The University of Chicago Press 2002), page 3

30. Jonah Goldberg, *Liberal Fascism, The Secret History of the American Left from Mussolini to the Politics of Meaning*, (Doubleday 2007), page 81

31. Jonah Goldberg, *Liberal Fascism, The Secret History of the American Left from Mussolini to the Politics of Meaning*, (Doubleday 2007), page 74

32. Jonah Goldberg, *Liberal Fascism, The Secret History of the American Left from Mussolini to the Politics of Meaning*, (Doubleday 2007), page 216

33. http://nobelprize.org

34. http://bioguide.congress.gov/scripts/biodisplay

35. http://www.worldroots.com

36. http://www.answers.com

37. http://www.bbc.co.uk/history/historicfigures/darwin_charles.shtml

38. http://www.aflcio.org/aboutus/history/history/debs.cfm

39. http://www.spartacuseducational.com

40. http://www.answers.com

41. http://www.spartacuseducational.com

42. http://www.ohiohistorycentral.org/entry.php?rec=159

43. http://www.u-s-history.com/pages/h1747.html

44. http://www.biographyathegel.net

45. http://www.webapps,jhu.edu/jhuniverse/information_about_hopkins/about_jhu/who_was_johns_hopkins

46. http://www.answers.com

47. http://www.marxistshistory.org/subject/use/eam/iss.html

48. http://www.us.history.wisc.edu/hist102/bios/21.html

49. http://www.questia.com

50. http://www.hyperhistory.com

51. http://www.spartacuseducational.com

52. http://www.spartacuseducational.com

53. http://www.historyguide.org/intellect/marx.html

54. http://www.bbc.co.uk/history/historic_figures/mussolini_benito.shtml

55. http://www.encyclopedia.com

56. http://www.kirjasto.sci.fi/johnreed.htm

57. http://www.spartacusschoolnet.co.uk/Jsanger.htm

58. http://www.kirjasto.sci.fi/sinclair.htm

59. http://www.pbs.org/redfiles/bios/all_bio_joseph_stalin.htm

60. http://www.bookrags.com/biography/lincoln_steffens/

61. http://www.pbs.org/wgbh/amex/rockefellers/peopleevents/p_tarbell.html

62. http://www.answers.com

63. http://www.ask.com

CHAPTER 2

1. Ronald K. Pestritto, William J. Atto, *American Progressivism,* (Lexington Books 2008), page 4

2. Jonah Goldberg, *Liberal Fascism, The Secret History of the American Left from Mussolini to the Politics of Meaning,* (Doubleday 2007), page 86

3. Jonah Goldberg, *Liberal Fascism, The Secret History of the American Left from Mussolini to the Politics of Meaning,* (Doubleday 2007), page 86

4. Jonah Goldberg, *Liberal Fascism, The Secret History of the American Left from Mussolini to the Politics of Meaning,* (Doubleday 2007), page 86

5. Jonah Goldberg, *Liberal Fascism, The Secret History of the American Left from Mussolini to the Politics of Meaning*, (Doubleday 2007), pages 88-89

6. Jonah Goldberg, *Liberal Fascism, The Secret History of the American Left from Mussolini to the Politics of Meaning*, (Doubleday 2007), page 100

7. Jonah Goldberg, *Liberal Fascism, The Secret History of the American Left from Mussolini to the Politics of Meaning*, (Doubleday 2007), page 95

8. http://www.presidency.ucsb.edu/data/orders.php

9. Jonah Goldberg, *Liberal Fascism, The Secret History of the American Left from Mussolini to the Politics of Meaning*, (Doubleday 2007), page 104

10. Ronald K. Pestritto, William J. Atto, *American Progressivism*, (Lexington Books 2008), page 208

11. Ronald K. Pestritto, William J. Atto, *American Progressivism*, (Lexington Books 2008), page 199

12. W. Cleon Skousen, *The Making of America; The Substance and Meaning of the Constitution*, (National Center for Constitutional Studies, 2007), page 254

13. W. Cleon Skousen, *The Making of America; The Substance and Meaning of the Constitution*, (National Center for Constitutional Studies, 2007), page 253

14. Ronald K. Pestritto, William J. Atto, *American Progressivism*, (Lexington Books 2008), page 17

15. Ronald K. Pestritto, William J. Atto, *American Progressivism*, (Lexington Books 2008), page 20

16. Ronald K. Pestritto, William J. Atto, *American Progressivism*, (Lexington Books 2008), page 50

17. Ronald K. Pestritto, William J. Atto, *American Progressivism*, (Lexington Books 2008), pages 50, 51

18. Glenn Beck, *Broke, The Plan to Restore our Trust, Truth and Treasure*, (Threshold Editions 2010), pages 48-52

19. W. Cleon Skousen, *The Making of America; The Substance and Meaning of the Constitution*, (National Center for Constitutional Studies, 2007), page 796

20. http://www.usgovernmentspending.com

21. W. Cleon Skousen, *The Making of America; The Substance and Meaning of the Constitution*, (National Center for Constitutional Studies, 2007), page 796

22. W. Cleon Skousen, *The Making of America; The Substance and Meaning of the Constitution*, (National Center for Constitutional Studies, 2007), page 260

23. W. Cleon Skousen, *The Making of America; The Substance and Meaning of the Constitution*, (National Center for Constitutional Studies, 2007), page 260

24. W. Cleon Skousen, *The Five Thousand Year Leap*, (American Documents Publishing, L.L.C., 2009), page 150

25. W. Cleon Skousen, *The Making of America; The Substance and Meaning of the Constitution*, (National Center for Constitutional Studies, 2007), page 795

26. William J. Bennett, *America, The Last Best Hope Volume II*, (Thomas Nelson, Inc. 2007), page 74

27. William J. Bennett, *America, The Last Best Hope Volume II*, (Thomas Nelson, Inc. 2007), page 84

28. Jonah Goldberg, *Liberal Fascism, The Secret History of the American Left from Mussolini to the Politics of Meaning*, (Doubleday 2007), page 114

29. Jonah Goldberg, *Liberal Fascism, The Secret History of the American Left from Mussolini to the Politics of Meaning,* (Doubleday 2007), pages 111, 112

30. Jonah Goldberg, *Liberal Fascism, The Secret History of the American Left from Mussolini to the Politics of Meaning,* (Doubleday 2007), page 88

31. Milton Friedman, *Capitalism and Freedom,* (The University of Chicago Press 2002), pages 43-47

32. W. Cleon Skousen, *The Making of America; The Substance and Meaning of the Constitution,* (National Center for Constitutional Studies, 2007), pages 420-426

33. Judge Andrew P. Napolitano, *Lies the Government told you; Myth, Power and Deception in American History,* (Thomas Nelson, Inc. 2010), page 141

34. Judge Andrew P. Napolitano, *Lies the Government told you; Myth, Power and Deception in American History,* (Thomas Nelson, Inc. 2010), page 149

35. Judge Andrew P. Napolitano, *Lies the Government told you; Myth, Power and Deception in American History,* (Thomas Nelson, Inc. 2010), page 150

36. W. Cleon Skousen, *The Making of America; The Substance and Meaning of the Constitution,* (National Center for Constitutional Studies, 2007), page 425

37. Judge Andrew P. Napolitano, *Lies the Government told you; Myth, Power and Deception in American History,* (Thomas Nelson, Inc. 2010), page 153

38. Ronald K. Pestritto, William J. Atto, *American Progressivism,* (Lexington Books 2008), page 321

39. W. Cleon Skousen, *The Making of America; The Substance and Meaning of the Constitution,* (National

Center for Constitutional Studies, 2007), pages 548, 549

40. Jonah Goldberg, *Liberal Fascism, The Secret History of the American Left from Mussolini to the Politics of Meaning,* (Doubleday 2007), page 85

41. Glenn Beck, *Broke, The Plan to Restore our Trust, Truth and Treasure,* (Threshold Editions 2010), page 50

42. http://nobelprize.org

43. http://bioguide.congress.gov/scripts/biodisplay

44. http://www.criticalthink.info/webindex/bernays/htm

45. http://www.worldroots.com

46. http://projects.vassar.edu/1896/bryan.html

47. http://www.answers.com

48. http://www.answers.com

49. http://www.bbc.co.uk/history/historicfigures/darwin_charles.shtml

50. http://www.aflcio.org/aboutus/history/history/debs.cfm

51. http://www.spartacuseducational.com

52. http://www.answers.com

53. http://www.spartacuseducational.com

54. http://www.ohiohistorycentral.org/entry.php?rec=159

55. http://www.u-s-history.com/pages/h1747.html

56. http://www.biographyathegel.net

57. http://www.webapps,jhu.edu/jhuniverse/
    information_about_hopkins/about_jhu/
    who_was_johns_hopkins

58. http://www.marxistshistory.org/subject/use/eam/iss.
    html

59. http://www.us.history.wisc.edu/hist102/bios/21.html

60. http://www.questia.com

61. http://www.hyperhistory.com

62. http://www.spartacuseducational.com

63. http://www.spartacuseducational.com

64. http://www.historyguide.org/intellect/marx.html

65. http://en.wikipedia.org/wiki/william_gibbs_mcadoo

66. http://www.bbc.co.uk/history/historic_figures/
    mussolini_benito.shtml

67. http://www.encyclopedia.com

68. http://www.kirjasto.sci.fi/johnreed.htm

69. http://www.spartacusschoolnet.co.uk/Jsanger.htm

70. http://www.kirjasto.sci.fi/sinclair.htm

71. http://www.pbs.org/redfiles/bios/all_bio_joseph_
    stalin.htm

72. http://www.bookrags.com/biography/lincoln_steffens/

73. http://www.pbs.org/wgbh/amex/rockefellers/
    peopleevents/p_tarbell.html

74. http://www.answers.com

75. http://www.ask.com

CHAPTER 3

1. Mark R. Levin, *Liberty and Tyranny, A Conservative Manifesto,* (Simon & Schuster, Inc. 2009), page 88

2. Newt Gingrich, *Real Change, From the World That Fails to the World That Works,* (Regnery Publishing 2008), page 82

3. Thomas A. Bailey, David M. Kennedy, Lizabeth Cohen, *The American Pageant,* (Houghton Mifflin Company 1998), page 795

4. Thomas A. Bailey, David M. Kennedy, Lizabeth Cohen, *The American Pageant,* (Houghton Mifflin Company 1998), pages 798, 799

5. Thomas A. Bailey, David M. Kennedy, Lizabeth Cohen, *The American Pageant,* (Houghton Mifflin Company 1998), page 821

6. Thomas A. Bailey, David M. Kennedy, Lizabeth Cohen, *The American Pageant,* (Houghton Mifflin Company 1998), pages 820, 821

7. Thomas A. Bailey, David M. Kennedy, Lizabeth Cohen, *The American Pageant,* (Houghton Mifflin Company 1998), page 821

8. Peter Jennings, Todd Brewster, *The Century,* (Doubleday 1998), page 157

9. Peter Jennings, Todd Brewster, *The Century,* (Doubleday 1998), page 159

10. Peter Jennings, Todd Brewster, *The Century,* (Doubleday 1998), page 157

11. Judge Andrew P. Napolitano, *Lies the Government told you; Myth, Power and Deception in American History,* (Thomas Nelson, Inc. 2010), page 176

12. Amity Shlaes, *The Forgotten Man,* (Harper Collins Publishers 2007), page 132

13. Amity Shlaes, *The Forgotten Man,* (Harper Collins Publishers 2007), page 39

14. Amity Shlaes, *The Forgotten Man,* (Harper Collins Publishers 2007), page 84

15. Amity Shlaes, *The Forgotten Man,* (Harper Collins Publishers 2007), page 105

16. Amity Shlaes, *The Forgotten Man,* (Harper Collins Publishers 2007), page 147

17. Mark R. Levin, *Liberty and Tyranny, A Conservative Manifesto,* (Simon & Schuster, Inc. 2009), page 88

18. Stephen Ambrose, Douglas Brinkley, *Witness to America,* (HarperCollins, 1999), page 359

19. Stephen Ambrose, Douglas Brinkley, *Witness to America,* (HarperCollins, 1999), page 360

20. Milton Friedman, *Capitalism and Freedom,* (The University of Chicago Press 2002), pages 43-50

21. Milton Friedman, *Capitalism and Freedom,* (The University of Chicago Press 2002), pages 38

22. Amity Shlaes, *The Forgotten Man,* (Harper Collins Publishers 2007), page 148

23. Amity Shlaes, *The Forgotten Man,* (Harper Collins Publishers 2007), pages 150-158

24. Amity Shlaes, *The Forgotten Man,* (Harper Collins Publishers 2007), pages 11

25. Glenn Beck, *Broke, The Plan to Restore our Trust, Truth and Treasure,* (Threshold Editions 2010), page 69

26. Glenn Beck, *Broke, The Plan to Restore our Trust, Truth and Treasure*, (Threshold Editions 2010), page 60

27. Mark R. Levin, *Liberty and Tyranny, A Conservative Manifesto*, (Simon & Schuster, Inc. 2009), page 89

28. Jonah Goldberg, *Liberal Fascism, The Secret History of the American Left from Mussolini to the Politics of Meaning*, (Doubleday 2007), page 152

29. Jonah Goldberg, *Liberal Fascism, The Secret History of the American Left from Mussolini to the Politics of Meaning*, (Doubleday 2007), page 153

30. Jonah Goldberg, *Liberal Fascism, The Secret History of the American Left from Mussolini to the Politics of Meaning*, (Doubleday 2007), page 87

31. William J. Bennett, *America, The Last Best Hope Volume II*, (Thomas Nelson, Inc. 2007), page 232

32. Stephen Ambrose, Douglas Brinkley, *Witness to America*, (HarperCollins, 1999), pages 361, 362

33. Amity Shlaes, *The Forgotten Man*, (Harper Collins Publishers 2007), pages 175

34. Amity Shlaes, *The Forgotten Man*, (Harper Collins Publishers 2007), pages 237

35. Jonah Goldberg, *Liberal Fascism, The Secret History of the American Left from Mussolini to the Politics of Meaning*, (Doubleday 2007), page 151

36. Jonah Goldberg, *Liberal Fascism, The Secret History of the American Left from Mussolini to the Politics of Meaning*, (Doubleday 2007), page 123

37. Amity Shlaes, *The Forgotten Man*, (Harper Collins Publishers 2007), page 8

38. Amity Shlaes, *The Forgotten Man,* (Harper Collins Publishers 2007), pages 153-155, 168

39. Milton Friedman, *Capitalism and Freedom,* (The University of Chicago Press 2002), page 182

40. Amity Shlaes, *The Forgotten Man,* (Harper Collins Publishers 2007), page 8

41. Amity Shlaes, *The Forgotten Man,* (Harper Collins Publishers 2007), page 151

42. Amity Shlaes, *The Forgotten Man,* (Harper Collins Publishers 2007), page 202

43. Amity Shlaes, *The Forgotten Man,* (Harper Collins Publishers 2007), page 222

44. Milton Friedman, *Capitalism and Freedom,* (The University of Chicago Press 2002), page 160

45. Milton Friedman, *Capitalism and Freedom,* (The University of Chicago Press 2002), page 109

46. Milton Friedman, *Capitalism and Freedom,* (The University of Chicago Press 2002), pages 13-16

47. Amity Shlaes, *The Forgotten Man,* (Harper Collins Publishers 2007), page 225

48. Amity Shlaes, *The Forgotten Man,* (Harper Collins Publishers 2007), page 242

49. Amity Shlaes, *The Forgotten Man,* (Harper Collins Publishers 2007), page 243

50. Amity Shlaes, *The Forgotten Man,* (Harper Collins Publishers 2007), page 244

51. Mark R. Levin, *Liberty and Tyranny, A Conservative Manifesto,* (Simon & Schuster, Inc. 2009), page 87

52. James M. McPherson, *To the Best of My Ability*, (Agincourt Press 2004), page 225

53. Amity Shlaes, *The Forgotten Man*, (Harper Collins Publishers 2007), page 259

54. Amity Shlaes, *The Forgotten Man*, (Harper Collins Publishers 2007), page 250

55. Judge Andrew P. Napolitano, *Lies the Government told you; Myth, Power and Deception in American History*, (Thomas Nelson, Inc. 2010), page 172

56. W. Cleon Skousen, *The Making of America; The Substance and Meaning of the Constitution*, (National Center for Constitutional Studies, 2007), pages 793, 794

57. Judge Andrew P. Napolitano, *Lies the Government told you; Myth, Power and Deception in American History*, (Thomas Nelson, Inc. 2010), page 175

58. Judge Andrew P. Napolitano, *Lies the Government told you; Myth, Power and Deception in American History*, (Thomas Nelson, Inc. 2010), page 139

59. Glenn Beck, *Broke, The Plan to Restore our Trust, Truth and Treasure*, (Threshold Editions 2010), page 204

60. Glenn Beck, *Broke, The Plan to Restore our Trust, Truth and Treasure*, (Threshold Editions 2010), page 205

61. Milton Friedman, *Capitalism and Freedom*, (The University of Chicago Press 2002), pages 182-189

62. Amity Shlaes, *The Forgotten Man*, (Harper Collins Publishers 2007), pages 249-254

63. Amity Shlaes, *The Forgotten Man*, (Harper Collins Publishers 2007), pages 282

64. Judge Andrew P. Napolitano, *Lies the Government told you; Myth, Power and Deception in American History,* (Thomas Nelson, Inc. 2010), page 176

65. http://www.presidency.ucsb.edu/data/orders.php

66. Perry, Allison, Skousen, *The Real George Washington; The True Story of America's Most Indispensable Man,* (National Center for Constitutional Studies 2009), page 669

67. Perry, Allison, Skousen, *The Real George Washington; The True Story of America's Most Indispensable Man,* (National Center for Constitutional Studies 2009), page 651

68. W. Cleon Skousen, *The Five Thousand Year Leap,* (American Documents Publishing, L.L.C., 2009), page 205

69. Amity Shlaes, *The Forgotten Man,* (Harper Collins Publishers 2007), page 31

70. Amity Shlaes, *The Forgotten Man,* (Harper Collins Publishers 2007), page 34

71. Amity Shlaes, *The Forgotten Man,* (Harper Collins Publishers 2007), page 35

72. Amity Shlaes, *The Forgotten Man,* (Harper Collins Publishers 2007), page 37

73. Amity Shlaes, *The Forgotten Man,* (Harper Collins Publishers 2007), page 39

74. Amity Shlaes, *The Forgotten Man,* (Harper Collins Publishers 2007), page 132

75. Amity Shlaes, *The Forgotten Man,* (Harper Collins Publishers 2007), page 132

76. Amity Shlaes, *The Forgotten Man,* (Harper Collins Publishers 2007), page 143

77. Amity Shlaes, *The Forgotten Man,* (Harper Collins Publishers 2007), page 8

78. Amity Shlaes, *The Forgotten Man,* (Harper Collins Publishers 2007), page 252

79. Amity Shlaes, *The Forgotten Man,* (Harper Collins Publishers 2007), pages 252,256

80. Amity Shlaes, *The Forgotten Man,* (Harper Collins Publishers 2007), page 334

81. Amity Shlaes, *The Forgotten Man,* (Harper Collins Publishers 2007), page 339

82. Glenn Beck, *Broke, The Plan to Restore our Trust, Truth and Treasure,* (Threshold Editions 2010), page 64

83. William J. Bennett, *America, The Last Best Hope Volume II,* (Thomas Nelson, Inc. 2007), page 241

84. Judge Andrew P. Napolitano, *Lies the Government told you; Myth, Power and Deception in American History,* (Thomas Nelson, Inc. 2010), page 124

85. Amity Shlaes, *The Forgotten Man,* (Harper Collins Publishers 2007), page 312

86. William J. Bennett, *America, The Last Best Hope Volume II,* (Thomas Nelson, Inc. 2007), page 200

87. Thomas A. Bailey, David M. Kennedy, Lizabeth Cohen, *The American Pageant,* (Houghton Mifflin Company 1998), page 849

88. James M. McPherson, *To the Best of My Ability,* (Agincourt Press 2004), page 230

89. Peter Jennings, Todd Brewster, *The Century,* (Doubleday 1998), page 239

90. Robert Gellately, *Lenin, Stalin, and Hitler, The Age of Social Catastrophe,* (Alfred A. Knopf 2007), page 557

91. William J. Bennett, *America, The Last Best Hope Volume II,* (Thomas Nelson, Inc. 2007), page 248

92. Robert Gellately, *Lenin, Stalin, and Hitler, The Age of Social Catastrophe,* (Alfred A. Knopf 2007), page 547

93. William J. Bennett, *America, The Last Best Hope Volume II,* (Thomas Nelson, Inc. 2007), page 249

94. Robert Gellately, *Lenin, Stalin, and Hitler, The Age of Social Catastrophe,* (Alfred A. Knopf 2007), page 547

95. Amity Shlaes, *The Forgotten Man,* (Harper Collins Publishers 2007), pages 296-317

96. Amity Shlaes, *The Forgotten Man,* (Harper Collins Publishers 2007), pages 3,5,7,11,334-339

97. Charles Gasparino, *The Sellout,* (HarperCollins, 2009), page 107

98. Charles Gasparino, *The Sellout,* (HarperCollins, 2009), page 4

99. Dick Morris, Eileen McGann, *Outrage,* (HarperCollins 2007), page 222

100. W. Cleon Skousen, *The Five Thousand Year Leap,* (American Documents Publishing, L.L.C., 2009), page 151

101. http://www.harvardsquarelibrary.org/unitarians/baldwin.html

102. www.answers.com

103. http://www.epuribusmedia.org/
features/2006/200609_FDR_pt3.html

104. http://www.heritagefoundation.org

105. http://en.wikipedia.org/wiki/Stuart_Chase

106. Paul Johnson, *Churchill,* (Penguin Group 2009),
pages 4,76,79,130

107. http://www.ushmm.org/wlc/en/article.
php?moduleID=10005516

108. http://www.answers.com/topic/herbert-croly

109. http://www.spartacuseducational.com

110. http://www.britannica.com/EBcheck/topic/266986/
Alger-Hiss

111. http://www.answers.com/topic/harold-ickes

112. http://digital.library.okstate.edu/encyclopedia/
entries/J/JO008.html

113. http://www.sparatucseducational.com

114. http://www.questia.com

115. http://www.spartacuseducational.com

116. http://ech.cwru.edu/ech-cgi/article.pl?id=MR1

117. http://www.jewishvirtuallibrary.rog/jsource/
biography/Morgenthau.html

118. http://bbc.co.uk/history/historic_figures/mussolini_
benito.shtml

119. http://www.answers.com

120. http://en.wikipedia.org/wiki/Georeg_Peek

121. http://www.aflcio.org/aboutus/history/history/perkins. cfm

122. http://www.facebook.com/pages/Samuel-Irving0Rosenman/108172879203364

123. http://www.spartacusschoolnet.co.uk/Jsanger.htm

124. http://www.kirjasto.sci.fi/sinclaie.htm

125. http://www.pbs.org/redfiles

126. http://www.answers.com

127. http://c250columbia.edu/c250.celebrates/remarkable. columbians/rexford_tugwell.html

128. http://www.spartacusschoolnet.co.uk/USARwallace. htm

129. http://www.gwu.edu/~erpapers/teachinger/glossary/ wilkie-wendell.cfm

CHAPTER 4

1. Perry, Allison, Skousen, *The Real George Washington; The True Story of America's Most Indispensable Man,* (National Center for Constitutional Studies 2009), page 10

2. Walter Isaacson, *Einstein, His Life and Universe* (Simon & Schuster 2007), page 8

3. Perry, Allison, Skousen, *The Real George Washington; The True Story of America's Most Indispensable Man,* (National Center for Constitutional Studies 2009), page 675

4. W. Cleon Skousen, *The Making of America; The Substance and Meaning of the Constitution,* (National

Center for Constitutional Studies, 2007), pages 393,394

5. Perry, Allison, Skousen, *The Real George Washington; The True Story of America's Most Indispensable Man,* (National Center for Constitutional Studies 2009), page 669

6. W. Cleon Skousen, *The Five Thousand Year Leap,* (American Documents Publishing, L.L.C., 2009), page 208

7. W. Cleon Skousen, *The Five Thousand Year Leap,* (American Documents Publishing, L.L.C., 2009), page 205

8. Dick Morris& Eileen McGann, *Catastrophe,* (HarperCollins 2009), pages 10-20

9. Dick Morris& Eileen McGann, *Catastrophe,* (HarperCollins 2009), pages 21,22

10. W. Cleon Skousen, *The Making of America; The Substance and Meaning of the Constitution,* (National Center for Constitutional Studies, 2007), pages 372,375

11. W. Cleon Skousen, *The Making of America; The Substance and Meaning of the Constitution,* (National Center for Constitutional Studies, 2007), pages 391

12. http://www.heritagefoundation.org

13. http://www.usgovernmentspending.com

14. Mark R. Levin, *Liberty and Tyranny, A Conservative Manifesto,* (Simon & Schuster, Inc. 2009), page 88

15. http://www.heritagefoundation.org

16. Milton Friedman, *Capitalism and Freedom,* (The University of Chicago Press 2002), page 16

17. Charles Gasparino, *The Sellout*, (HarperCollins 2009), pages 279,386

18. Charles Gasparino, *The Sellout*, (HarperCollins 2009), page 423

19. Charles Gasparino, *The Sellout*, (HarperCollins 2009), page 111

20. Charles Gasparino, *The Sellout*, (HarperCollins 2009), page 157

21. Charles Gasparino, *The Sellout*, (HarperCollins 2009), page 233

22. Charles Gasparino, *The Sellout*, (HarperCollins 2009), page 424

23. Dick Morris& Eileen McGann, *Catastrophe*, (HarperCollins 2009), page 181

24. Dick Morris& Eileen McGann, *Catastrophe*, (HarperCollins 2009), page 183

25. Dick Morris& Eileen McGann, *Catastrophe*, (HarperCollins 2009), page 184

26. http://www.bloomberg.com

27. http://www.spigel.de/international/world/0,1518,613330,00.html

28. http://www.foxnews.com/story/0,2933,524139,00.html

29. http://www.nytimes.com/2010/04/24/nyregion/24zarien.html

30. http://bbsnews24.blogspot.com/2011/03/court-martial-recommended-for-fort-hood.html

31. http://abcnews.go.com/m/story2id=9426085

32. http://www.reutersreprints.com

33. Glenn Beck, *Arguing with Idiots,* (Threshold Editions, 2009), page 93

34. Glenn Beck, *An Inconvenient Book,* (Threshold Editions, 2007), page 105

35. Glenn Beck, *An Inconvenient Book,* (Threshold Editions, 2007), page 105

36. Glenn Beck, *Arguing with Idiots,* (Threshold Editions, 2009), page 94

37. Christopher C. Horner, *Red Hot Lies,* (Regnery Publishing, Inc. 2008), page 297

38. Dick Morris & Eileen McGann, *2010 Take Back America,*(HarperCollins 2010)page 127

39. Dick Morris & Eileen McGann, *2010 Take Back America,*(HarperCollins 2010)page 130

40. Dick Morris & Eileen McGann, *2010 Take Back America,*(HarperCollins 2010)page 132

41. http://articles.latimes.com/2008/nov/03/nation/na-trailcoal3

42. http://www.thenewamerican.com/12/02/10

43. http://townhall.com/columnists/debrajsaunders/2011/02/06/green_jobs_are_not_evergreen_jobs

44. http://www.thenewamerican.com/12/02/10

45. Glenn Beck, *Arguing with Idiots,* (Threshold Editions, 2009), page 89

46. http://www.api.org/Newsroom/taxes-hurt-oil-prod.cfm

47. http://www.thehill.com/blogs/congress-blog/ energy/2010/07/08

48. http://www.api.org/Newsroom/taxes-hurt-oil-prod. cfm

49. Glenn Beck, *Arguing with Idiots*, (Threshold Editions, 2009), page 102

50. http://townhall.com/columnists/ debrajsaunders/2011/02/06/ green_jobs_are_not_evergreen_jobs

51. http://townhall.com/columnists/ debrajsaunders/2011/02/06/ green_jobs_are_not_evergreen_jobs

52. http://townhall.com/columnists/ johnstossel/2011/03/09/obamas_grre_job_fantasies

53. http://www.dickmorris.com/blog/obama-using- executive-orders-to-implement-radical-agenda/

54. http://townhall.com/columnists/ thomassowell/2011/03/08/union_myths

55. http://townhall.com/columnists/ johnhawkins/2011/03/08/5_reasons_unions_are_ bad_for_America

56. http://townhall.com/columnists/ howardrich/2011/03/03/ why_collective_bargaining_is_bad

57. http://townhall.com/columnists/ walterwilliams/2011/03/03/public_employee_unions

58. http://townhall.com/columnists/ howardrich/2011/03/03/ why_collective_bargaining_is_bad

59. Milton Friedman, *Capitalism and Freedom,* (The University of Chicago Press 2002), pages 124, 125

60. http://townhall.com/columnists/ debrajsaunders/2011/02/06/ green_jobs_are_not_evergreen_jobs

61. Michelle Malkin, *Culture of Corruption, Obama and His Team of Tax Cheats, Crooks and Cronies* (Regnery Publishing, Inc, 2009), page 31

62. Michelle Malkin, *Culture of Corruption, Obama and His Team of Tax Cheats, Crooks and Cronies* (Regnery Publishing, Inc, 2009), page 31

63. Michelle Malkin, *Culture of Corruption, Obama and His Team of Tax Cheats, Crooks and Cronies* (Regnery Publishing, Inc, 2009), pages 32-35

64. http://townhall.com/columnists/ luritadoan/2011/02/21/ obamas_2012_budget_gimmicks

65. http://townhall.com/columnists/ phylissschafly/2011/03/15/ bachman_exposes_$105billion_secret

66. http://www.weeklystandard.com/print/ blogs/2011/03/21/obamacare-one-year-later-even-less-popular

67. http://townhall.com/columnists/ leehabeeb/2011/02/03/obamacare_and_the_bench_ why_federal_judges_matter_more_now_than_ever

68. W. Cleon Skousen, *The Making of America; The Substance and Meaning of the Constitution,* (National Center for Constitutional Studies, 2007), page 787

69. W. Cleon Skousen, *The Making of America; The Substance and Meaning of the Constitution,* (National Center for Constitutional Studies, 2007), page 401

70. http://www.dickmorris.com/blog/2011/02/01

71. http://townhall.com/columnists/larryelder/2011/02/24/dem_congresswoman_declares_obamacare_a_disparing_reference

72. http://townhall.com/columnists/larryelder/2011/02/24/dem_congresswoman_declares_obamacare_a_disparing_reference

73. http://townhall.com/columnists/garrettmurch/2011/02/26/and_so_rationing_begins_obamacare_vs_breast_cancer_patients

74. http://townhall.com/columnists/jasonfodeman/2011/02/26/obamacare_on_the_front_lines

75. http://townhall.com/columnists/larryelder/2011/02/24/dem_congresswoman_declares_obamacare_a_disparing_reference

76. http://www.weeklystandard.com/blogs/starbucks-ceo-and-obamacare-supporter-now-decries-laws-small-business-impact 555346.html

77. http://www.foxnews.com/politics/2011/03/23/health-care-law-looms-large-2012-race

78. http://townhall.com/columnists/2011/02/23/unhappy_anniversary_obamacare

79. http://washingtonexaminer.com/opinion/editorials/2011/03/what-difference-year-has-made

80. http://washingtonexaminer.com/opinion/editorials/2011/03/what-difference-year-has-made

81. Dick Morris & Eileen McGann, *2010 Take Back America,*(HarperCollins 2010)pages 69,70

82. http://assets.open.crs.com/rpts/RL34175

83. Michael Tanner, *The Grass is not Always Greener, A Look at National Health Care Systems Around the World,* (Cato Institute 03/18/2008) page 35

84. Michael Tanner, *The Grass is not Always Greener, A Look at National Health Care Systems Around the World,* (Cato Institute 03/18/2008) page 4

85. Michael Tanner, *The Grass is not Always Greener, A Look at National Health Care Systems Around the World,* (Cato Institute 03/18/2008) pages 7,18,19,20,24,25,29,31

86. Michael Tanner, *The Grass is not Always Greener, A Look at National Health Care Systems Around the World,* (Cato Institute 03/18/2008) page 4

87. http://assets.open.crs.com/rpts/RL34175

88. Michael Tanner, *The Grass is not Always Greener, A Look at National Health Care Systems Around the World,* (Cato Institute 03/18/2008) page 5

89. Michael Tanner, *The Grass is not Always Greener, A Look at National Health Care Systems Around the World,* (Cato Institute 03/18/2008) page 6

90. Dick Morris & Eileen McGann, *Catastrophe,* (HarperCollins 2009), page 109

91. Michael Tanner, *The Grass is not Always Greener, A Look at National Health Care Systems Around the World,* (Cato Institute 03/18/2008) page 5

92. http://mjperry.blogspot.com/2009/08/5-yr-cancer-survival-rates-us-dominates.html

93. http://mjperry.blogspot.com/2009/08/5-yr-cancer-survival-rates-us-dominates.html

94. http://www.ncpa.org/scottatlas/2009/03/24

95. http://www.ncpa.org/scottatlas/2009/03/24

96. http://www.fair.us/site/docserver/uscoststudy

97. http://www.balancedpolitics.org/universal.health

98. http://www.balancedpolitics.org/universal.health

99. Newt Gingrich, *Real Change, From the World That Fails to the World That Works* (Regnery Publishing, Inc 2008), page 82

100. http://www.realclearpolitics.com/articles/2011/01/26/regulations_and_rhetoric_108664.html

101. http://www.townhall.com/columnists/donaldlambro/2011/03/04/obama_does_not_walk_his_talk

102. http://www.investors.com/NewsAndAnalysis/Article/566837/201103221841/Crony_In_Chief.aspx

103. http://www.investors.com/NewsAndAnalysis/Article/566837/201103221841/Crony_In_Chief.aspx

104. http://www.washingtonpost.com/wp-dyn/content/article/2011/01/10/AR2011011003685_pf.html

105. Ann Coulter, *Demonic, How the Liberal Mob is Endangering America* (Crown Forum, 2011) page 198

106. William J. Bennett, *America, The Last Best Hope Volume I,* (Thomas Nelson, Inc. 2007), page 40

107. Barack Obama, *Dreams From my Father,* (Three Rivers press, 1995, 2004), pages 80,142,186

108. Barack Obama, *The Audacity of Hope,* (Crown Publishers, 2006), pages 39,40,81,89-92,109-115,118,119,167-169,187-189

109. http://www.u-s-history.com/h1747.html

110. http://www.sourcewatch.org

111. http://www.DiscvoerTheNetwork.org

112. http://www.foxnews.com/politics/2011/01/24/obamas-energy-advisor-step/

113. http://www.DiscoverTheNework.org

114. http://www.conservadepedia.com/Steven_Chu

115. http://www.DiscoverTheNetwork.org

116. http://www.DiscoverTheNetwork.org

117. http://www.DiscoverTheNetwork.org

118. http://www.DiscoverTheNetwork.org

119. http://www.wikipedia.com/Robert_Gibbs

120. http://DiscoverTheNetwork.org

121. http://DiscoverTheNetwork.org

122. http://www.wikipedia.com/Jeffrey_Immelt

123. http://www.wikipedia.com/Valerie_Jarrett

124. http://wwwDiscoverTheNetwork.org

125. http://www.DiscoverTheNetwork.org

126. http://www.DiscoverTheNetwork.org

127. http://washingtonexaminer.com/blogs/beltway-confidential/2011/03/seiu-leader-plots-economic-sabotage-time-put-boot-wheel-capitalis

128. http://www.DiscoverTheNetwork.org

129. http://www.americanthinker.com/blog/2011/02/
david_plouffes_ties_to_ge_and.html

130. http://www.DiscoverTheNetwork.org

131. http://www.wikipedia.com/Samantha_Power

132. http://www.DiscoverTheNetwork.org

133. http://www.DiscoverTheNetwork.org

134. http://www.realclearpolitics.com/articles/2011/03/23/
drilling_ken_salazar_109322.html

135. http://www.conservapedia.com/SEIU

136. http://www.conservapedia.com/George_Soros

137. http://www.DiscoverTheNetwork.org

138. http://www.DiscoverTheNetwork.org

139. http://www.DiscoverTheNetwork.org

140. http://www.DiscoverTheNetwork.org

141. http://www.DiscoverTheNetwork.org

142. http://www.DiscoverTheNetwork.org

143. http://www.DiscoverTheNetwork.org

CHAPTER 5

1. Perry, Allison, Skousen, *The Real George Washington;
The True Story of America's Most Indispensable Man*,
(National Center for Constitutional Studies 2009),
page 819

2.   Perry, Allison, Skousen, *The Real George Washington;*
      The True Story of America's Most Indispensable Man,
      (National Center for Constitutional Studies 2009),
      page xix

3.   Perry, Allison, Skousen, *The Real George Washington;*
      The True Story of America's Most Indispensable Man,
      (National Center for Constitutional Studies 2009),
      page 520

4.   Perry, Allison, Skousen, *The Real George Washington;*
      The True Story of America's Most Indispensable Man,
      (National Center for Constitutional Studies 2009),
      page 522

5.   W. Cleon Skousen, *The Five Thousand Year Leap,*
      (American Documents Publishing, Inc. 1981, 2009),
      page 45

6.   Perry, Allison, Skousen, *The Real George Washington;*
      The True Story of America's Most Indispensable Man,
      (National Center for Constitutional Studies 2009),
      page 522

7.   Perry, Allison, Skousen, *The Real George Washington;*
      The True Story of America's Most Indispensable Man,
      (National Center for Constitutional Studies 2009),
      page 680

8.   William J. Bennett, *America, The Last Best Hope*
      Volume I, (Thomas Nelson, Inc. 2007), page 215

9.   James M. McPherson, *To the Best of My Ability,*
      (Agincourt Press 2004), page 120

10.   William J. Bennett, *America, The Last Best Hope*
      Volume I, (Thomas Nelson, Inc. 2007), pages 286-
      306

11.   William J. Bennett, *America, The Last Best Hope*
      Volume I, (Thomas Nelson, Inc. 2007), page 308

12. William J. Bennett, *America, The Last Best Hope Volume I,* (Thomas Nelson, Inc. 2007), page 316

13. William J. Bennett, John T.E. Cribb, *The American Patriot's Almanac,* (Thomas Nelson, Inc. 2008), page 330

14. William J. Bennett, John T.E. Cribb, *The American Patriot's Almanac,* (Thomas Nelson, Inc. 2008), page 330

15. William J. Bennett, *America, The Last Best Hope Volume I,* (Thomas Nelson, Inc. 2007), page 371

16. William J. Bennett, *America, The Last Best Hope Volume I,* (Thomas Nelson, Inc. 2007), pages 385, 386

17. William J. Bennett, *America, The Last Best Hope Volume I,* (Thomas Nelson, Inc. 2007), page 389

18. William J. Bennett, *America, The Last Best Hope Volume I,* (Thomas Nelson, Inc. 2007), pages 288, 289

19. Judge Andrew P. Napolitano, *Lies The Government Told You, Myth, Power, and Deception in American History,* (Thomas Nelson 2010), page 316

20. William J. Bennett, *America, The Last Best Hope Volume I,* (Thomas Nelson, Inc. 2007), page 83

21. Matthew Spalding, *We Hold These Truths, Rediscovering our Principles, Reclaiming our Future,* (ISI Books, 2009), page 92

22. Matthew Spalding, *We Hold These Truths, Rediscovering our Principles, Reclaiming our Future,* (ISI Books, 2009), page 35

23. Matthew Spalding, *We Hold These Truths, Rediscovering our Principles, Reclaiming our Future,* (ISI Books, 2009), page 39

24. Matthew Spalding, *We Hold These Truths, Rediscovering our Principles, Reclaiming our Future,* (ISI Books, 2009), page 40

25. Matthew Spalding, *We Hold These Truths, Rediscovering our Principles, Reclaiming our Future,* (ISI Books, 2009), page 52

26. William J. Bennett, John T.E. Cribb, *The American Patriot's Almanac,* (Thomas Nelson, Inc. 2008), page 229

27. William J. Bennett, *America, The Last Best Hope Volume I,* (Thomas Nelson, Inc. 2007), page 179

28. William J. Bennett, *America, The Last Best Hope Volume I,* (Thomas Nelson, Inc. 2007), page 185

29. William J. Bennett, *America, The Last Best Hope Volume I,* (Thomas Nelson, Inc. 2007), page 188

30. James M. McPherson, *To the Best of My Ability,* (Agincourt Press 2004), page 31

31. W. Cleon Skousen, *The Five Thousand Year Leap,* (American Documents Publishing, Inc. 1981, 2009), pages 18, 28, 59, 62, 68, 70, 119, 138, 171, 172, 206

32. William J. Bennett, *America, The Last Best Hope Volume I,* (Thomas Nelson, Inc. 2007), page 85

33. W. Cleon Skousen, *The Making of America; The Substance and Meaning of the Constitution,* (National Center for Constitutional Studies, 2007), page 16

34. W. Cleon Skousen, *The Making of America; The Substance and Meaning of the Constitution,* (National Center for Constitutional Studies, 2007), page 20

35. W. Cleon Skousen, *The Making of America; The Substance and Meaning of the Constitution,* (National Center for Constitutional Studies, 2007), pages 15-37

36. William J. Bennett, John T.E. Cribb, *The American Patriot's Almanac,* (Thomas Nelson, Inc. 2008), page 43

37. William J. Bennett, *America, The Last Best Hope Volume II,* (Thomas Nelson, Inc. 2007), page 485

38. William J. Bennett, *America, The Last Best Hope Volume II,* (Thomas Nelson, Inc. 2007), page 515

39. William J. Bennett, *America, The Last Best Hope Volume II,* (Thomas Nelson, Inc. 2007), page 490

40. James M. McPherson, *To the Best of My Ability,* (Agincourt Press 2004), page 448

41. James M. McPherson, *To the Best of My Ability,* (Agincourt Press 2004), page 449, 450

42. William J. Bennett, *America, The Last Best Hope Volume II,* (Thomas Nelson, Inc. 2007), page 481

43. James M. McPherson, *To the Best of My Ability,* (Agincourt Press 2004), page 451

44. James M. McPherson, *To the Best of My Ability,* (Agincourt Press 2004), page 452, 453

45. James M. McPherson, *To the Best of My Ability,* (Agincourt Press 2004), page 453

46. http://www.skymachine.com/US-National-Debt-Per-Capita-Percent-of-GDP-and-by-Presidential

47. http://www.InflationData.com

48. William J. Bennett, *America, The Last Best Hope Volume II,* (Thomas Nelson, Inc. 2007), page 533

49. Amity Shlaes, *The Forgotten Man,* (Harper Collins Publishers 2007), page 37

50. James M. McPherson, *To the Best of My Ability,* (Agincourt Press 2004), page 213

51. Amity Shlaes, *The Forgotten Man,* (Harper Collins Publishers 2007), page 37

52. Amity Shlaes, *The Forgotten Man,* (Harper Collins Publishers 2007), page 39

53. http://www.USGovernmentspending.org

54. Amity Shlaes, *The Forgotten Man,* (Harper Collins Publishers 2007), page 5

55. Amity Shlaes, *The Forgotten Man,* (Harper Collins Publishers 2007), page 18

56. Amity Shlaes, *The Forgotten Man,* (Harper Collins Publishers 2007), page 18

57. Amity Shlaes, *The Forgotten Man,* (Harper Collins Publishers 2007), page 24

58. Amity Shlaes, *The Forgotten Man,* (Harper Collins Publishers 2007), page 32

59. Amity Shlaes, *The Forgotten Man,* (Harper Collins Publishers 2007), page 37

CHAPTER 6

1. Thomas A. Bailey, David M. Kennedy, Lizabeth Cohen, *The American Pageant,* (Houghton Mifflin Company, 1998), page 795

2. Paul Johnson, *Churchill,* (Penguin Group, 2009), page 118

3. W. Cleon Skousen, *The Five Thousand Year Leap,* (American Documents Publishing, Inc. 1981, 2009), page 212

4. http://www.presidency.ucsb.edu/data/orders.php

5. Ronald K. Pestritto, William J. Atto, *American Progressivism,* (Lexington Books 2008), page 4

6. http://www.presidency.ucsb.edu/data/orders.php

7. Jonah Goldberg, *Liberal Fascism, The Secret History of the American Left from Mussolini to the Politics of Meaning,* (Doubleday 2007), page 255

8. Charles Gasparino, *The Sellout,* (HarperCollins, 2009) pages 107-110

9. Charles Gasparino, *The Sellout,* (HarperCollins, 2009) page 111

10. Charles Gasparino, *The Sellout,* (HarperCollins, 2009) page 503

11. David N. Bossie, *Intelligence Failure,* (WorldNetDaily Books, 2004), page 133

12. David N. Bossie, *Intelligence Failure,* (WorldNetDaily Books, 2004), page 146

13. David N. Bossie, *Intelligence Failure,* (WorldNetDaily Books, 2004), page 161

14. David N. Bossie, *Intelligence Failure,* (WorldNetDaily Books, 2004), page 178

15. David N. Bossie, *Intelligence Failure,* (WorldNetDaily Books, 2004), page 194

16. David N. Bossie, *Intelligence Failure,* (WorldNetDaily Books, 2004), page 88

17. http://www.prorev.com/legacy.htm

18. Peter Jennings, Todd Brewster, *The Century*, (Doubleday 1998), page 29

19. F.A.Hayek, *The Road To Serfdom*, (The University of Chicago Press, 2007), page 180

CONCLUSION

1. Perry, Allison, Skousen, *The Real George Washington; The True Story of America's Most Indispensable Man*, (National Center for Constitutional Studies 2009), pages 201,202